THE ASSIGNATS

BY

S. E. HARRIS

AMS PRESS
NEW YORK

Reprinted from the edition of 1930, Cambridge, Mass.
First AMS EDITION published 1969
Manufactured in the United States of America

Library of Congress Catalogue Card Number: 74-98625

AMS PRESS, INC.
New York, N.Y. 10003

TO THE MEMORY OF

MY FATHER

PREFATORY NOTE

I OWE my interest in the Assignats to a stimulating essay in Mr. Hawtrey's *Currency and Credit*. The very capable studies of Gomel and Marion on French financial history, and the vast materials on the economic history of the Revolution recently assembled by Aulard, Mathiez, Schmidt, Bloch and others, have been invaluable to me.

Professor E. R. A. Seligman of Columbia University generously allowed me to use his excellent collection on the eighteenth century, and Mr. Willis of the Cornell University Library put at my disposal the Andrew D. White Collection on the French Revolution. My student, V. M. Longstreet (Harvard, 1930) and I have spent several weary weeks checking footnotes. We hope that we have eliminated all errors. Mr. Joseph Wright kindly read the proofs.

My friends and colleagues, Professors John H. Williams and Crane Brinton, and Drs. Arthur E. Monroe and Overton H. Taylor have made many helpful suggestions. Dr. Monroe and Dr. Taylor have read the entire manuscript with great care.

I first became interested in monetary problems in Professor Edwin Walter Kemmerer's Seminar at Princeton. Professors Frank A. Fetter and David A. McCabe of Princeton University also gave me much excellent instruction and sound advice.

To my first teacher of Economics, Professor Harold H. Burbank, I acknowledge a great indebtedness. As my tutor he taught me how to read with discrimination. I received an orientation in economic literature from him which has been of inestimable value. In the late Professor Allyn A. Young's Economics 38 I learned much about monetary theory. He helped me at every stage of this work, and gave unselfishly of his time in an attempt to make a poorly written manuscript presentable.

My wife assembled the statistical material in Chapter V and read the manuscript and proofs. But the entire work is in truth

hers. Every page has profited from her interest and encouragement.

This study was completed as a Doctorate thesis in 1926. Other
interests and responsibilities have kept me from publishing it
earlier. Although I believe that I have improved it at a number of
points in the intervening three years, it remains substantially the
work completed in 1926.

S. E. Harris

Harvard University
    December, 1929

CONTENTS

INTRODUCTION . . . . **xiii–xix**

I. ORIGIN AND EARLY HISTORY 3
  1. Monetary Conditions at the Outbreak of the Revolution . 3
  2. Origin of the Assignats 8
  3. Assignats versus Quittances de Finance 13
  4. Other Discussions 18
  5. Billets de Confiance 24
  6. Numéraire 26

II. TAXATION VERSUS ASSIGNATS 28
  1. Introduction 28
  2. Debt Payments 29
  3. Deficits 34
  4. Taxation 41
  5. Taxation versus Assignats 47
  6. Emissions 53
  7. Summary. 59
  8. Note on Deficits of 1791 60

III. LAND AND THE ASSIGNAT 62
  1. Land versus Assignat 62
  2. Land, a General Security, versus Land, a Special Security 65
  3. Land and the Value of the Assignat 68
  4. The Waste of the National Resources 73
  5. Summary 90

IV. MEASURES AND EXTENT OF DEPRECIATION 92
  1. Previous Consideration of the Choice of a Measure . . . 92
  2. An Analysis of the Possible Measures 95
  3. Extent of Depreciation 102
  4. Note on Treasury Tables 108

V. LOCAL DEPRECIATION 111
  1. Introduction 111
  2. Construction of the Tables 112
  3. Analysis of the Local Tables 120

VI. THE CONTROL OF PRICES AND SUPPLIES 133
  1. Legislative History 133
  2. Opinions of Historians 147
  3. Results of Control 148
  4. Significance for the Assignats 158

VII. CAUSES OF DEPRECIATION (THROUGH THE TERROR) 163
 1. Opinions of Present-Day Writers 163
 2. An Explanation of Depreciation 166
  A. First Period, 1790–91 166
  B. Second Period, January–May, 1792 171
  C. Third Period, June–December, 1792 175
  D. Fourth Period, January–August, 1793 176
  E. Fifth Period, September, 1793–July, 1794 181

VIII. CAUSES OF DEPRECIATION (AFTER THE TERROR) 186
 1. An Explanation of Depreciation 186
  F. Sixth Period, August, 1794–December, 1795 186
 2. Summary. 201

IX. SOME EFFECTS OF DEPRECIATION 206
 1. Debtor — Creditor Relations 206
 2. Transition to a Metallic Standard 218

X. FOREIGN EXCHANGES 235
 1. Explanations of the Depreciation of the Exchanges . . . 235
 2. Capital Movements 238
 3. Foreign Trade 240
 4. Control of the Gold and Silver Market 243
 5. Exchange Control 245
 6. Control of Trade 247
 7. Comprehensive Analysis 255

XI. SUMMARY 262

BIBLIOGRAPHY 268

CHARTS

1. Emissions according to Deficits and Financial Reports 38
2. Monthly Tax Revenues, Nominal and Stable. 48
3. Proportion of Total Revenues raised by Taxation; Monthly Tax Revenues (Stable Values) 49
4. Percentage of Assignats destroyed to Totals in Circulation . . 71
4A. Ratio of Sales Value to "Prix d'Estimation" 74
    (1) Department of Yonne.
    (2) Department of Ille-et-Vilaine.
5. Percentage of Monthly Payments received to Payments Due for Land 75
    Department of Yonne
6. Émigré Lands. Proportion of Sales Prices to "Prix d'Estimation" 83
    (1) Department of Yonne.
    (2) Department of Ille-et-Vilaine.
7. Price of Wheat and Depreciation of Assignat in District of Bergues 106
8. Treasury Values and the Price of Gold 109
9. Value of Assignat According to Local Tables and Treasury Tables 121
10. Local Depreciation: Monthly Dispersion. 122
11. Territorial Depreciation: Nine Sections of France 124
12. Territorial Depreciation: East, Center, and West 125
13. Territorial Depreciation: North, Center, and South 126
    Monthly Depreciation
14.   (1) Seine, Seine-et-Marne, Seine-et-Oise, Oise 127
15.   (2) Seine, Northern Departments, all Departments 127
16.   (3) Cher, Indre, Loire-et-Cher 128
17.   (4) Vosges, Marne-Haute, Sâone-Haute 128
18.   (5) Vendée, Maine-et-Loire, Sèvres (Deux), Charente-Inférieure 129
19.   (6) Côte-d'Or, Jura, Sâone-et-Loire 129
20.   (7) Garonne-Haute, Gers, Pyrénées-Haute 130
21.   (8) Gironde, Lot-et-Garonne, Dordogne 130
22. Assignats in Circulation and their Stable Value 221
23. Foreign Exchange Quotations to the Reign of Terror — Bâle, Hamburg and London 256
24. Bâle Exchanges and Treasury Tables 1790–94 256
25. Foreign Exchanges (Bâle and Hamburg) and the Price of Gold and Silver by 10-Day Periods, February 1795–February 1796. 257

INTRODUCTION

THERE are two circumstances which appear to justify this new study of a familiar episode. The first is, that in the last fifteen years the industrious scholars of France have unearthed an incredible quantity of documentary material, hitherto unobtainable, and to a large extent unknown. Through the *Collection de Documents Inédits sur l'Histoire de France pendant la Révolution*, the *Collection de Documents Inédits sur l'Histoire de Paris pendant la Révolution*, the *Collection de Documents sur l'Histoire Économique de la Révolution*, and finally the annual publications of the *Commission de Recherche*, these documents have been made accessible.

These volumes include such indispensable collections as the letters, decrees and rulings of the Committee of Public Safety, the local documents relative to the subsistence question and to the administration of the public lands (the security of the Assignats), and the police reports of Paris, which last give invaluable clues to the attitude of the man in the street toward the Assignat. These indefatigable workers have also made accessible for the Revolutionary period the laws, decrees, administrative rulings and the like pertaining to monetary matters, to agriculture and rural economy, and to industry and commerce; the acts, decrees and rulings of the Directory; the communications of the Minister of Interior; the correspondence of Carnot; the procès-verbal of the Committees of Agriculture and Commerce and of Finance; the Cahiers, communal decrees, circulars and deliberations of the Paris authorities; and many other valuable documents. (They are listed in the bibliography appended to this study.) The *Archives Parliamentaires*, *1789–1797*, were completed through 1793 just prior to the outbreak of the recent war; work has not been continued on them to my knowledge. These seventy-eight volumes contain not only a painstaking and thoughtful edition of the parliamentary debates, but also valuable commentaries from contemporary journals, many of which are difficult or impossible to find elsewhere.

The other circumstance referred to is the recent advance of monetary theory. Just as the restriction of payments by the Bank of England during the Napoleonic Wars led to a notable development of the theory of inconvertible paper money, so the recourse to such money since 1914 has led to much speculation about its necessity, functioning and results. Writers have dwelt in particular on the inevitableness of the creation of paper money in the course of a costly war, on psychological explanations of the fluctuations in its value, on the relation between internal and external depreciation, and on the repercussions of depreciation on the movements of foreign trade; and they have tended, in contrast with the older writers, to justify, or at least to excuse, resort to such money under some conditions. They have elaborated the treatment of these problems with a nicety and precision hitherto unknown. In monetary theory in its present state one finds an instrument for the analysis of France's experience with the Assignats, which is of greater precision than any that has been available until recent years. Peculiarly important has been the attention in recent years given to the problems of the movements of balances and hoards.

Marion, Falkner and Hawtrey have of late done some creditable work with this subject.[1] Marion devotes two volumes of his pretentious work on French financial history to the Revolutionary period. Concerned primarily with the public finances of the Revolution, he devotes much space to the Assignats. But he has not kept up with recent developments in monetary theory; and he is unable to divest himself of strong prejudices against inconvertible paper money. He is uncompromising in his adherence to the traditional attitude. Had he assumed a more detached attitude, he could not have been blind to some of its compensating advantages. Falkner's treatise constitutes a meritorious treatment of the subject. He offers several ingenious and even brilliant suggestions in explanation of the depreciation of the Assignat. Unfortu-

---

[1] M. Marion, *Histoire Financière de la France depuis 1715*, Vol. II, 1789 à 1792; Vol. III, 1792 à 1797; S. V. Falkner, " Das Papiergeld der französischen Revolution 1789-1797 "; Schriften des Vereins für Sozialpolitik, Vol. CLXV; R. G. Hawtrey, *Currency and Credit*, 2d ed., Ch. XV.

nately, he had access to relatively few of the documents enumerated above.

Hawtrey's chapter on the Assignats should be considered with a thought as to its purpose. He finds in the Assignats an opportunity to test his ingeniously elaborated monetary theory. The principal ground of my criticisms of Hawtrey's interpretation lies in his failure to study this particular experience more intensively. To evolve a profound theory is one task; to seek in the world of facts for its verification is another; and the danger lies in not devoting sufficient energy to the empirical test. Nevertheless, Hawtrey's chapter is a conspicuous contribution. One cannot read it without being impressed by the brilliant way in which an eighteenth century episode is construed in terms of present-day monetary theory. While differing from Hawtrey's interpretation on a number of points, I am, nevertheless, conscious of my indebtedness to one who, in my opinion, more than any one else, has contributed to that improvement of monetary theory which makes the rewriting of the Assignat episode expedient.

The more important arguments are presented in Chapter III and the following chapters.

My first chapter summarizes the pamphlets and legislative debates which were influential in bringing about the confiscation of church lands and the creation of the Assignats, and which throw light upon their early history. Gomel, Marion and Stourm (named in order of the importance of their contributions) have done pioneer work on the finances of the Revolution. I have not attempted to explore again the ground traversed by them. My second chapter is devoted to a summary of the Revolutionary finances and to the investigations of a few problems of special significance for the history of the Assignats, such as the amount of the monthly deficits, the public debt, and the rate of repayment. These aspects concern us because they shed some light on the disbursements of the Assignats. The issues, burnings and circulation of Assignats and, finally, the relative contributions of taxes and of paper money are also considered. The mistakes and inconsistencies of the authorities, and many instances of official dishonesty are duly noted. I have attempted to construct some new statistical series, but some of the results are only provisional because of the scarcity of reliable data.

The problem of the relation of the land security to the value of the Assignat, which has generally been regarded as definitely solved, requires further study in my opinion, and I have dealt with it in Chapter III. Although adherents to the Assignat system erred (1) in overestimating the importance of the land security, and (2) in proclaiming the immediate redeemability of the Assignat, I am satisfied, nevertheless, that the existence of the land security contributed materially to the maintenance of the value of the Assignat. In Chapter III, I develop the theses that the land security (the confiscated property of the Church and Émigrés) by helping to create confidence in the Assignats helped to retard their depreciation, and that fluctuations in the value of the Assignats were, to an appreciable extent, determined by the operations of the public land officers. The value of these resources, the total of Assignats realised (and incinerated) as a result of the sales of land, the wasted opportunities — resulting largely from the insecurity and the depression of controlled commodity prices below market prices, both responsible for a marked contraction of land sales — are all, therefore, relevant problems for a study of the Assignats, and are pursued at length. The prevalence and danger of the land fallacy popularized by Mirabeau and others and since condemned by Mill, Levasseur and Hawtrey, are not questioned; but it is maintained that since the fallacy was accepted by the gullible and ignorant, their credulity contributed appreciably to the maintenance of the value of the paper money. The fact that most of France was cajoled into believing that the land security transformed an otherwise valueless paper money into "circulating land", certainly added to the confidence in the Assignat.

Chapter IV, like the chapters which precede it, helps to prepare the ground for the comprehensive treatment of depreciation offered in Chapters VII–VIII. The preliminary problems of the measures and extent of depreciation are examined at this point. I have considered four aspects of these related problems: the failure of earlier writers to employ such measures judiciously; the theoretical and practical difficulties of each of the available measures; the selection of the one most appropriate for this particular study; and, finally, the extent of depreciation.

In an attempt to adjust contracts made during the paper money régime, the Central Government in 1797 ordered each of the eighty or more departments to prepare a monthly table of depreciation. In Chapter V, I have analyzed these tables and attempted to account for the marked discrepancies found in them. Although these tables are unique in the annals of the history of paper money and offer an unusual opportunity for an analysis of the geographical distribution of depreciation, they have been virtually disregarded by all writers on the subject.

The next chapter (VI) may appear to be a digression, but it also helps to clear the ground for the chapters which follow. Even the lengthy summary of the legislative history of price control is not without significance for the history of the Assignat. Was the system of price control introduced, as many writers have thought, to bolster up the value of the Assignat? Were the high prices of subsistence caused by excessive issues of Assignats, or are they explicable in terms of curtailed production and impeded circulation of commodities? In any case, the repercussions of changes in the condition of the subsistence market and in the success of price control on the value of the Assignats, were significant. Are we to agree with Marion that, "The maximum had been only a procedure to stop or rather conceal the progress of the depreciation, a procedure badly conceived, soon revealed powerless, even injurious", or with Hawtrey, who includes price control among the causes of a significant rise in the value of the Assignat? A careful consideration of price control is relevant in the selection of the right measure of depreciation. Just what is the meaning of a rise or a fall in the value of a paper money when the Government, through an effective system of rationing, compels the public to hoard a large proportion of its money? Failure to use the available measures of depreciation judiciously results in confusion in studies of the period of maximum prices. The kaleidoscopic (yet in the main effective) changes in the legislation against the precious metals, the violent movements of the gold points, and the varying effectiveness of price control, demand at least a realisation of the difficulties of the choice of a suitable measure.

Many of the conclusions of the first six chapters are reviewed and evaluated in Chapters VII and VIII. But in these latter chapters I have also tried to weigh supplementary material gleaned from every accessible source. After dividing the entire history of the Assignats into convenient periods, I delved into each period with a view to giving each contributory cause of depreciation its proper weight. Among these factors are not only such outstanding factors as the effects of the land security, the state of the subsistence market and the finances, but also many other influences, such as the varying competition of gold and silver, the quantities of Assignats in circulation, the demonetisations, the attempts of the Government to enhance the value of the paper money, the inordinate issues of "billets de confiance," the prevalence of counterfeiting, and "au cours" payments.

When the Assignat began to depreciate rapidly, debtors hastened to repay their debts; when the Government decided to withdraw the Assignat in favor of the Mandat, and finally to renounce both in favor of a return to metallic payments, the debtors found themselves in a trying position: the creditors demanded payments in gold and silver at the face value for debts contracted in a depreciated currency. The Government, by making anticipatory reimbursements illegal during the period of rapid depreciation, intervened in behalf of the creditor; later, by sponsoring the construction and use of the local tables of depreciation, it intervened in behalf of the debtors. The local tables of depreciation formed but one incident in this conspicuous attempt to modify the terms of private contracts. The history of this paternal interest in private contracts forms the subject matter of the first section of Chapter IX.

The second section of the same chapter concerns itself with the obstacles encountered in the attempt to return to a metallic standard. This is an aspect of the history of the Assignats that has received little attention, although the attempt to return to a metallic standard encountered difficulties that for many years proved virtually insurmountable.

I have found it convenient to collect most of the facts pertaining to the foreign exchanges in a separate chapter. The Revolutionary exchanges have never been examined adequately, nor has the heterogeneous collection of accessible facts been presented as a unit. In Chapter X I am concerned with the large movements in the exchanges resulting from internal fluctuations in the value of the Assignat and with the explanation of the marked deviations from the internal values. Capital movements, control of exports and imports — extending to the virtual nationalisation of foreign trade — control of the exchanges and of the movements of gold and silver were the most potent of the independent forces affecting the exchanges. Movements in the exchanges resulted in part from changes in the internal value of the Assignats; but independent changes in the external value of the Assignats had far-reaching effects on their internal value.

THE ASSIGNATS

CHAPTER I

ORIGIN AND EARLY HISTORY

1. Monetary Conditions at the Outbreak
of the Revolution

In 1789 less than one-quarter of the population of France resided in the cities.[1] Agriculture was the most important occupation. Hence the state of agriculture at any particular time might be an excellent index of the demand for money. At the outbreak of the Revolution, Arthur Young found French agriculture in a deplorable condition: it suffered from a deficiency of capital which he put at four hundred and fifty million pounds sterling; the average yield of rye and wheat was eighteen bushels per acre, as compared to twenty-five bushels for England; the system of small farms received Young's unqualified condemnation.[2] The crops of 1788 were severely damaged by a hail storm, so that the Revolutionary era opened under unfavorable conditions in the subsistence markets.[3]

Depression was prevalent also in industrial pursuits. The disappearance of *numéraire*,[4] the evil transitory effects of the Treaty of 1786, and the weakened condition of the Government, all contributed to the low ebb of industry.[5] Foreign trade consisted in the main of exports of manufactured and colonial products, and of importations of raw materials and food products. The dangers of a famine in raw materials or in the means of sub-

---

[1] M. Lavoisier, *Résultats Extraits d'un Ouvrage Intitulé de la Richesse territoriale,* Oeuvres, Vol. VI, p. 457.

[2] A. Young, *Travels in France*, 2d ed., Vol. I, pp. 355, 404–417, 435.

[3] See Actes de Commune, Vol. I, pp. 226, 232, 297, 462–463, 674, for a description of the heroic measures taken by the city of Paris. A national decree of September 7, 1788 suspended the exportation of grains. Archives Parliamentaires, Vol. I, pp. 358–359. (Hereafter given as Arch. Parl.)

[4] The French word *numéraire* is not easily translated. As a rule, it includes metallic money only, but infrequently, the term refers to paper money in addition.

[5] See *L'État de Paris en 1789*, p. 43.

sistence were often averted by reco irse to importations. The decline of manufacturing jeopardized the continuance of France's importation of necessities. (Authorities agreed only roughly on the magnitude of France's foreign trade: Arnould estimated the aggregate annual foreign trade at seven hundred and fifty million livres, Necker at five hundred and thirty, and Young at six hundred and sixty millions.[1])

Countless witnesses of the momentous events at the eve of the Revolution attested to a partial or even to a complete loss of metallic money. The unsettled political and economic conditions made the people wary of the future, and hence resulted in increased monetary hoardings, and even metallic exportations. A decrease in the amount of circulating media, according to orthodox monetary theory in its more rigid form, should result in a fall of prices. But no evidence is to be found that a drop in prices occurred. Although a tendency to hoard commodities was probably present in these uncertain times, the absence of complaints in the Cahiers and other documents of the period against hoarding (such as were heard in 1792–93) points to the absence of any marked or concerted hoardings. The languishing state of manufacturing and the recent crop failures probably accounted for some decrease in the demand for money, but one hardly commensurate with the decrease of the circulating media.

If prices had reacted promptly to the reduction in the circulating media, complaints of the shortage of money would not have been so numerous. Prices moved sluggishly; they did not yield to the pressure of the reduction of the quantity of circulating media. The reduction did not make itself felt throughout the economic system. Rather, the system was prone to collapse at its weakest points: a manufacturer who was not efficient enough to meet the added burden of paying a premium for the purchase of precious metals for his wage bill without the compensation of increased prices for his wares, had to close his shop; and he was soon followed by other inefficient managers. The reduction in the

[1] J. Necker, *Treatise on the Administration of the Finances of France*, 3d ed., Vol. II, pp. 123–130; M. Arnould, *De la Balance du Commerce*, pp. 208–212; A. Young, *op. cit.*, Vol. I, p. 502.

quantity of money resulted in a decrease in production and hence in a decrease in the demand for money, instead of in a reduction of prices.[1]

The amount of currency, in existence, it should be observed, was not equivalent to the amount in circulation, even in normal times. Barbaroux, a member of the Convention, asserted in 1792 that six hundred million livres of the aggregate of twenty-two hundred millions of money had been regularly hoarded before the Revolution.[2] The proportion of cash hoarded increased during unsettled times. Writers often fail to distinguish between the aggregate quantity of money, and the aggregate of circulating media. A comparison of the amount of Assignats later in circulation with the pre-Revolutionary supplies of metals is misleading: the former was held with a view to spending; a large proportion of the latter was hoarded. (In the later years of the Revolution, a large proportion of all Assignats were necessarily hoarded for long periods of time.)

Many of the estimates of the pre-Revolutionary monetary supplies are based on Necker's calculations of 1784. He collected annual figures of coinage from the recoinage of 1726 until 1784; and from a study of the statistics of foreign trade, foreign payments, and the like, he estimated the aggregate exportations of specie. One possible source of error was eliminated for later investigators by the recoinage of 1785; the available supplies of gold coin then became known with a great degree of accuracy. Since silver was the overvalued metal until 1785, no appreciable exportation of silver occurred before that date. Therefore the only uncertain element in the later calculations lies in the annual coinage of silver from 1727-1785. Necker, Young, Calonne, Clavière, Arnould, and the First Committee on Money all studied the problem, and they were closely in accord; the estimates were from two thousand to twenty-two hundred million livres.[3] We

[1] Evidence of the failure of businesses as a result of the inability to obtain numéraire except at a great sacrifice, is furnished by C. Schmidt, *Un Essai de Statistique Industrielle, Commission de Recherche et de Publication des Documents*, 1908, pp. 11-205.

[2] *Moniteur*, Vol. XVI, p. 244.

[3] J. Necker, *Treatise on the Administration of the Finances of France*, Vol. III, pp. 59-67; A. Young, *op. cit.*, Vol. I, pp. 581-582; "First Report on Money," Procès

must not place too much faith in these figures, however, because the virtual agreement is due largely to the common reliance on Necker's calculations (aside from some independent contributions from Clavière and Calonne), and because the margin of error in the annual coinage of silver cannot be neglected. The results, however, may be accepted as a rough estimate.

The recoinage of 1785 approximately doubled the seigniorage on gold; the mint ratio of gold to silver was changed from 14.5 to 15.5.[1] The mint ratio in England at the time was 15 to 1. Hawtrey, finding that France did not lose her silver, explains the apparent failure of Gresham's law to operate by the fact that a coinage charge of 2 per cent for gold at the French mints, together with the remedy allowed in fineness, reduced the actual ratio to 15 to 1.[2] But the ratio of 15.5 to 1 is derived from the actual money coined after the coinage charge is deducted: the mark of gold was coined into 768 livres, and the mark of silver into 49 livres and 16 sous, a ratio of 15-30/59 to 1.[3]

In actual fact silver was exported. The Cahiers contained many complaints from the people of the loss of coins — and silver was their coin.[4] The French received many communications from England which informed them of the plentiful importations of the silver écu (3 livres) rather than the gold louis.[5] Necker offered 54 livres for a mark of silver in September 1789, or 58 livres if the silver were employed as a subscription to the current loan — instead of the mint price of 49-4/5 livres.[6] Crowds interfered with the passage of conveyances of silver.[7] The crowding of the streets that resulted from the attempts to obtain both silver and gold

Verbal, Vol. XXXVIII, p. 22; F. Clavière, *Opinion d'un Créancier de l'Etat*, pp. 10–20; M. Arnould, *De la Balance du Commerce*, Vol. II, pp. 208–212. (Hereafter Procès Verbal will be designated P. V. The pagination is annoying.)

[1] It is difficult to reconcile this with Shaw's statement that the recoinage of 1785 practically eliminated seigniorage from French currency. W. A. Shaw, *The History of Currency 1252–1894*, p. 173. Compare "The First Report on Money," P. V., Vol. XXXVIII, p. 10.

[2] R. G. Hawtrey, *op. cit.*, p. 307.

[3] "First Report on Money," P. V., Vol. XXXVIII, p. 10.

[4] Arch. Parl., Vol. III, pp. 11, 169; Vol. IV, p. 285.

[5] *Journal Political National*, Vol. I, pp. 3, 143; Prudhomme, *Révolution de Paris*, Vol. I, p. 52.

[6] P. V., Vol. V, 85. If "p." is omitted, the number relates to a *Débat et Décret*.

[7] Actes de Commune, Vol. III, pp. 325–326.

from the Caisse d'Escompte forced the police to limit these exchanges to three days a week. Necker granted the City of Bordeaux a remission of the seigniorage in order to make it profitable to import Spanish piastres, and to recoin them into écus.[1] The Committee on Money in its first report proposed to reduce the relative value of gold, and (showing respect for an English precedent) proposed to effect this by a reduction of the monetary value of the louis from 24 to 23 livres.[2] In its second report the Committee dwelt on the profitableness of shipping silver in place of gold to London.[3] Baring asserted that the French Government's attempts to obtain metals in England were frustrated by the English Government.[4]

The Caisse d'Escompte added to the supplies of circulating media; this is, therefore, an appropriate place to say that most of the criticism suffered by the Caisse d'Escompte was wholly unwarranted. For example, Blanc's charge that the Bank was improvident is not justified.[5] A despairing financial minister embarrassed the Bank in order to save the tottering Government. In December, 1789, loans to the Government formed more than two-thirds of the Caisse's assets, and those assets were notoriously thrust upon the Caisse d'Escompte:[6]

STATEMENT OF DECEMBER 5, 1789

ASSETS (Millions of Livres)		LIABILITIES (Millions of Livres)	
Loans to the King	70	Capital	100
Anticipations on the Patriotic Tax	90	Notes	112
Letters of Exchange, etc.	40	Current Accounts	8
Coin in the Vaults	10		
Coin in the Process of Manufacture	6		
	216		220

[1] M. E. de Fayolé, "Documents Relatifs à la Rareté du Numéraire en Guyenne en 1789 et 1790," *Archives Historiques du Département de la Gironde*, Vol. XXXVI, pp. 470–476.
[2] "First Report on Money," P. V., Vol. XXXVIII, pp. 13–14.
[3] "Second Report on Money," P. V., Vol. XXXVIII, pp. 11–13.
[4] Sir F. Baring, *Observations on the Establishment of the Bank of England*, 2d ed., pp. 29–30.
[5] L. Blanc, *Histoire de la Révolution Française*, Vol. I, pp. 348–350.
[6] M. Laborde's "Mémoire," P. V., Vol. VIII, 144, p. 32.

2. ORIGIN OF THE ASSIGNATS

We cannot doubt that the disasters brought about by Law's activities were well remembered on the eve of the French Revolution. The country was prepared to oppose any suggestion for the introduction of a paper money. On August 16, 1788, a king's edict proclaimed the creation of a new interest-bearing paper money. The paper was to be withdrawn by December 31; its purpose was to effect a number of urgent payments. The storm of disapproval gathered so ominously that the Government revoked the edict on September 14.[1] Parlement, in a session of January 30, 1789, expressed the fear that the "billet noir" of the Caisse d'Escompte, already protected by the Government and therefore really issued by it, might be appropriated by the Treasury for its own use.[2] According to one Cahier, one parish argued, "above all, we will not countenance the introduction of a paper money or a national bank, either of which can only produce a great evil, and of which the memories alone are capable of frightening us because of the abuse and speculation that they occasioned in the past."[3] A Cahier of Paris demanded a rigid maintenance of the purity of the circulation; every suggestion for a new money, regardless of form or manner, is for a veritable paper money.[4] A few attributed the disastrous effects of paper money to the arbitrary nature of the Government, however, and were willing to try again at the solicitation of the Estates General. But these were a very small minority.[5]

Then came the Revolution, and with it a remarkable change in the attitude toward paper money. Expediency demanded paper money; the success of the people's Revolution was impossible without it. The Revolution was accompanied by a reaction against the old obnoxious and oppressive taxes, and by a demoralization of the economic and political organization that made the collection of taxes impossible. Loans were not forthcoming, perhaps because of a dearth of savings, or the uncertainty of the future, or

[1] Arch. Parl., Vol. I, pp. 354–357.
[2] *L'État de Paris*, p. 48.
[3] Arch. Parl., Vol. V, p. 59; see also Vol. I, pp. 676, 717, 720; Vol. II, p. 567.
[4] *Cahiers de Paris*, Vol. III, p. 175.
[5] Arch. Parl., Vol. III, pp. 626, 727; Vol. VI, pp. 34, 40.

mere administrative weaknesses. A comprehensive system of education that purported to demonstrate the uniqueness of the new paper money — especially as regards the peculiar land security that emphatically differentiated the Assignat from Law's paper — aided in the complete transformation of public opinion.

Clavière by his writings, and Mirabeau by his oratory, probably had more to do with the origin of the Assignat than any other individual.[1] Brissot, a most influential journalist, commended Clavière for his proposals, and recommended them to his readers.[2] Mirabeau called Clavière "l'auteur des Assignats."[3]

The Committee of Finance proposed in September, 1789, to force the Church to pay its fair proportion of taxes for the last six months of 1789.[4] As early as September 30, Mirabeau plagued the Church with a remark that the ecclesiastics' display of anxiety over discussions of paper money was only explicable by their fear that paper money might be issued on the security of church lands. Mirabeau's famous description, "Le papier-monnaie est un vol ou un emprunt fait le sabre à la main," however, came on the next day; this pronouncement was later adopted by Mirabeau's adversaries, much to his embarrassment.[5] A book by Sennebier, off the press on October 7, presented a plan for a bank with a capital of two milliards, secured by the possessions of the Church.[6]

The alienation of the church domains was beginning to attract much attention. Condorcet had suggested in 1788 that the present owners of domains should only enjoy the usufruct for life, and that they should then revert to the State.[7] Talleyrand's bold proposal on October 10, 1789 to confiscate the possessions of the Church, was fruitful indeed. He maintained that the expropriation of the Church was not incompatible with the maintenance of property rights; and he estimated that the Treasury would profit to the extent of fifty or sixty million livres annually even if the State

---

[1] E. Clavière, *Opinion d'un Créancier de l'État.*
[2] *Le Patriote François*, Vol. I, August 10, 1789.
[3] *Les Lettres au Comte Marck*, Vol. II, p. 156.
[4] P. V., Vol. IV, 69.
[5] *Moniteur*, Vol. I, p. 541.
[6] P. J. B. Buchez et P. C. Roux, *Histoire Parlémentaire*, Vol. III, p. 351.
[7] J. A. N. Condorcet, *Des Biens Appurtenant au Public*, Oeuvres, Vol. VIII, p. 446.

maintained the "culte."[1] Mirabeau elaborated on Talleyrand's arguments on October 30. His masterly discourse carried much weight, and the Assembly took the momentous step of appropriating the possessions of the Church on November 2.[2] Thus the "gage" for the future Assignats became available.

The need for haste was evident, and many suggestions for the utilization of the church lands were offered. In November, d'Arcy proposed a sale of 472 million livres of land to help liquidate the debt.[3] Many advocated the issuance of paper money, and Necker took the opportunity on November 14 to criticise many of these proposals. But Necker's opposition was not altogether uncompromising. He was not blind to the possibilities of a restricted issue, and even intimated that larger issues might be feasible later.[4] Anticipating a deficit of 170 million livres, Necker asked that the Caisse d'Escompte be permitted to increase its note issues in order to enable it to increase its advances to the Government. With this suggestion, Necker innocently strengthened the position of the adherents of paper money. Mirabeau was quick to discern the vulnerability of Necker's position; he dwelt upon the absurdity of asking the Government to lend to itself.[5] Mirabeau remained the inveterate opponent of Necker.[6]

The Viscount of Macaye proposed, in the session of November 21, the issuance of 600 million livres of national notes.[7] Another member suggested on the same day the creation of a bank, which was to receive the receipts from the Patriotic Contribution and the sale of church lands, and which was to manufacture 500 millions of notes. The Caisse de l'Extraordinaire, created by the provisions of the first Assignat law, answered the description of

---

[1] *Choix de Rapports*, Vol. I, pp. 89–101; P. V., Vol. VI, *Déb. et Déc.* 62.
[2] *Moniteur*, Vol. II, pp. 109–112.
[3] P. V., Vol. VII, 131.
[4] *Ibid.*, 126.
[5] *Ibid.*, 130.
[6] He wrote on January 20, 1790 to Count Marck, "if Necker remains another month, the écu will entirely disappear, and you will know the mistake of the sublime invention of paper money"; and previously, "It is a strange destiny that allows a mortal to advance to glory on the double crutch of famine and paper money." *Lettres au Comte Marck*, Vol. I, pp. 433, 455. Mirabeau's insincerity in his advocacy of paper money, is evident.
[7] P. V., Vol. VIII, 100.

this bank.[1] Du Pont de Nemours, the Physiocrat, attacked the proposal to issue paper money; he declared it an avowal of bankruptcy, the substitution of a non-interest-paying for an interest-paying debt.[2] The vast majority of the plans submitted carried some suggestions of note issues on the security of the church lands, or at least, of loans secured by the church lands. The Abbot of Abbecourt advocated a loan secured by the church lands.[3] Interested in reducing the arrears of debt payments, the Bishop d'Aûtun (Talleyrand) championed the creation of a new national bank, and the sale of church lands.[4] The Abbot of Coulmier, also, regarded with favor a loan supported by a lien on the possessions of the Church.[5] The non-churchmen were not satisfied with half-way measures: Anson, later an ardent champion of the Assignat, spoke strongly in favor of an issue of notes on the security of the church domains.[6]

Another step toward the inevitable was taken on December 5 when d'Angely and de Montlosier emphasized the necessity of a sale of church lands as a guarantee for additional issues of paper money.[7] The former made the novel suggestion that the paper money be employed to purchase the new domains, and thus be redeemed.[8]

The Commissioners appointed to examine the plans for a bank consulted with Necker. Their report, issued on December 19, called for a public loan of 80 million livres from the Caisse d'Escompte. The Government was to repay all of its advances from the Caisse d'Escompte by an issue of 70 millions of annuities and of 170 millions of Assignats, the latter redeemable in 5 years. A sale of church lands of a maximum value of 250 million livres was also recommended.[9] The plan represented a fusion of various plans already proposed.

[1] P. V., Vol. VIII, 131.
[2] Ibid., 130.
[3] Moniteur, Vol. II, p. 302.
[4] Ibid., pp. 303–304.
[5] P. V., Vol. VIII, 141.
[6] Ibid., 142.
[7] P. V., Vol. IX, 142.
[8] Moniteur, Vol. II, p. 310.
[9] "Report of the Commissioners," P. V., Vol. X, 153; Necker had already mentioned Assignats on December 17.

The sustained debates came to an end with the authorization of an issue of paper money on the same day. The decree closely followed the plans of the Commissioners. The Treasury was to repay the Caisse d'Escompte with Assignats; the Government was to issue 400 millions of these interest-bearing Assignats, which were to be supported by the sale of crown and church lands valued at 400 million livres; the notes were to be redeemed systematically within 5 years, and were to be given special privileges in the purchase of lands, but were not, be it noted, to be legal tender.[1]

The Assignat was the product of a gradual development, from the first attacks on the financial privileges of the Church until the confiscation, and then on to the successful plan of an issue of notes on the security of the land. Burke's contention that the Assignats were issued to keep the ecclesiastical lands out of the hands of Paris can find little support in parliamentary debates, or in the literature of the period.[2] And I wonder whether Jaurès, Marion, and others are justified in their contention that the Government created the Assignat to make the sale of lands possible. Looking backward, it is easy to see that the creation of the Assignats did contribute to the sale of the lands, but there is no evidence that the zealous supporters of paper money had this service in mind. Certainly no attention was paid to this particular service of the proposed paper money by the parliamentary leaders. However, the issue of Assignats was generally considered equivalent to the issue of circulating land. But this argument was employed later. Paper money was a financial expedient.[3] Fortunately, the land was available for use in bolstering up the Assignat. It is doubtful whether the issues of paper money could have been avoided even if the land had not been available. The fact that special advantages in the purchase of lands were to be attached to the Assignat may be construed as a recognition of the possibility of increasing the sales of lands by an issue of Assignats; but it may

---

[1] P. V., Vol. X, 153.
[2] E. Burke, *Reflections on the French Revolution*, Everyman's Edition, pp. 117–118.
[3] Subercaseaux, on the basis of a study of numerous paper money experiences, concludes that "there has never existed a cause more powerful and more general for the issue of paper money than the financial cause." G. Subercaseaux, *Le Papier Monnaie*, p. 53.

ceeds of future sales; and that the lesson taught by Law's experience, that paper money should be convertible into gold and silver,
had been lost on the Assembly.[1]

The members of the National Assembly rallied to the support of
nson and his colleagues. Roederer, Aiguillin, Pétion and La
ochefoucauld all argued in behalf of the new issues. Pétion con-
asted the new paper money, secured by specially designated
operty, with the type, secured by property in general.[2] La
chefoucauld preferred the Assignats, which were supported by
ls actually on sale, to Law's money, which was secured by
e gold mines yet to be discovered.[3]

he Assembly approved a decree in April that incorporated the
submitted by Anson: creditors of the clergy were designated
ors of the nation; the Assignats were to be legal tender; an
onal issue of four hundred million livres was to replace the
of the Caisse d'Escompte.[4]

abeau gave the opening discourse on August 27 in favor of
of the Assignat for the payment of debt. He asserted that
nsion of the use of the Assignat would materially increase
ks of the defenders of the Constitution, and would facili-
sale of land. By favoring a non-interest-bearing note,
u aided the movement toward a one-hundred-per-cent
money. He proposed to make the Assignat a land paper
se that the paper was to be issued on the security of land,
redeemed by the purchase of land, and was to have the
ight to be used in the purchase of the land. In advocat-
denominations, however, he was inconsistent; for the
e introduction of smaller denominations would be to
he circulation of the Assignats in the regular channels
tead of inducing their rapid redemption through land

cy was attracted by the need of numé
of circulation. In his opinion, it

l. IV, p. 125.
135.

II, 246, 247.
M. Mirabeau," P.V, Vo

more easily be construed as a measure for reduci
Assignats in circulation.

3. ASSIGNATS VERSUS QUITTANCES D

In the fall of 1790 there was an intense s
pediency of extending the use of the Assigna
debt. Should the reimbursement of debt be
employment of the Assignat, or by an issue
ing paper of a non-monetary nature, the (

A preliminary struggle occurred in the s
Necker conceded the necessity of a lin
nats; but he expressed skepticism as to
tion outside of Paris.[1] Anson, for the
ported unreservedly in favor of an in
is a money (signe) that represents a
This new numéraire will have the
must obey the general will." Ar
would be divided into small par
holders of the Assignats.[2]

De Cernon maintained that s
real wealth, the creation of the
able. In his opinion, the Assig
capital value of the rentes, th
its debts, and to profit from t
depreciate because the sur

The Committee of Finan
an early issue of legal ten
a bill for the Committee
hundred million livres a
all the newly acquired
Maury and Cazalès op
that the Assignat wa

1 "Necker's Report of
2 "Report of the Com
  (*Déb. et Déc.* are
  Plan for the Libera
  rocès-Verbal of
  ., Vol. XVII
  iteur, Vol.

R
tr
pr
Ro
lan
son

T
plan
credi
addit
notes

Mir
the us
the ext
the ran
tate the
Mirabea
fiat pape
in the ser
was to be
exclusive
ing smalle
result of t
encourage t
of trade, ins
purchases.[5]

Gouy d'A
new channels

1 *Moniteur*, V
2 *Ibid.*, pp. 134
3 *Ibid.*, p. 125.
4 P. V., Vol. XV
5 "Discourse of

to exchange circulating Assignats for non-circulating public securities.[1] Within the next month, thirty-seven sections of Paris declared themselves in favor of increased issues of Assignats, and only one section was opposed.[2] The sections, in general, favored small denominations, the legal tender quality, and the exclusive privilege of exchangeability for public lands for the Assignat. Pétion proved himself an able disciple of Mirabeau's. He advocated, especially, the representation of each Assignat by a designated parcel of land; he was, however, not blind to the practical difficulties involved. In order to encourage speedy redemption through land purchases, Pétion proposed the discontinuance of interest payments, because they were an incentive to the hoarding of the Assignats.[3]

"Every nation has the right to manufacture money, to substitute territorial numéraire for metallic numéraire," said Anson. He believed, also, that the long lapse of time between the manufacture of the first and the last Assignat, as well as the investment in lands, would reduce the Assignats in circulation to the minimum necessary amount. The fact that the utilization of Assignats for the payment of debt would save heavy interest charges was a deciding factor for Anson — and many others. To the argument that increased prices would result in an unfavorable balance of trade, Anson retorted that the foreigner could afford to pay more livres since each livre would be cheaper.[4]

Chapelier, one of the most influential members of the National Assembly, shifted the attention of the Assembly from the financial aspects of the problem to the political aspect: the sale of the lands, and the issuance of more Assignats were necessary to insure the success of the Revolution.[5] He merely elaborated an argument previously presented by Mirabeau.

In his reply of September 27, Mirabeau conceded several points to his opponents, and he also dealt with several of his opponents' criticisms. In his opinion, an Assignat and a parcel of land of

---

[1] P. V., Vol. XXVIII, 407; Moniteur, Vol. V, pp. 505–506.
[2] Actes de Commune, Vol. VII, pp. 81–111.
[3] Reprint of Pétion's speech, P. V., Vol. XXIX, 400.
[4] P. V., Vol. XXX, 414.
[5] Moniteur, Vol. V, p. 769.

equal value were interchangeable — they were almost identities; an Assignat was a bill of exchange, payable on sight in land. To the criticism that several banks with territorial securities had become insolvent in the past, he responded that those institutions had not actually put lands on sale. He bitterly assailed the interest-bearing note, the Quittance de Finance. It would become a subject of speculation; and the interest payments would ruin the Treasury.[1] Barnave added to the criticism of the Quittance: its creation would result in the acquisition of lands by the large landed interests. A few days later, the Assembly approved an issue of eight hundred million livres of non-interest-bearing Assignats. The remaining provisions of the law were in close agreement with Mirabeau's proposals.[2]

Let us turn to the more influential opponents now: Beaumez objected to the exchange of four and one-half milliards of public script for three milliards of lands; the result would be either that some creditors would be eliminated from the competition for the lands, or the paper money would depreciate.[3] Lablanche was of the opinion that extending the use of the Assignat was equivalent to sacrificing France as a whole to the interests of her creditors, for the people would exchange their Assignats largely for goods, not for lands; and prices would increase as debt holders were paid in Assignats.[4] An American citizen warned the Assembly of the dangers of paper money. Since most of the business of the nation was done on credit, he feared that issuing an unstable currency would depress trade. Moreover, he realized that people would make only indispensable purchases with their gold and silver, and would use the Assignats for all other purposes; the Assignats, when issued, would therefore circulate rapidly, and depreciate long before a volume of circulation equivalent to the pre-Revolutionary circulation of money was reached.[5]

The Provinces were not nearly so enthusiastic as Paris about the paper money. A delegation of officials from the Department

[1] Mirabeau's reply, September 27, 1790, P. V., Vol. XXXI, 450.
[2] P. V., Vol. XXXII, p. 451.
[3] Beaumez's opinion in P. V., Vol. XXXI, 147.
[4] Opinion of M. Lablanche, P. V., Vol. XXIX, 403.
[5] "Advice on the Assignats by a citizen of the United States," *ibid*.

of Seine-Inférieure protested against further issues on the ground that the Assignats would force the metals out of circulation, and that the public would expend its Assignats for purposes other than the purchase of land.[1] A delegation from the City of Lille feared the over abundance of paper money.[2] The citizens and business men of Lyons informed the Assembly that since May, when the Assignats first began to circulate in the Provinces, numéraire had disappeared; and that the silk merchants of Piedmont now refused to sell their raw silk except for cash.[3] Protests against Mirabeau's proposals came from many of the principal cities of France.[4]

Dupont preferred the interest-bearing notes (Quittances de Finance) because they would not be forced into circulation, and therefore would not affect prices. An exchange of Assignats for "debt papers" would not really be a payment of the debt, for the Assignat would remain an obligation of the Government until redeemed. The repudiation of the interest on rentes by paying in Assignats, would constitute an exploitation of the rights of creditors. Because many of the holders of the Assignats would be unable or unwilling to invest in lands, large quantities would remain in circulation. In spite of all of these objections, Dupont saw the practical necessity of a limited issue to meet the most pressing needs, including the payment of the arrears due on the rentes.[5]

Talleyrand made a plea for the Quittance on September 18 that had little acute analysis in it, but within a few days he made a more impressive discourse. The Assignat, which only represents the metals, he said, can never have the value of its model. He maintained that the Assignat would depreciate because of doubt as to the correspondence of the value of the Assignat with the value of the land, because of the time required to sell the lands, and because of the increased quantity of money. The State would

---

1 "Address to the National Assembly by the Administrators of the Department of Seine-Inférieure," P. V., Vol. XXIX, 402.
2 "Address of the City of Lille," ibid.
3 "Address of the Citizens and Business Men of Lyons," ibid.
4 Ibid., 426.
5 "Effects of the Assignats on the Price of Bread by a Friend of the People," ibid.; also Moniteur, Vol. V, pp. 742–743.

lose by accepting depreciated Assignats and disbursing metals. Finally, Talleyrand expressed skepticism as to the possibility of even measuring the eventual depreciation.[1]

4. OTHER DISCUSSIONS

Many pamphlets of the period were concerned with the financial situation, and in particular, with the Assignats. Some of this literature had an important influence on the trend of monetary legislation — Clavière's writings, for example — and some of it has some significance for monetary theory. Space permits only a summary account of a few of the contributions.

An interesting compilation of remedies was contained in the "Rapport des Plans et Projets Preséntées au Comité des Finances en 1789." The suppression of all taxes and the substitution of voluntary taxes; the introduction of a personal tax; the nationalization of the shoe manufacturing industry; the adoption of universal peace; the creation of a few hundred million livres of notes, each note to lose one per cent of its value at each change of hands; the reimbursement of the capital and interest of the public debt by the gradual reduction of interest payments — these were a few of the specifics offered.

Le Sage Citoyen suggested a single tax on the wealthy, as well as voluntary gifts to the Government.[2] One writer proposed the creation of a Caisse d'Amortissement which was to have the privilege of issuing two milliards of notes.[3] An opponent of the Clergy recommended that the Clergy be deprived of their lands — this before the confiscation took place — and be given a life annuity.[4] Estimating the value of all lands at fifty milliards and of other forms of wealth at twenty-five milliards, Dubernet proposed a forced loan of two per cent. Realizing the impossibility of lending in cash, he would allow the Provinces to issue circulating notes guaranteed by the subscribers.[5] Linguet favored a public bank

---

[1] "Opinion of the Bishop of Aûtun," P. V., Vol. XXXI, 421.
[2] Le Sage Citoyen, pp. 5–9, 16–19.
[3] Plan Proposé pour l'Extinction de la Dette Nationale, p. 2.
[4] L'État Libéré et l'Impôt Diminué, p. 12.
[5] Dubernet, Projet de Finances ou Moyen pour les Rétablir dans le Royaume, pp. 7–8, 14–17.

with the privilege of issuing notes, which were to be convertible into gold, but were not to be legal tender between individuals. Thus the Government would be enabled to fulfill its engagements without cost.[1] Finally, an anonymous pamphleteer proposed a loan secured by the receipts from the sales of lands; the subscribers were to obtain the privilege of attaching any particular parcel of land of equal value in case of a default on the part of the Government.[2]

Some of the better pamphleteers were surprisingly hostile toward the Assignat — surprising when one considers the stability of the Assignat during this period (1790–91).[3] Ex-Minister Calonne chided the Government for its failure to profit from the experiences of Law. Calonne believed that the investment of the Assignats in land was contingent upon an appreciable cheapening of the paper money: the depreciation of the Assignat would finally reach a point where investment in land would become highly profitable.[4]

The author of "La Fameuse Semaine" mercilessly attacked the Assignats: "Every man in France who owes nothing, and to whom everything is due, is ruined by paper money." The State, in his opinion, declares itself bankrupt when it pays with paper that may depreciate. The Government does not inspire great confidence.[5] The "Examen Impartial" presented two major criticisms of the Assignats, viz · (1) they might easily be counterfeited; (2) they would remain in circulation long after the land was sold.[6]

The Chamber of Commerce of Lyons entered a violent protest: "Effective numéraire is representative of all other values only because it has a value independent of this representation; paper money can never fulfill this function adequately. The Assignat, redeemable in a distant future, is not likely to retain our confidence, as is a paper money daily redeemable in silver."[7]

[1] M. Linguet, *Point de Banqueroute, Plus d'Emprunts.*
[2] *Parallèle entre les Effets de la Nouvelle Emissions d'Assignats et les Billets du Caisse Nationale.* Page references are omitted for small pamphlets.
[3] In Chapter VII, I refer again to some of this literature.
[4] C. A. Calonne, *De l'État de France*, pp. 86, 90.
[5] *La Fameuse Semaine ou le Peuple de Paris Sept Fois Heureux*, pp. 11–15.
[6] *Examen Impartial du Projet d'une Nouvelle Emission d'Assignats par un Négociant de Bordeaux*, pp. 4–5, 14.
[7] *Opinion de la Chambre du Commerce de Lyon*, pp. 10–12.

Another critic pointed out the inconsistency involved in creating a land paper, and then encouraging its circulation by issuing it as legal tender in small denominations.[1] Bergasse was the most indomitable opponent of all. Since the land was heavily mortgaged, and since the Government had a prior lien on the net revenues from the land for the maintenance of the "culte" and the care of the poor, he contended that the church lands constituted an inadequate security for the Assignats.[2] The Assignat, he thought, would result in the destruction of commerce because an uncertain element would be introduced into business.[3] Because Law's money had a more solid security — the revenue farms, and the monopoly of certain trading rights — Bergasse preferred it to the Assignat. He found counterfeiting to be a real evil that increased with time.[4] He ridiculed Montesquiou's suggestion that the value of the money be increased by reducing the quantity. The value of paper money depends on the difficulty of counterfeiting and the invariability of the security. Then followed an ingenious refutation of the quantity theory: when every individual possesses Assignats, there results a general effort to sustain the Assignat against a multiplicity of causes tending to cheapen it. But not so when there are few holders.[5] In both his *Réplique* and *Réponse* to Montesquiou, Bergasse made some damaging criticisms of the official estimates of the circulation, the debt, and the value of the security; Montesquiou's rejoinders were weak, indeed.[6]

Cerutti expressed himself strongly: "This money is an 'effet éventuel,' which relies on good fortune, which advances with public opinion, of which the redemption and convertibility are arbitrary and doubtful, and to which finally the sovereign wish com-

[1] *Courtes Réflexions sur l'Emission de Près de Deux Milliards d'Assignats-Monnaie,* pp. 2–3.
[2] *Protestation de M. Bergasse, contre les Assignats-Monnaie,* 2d ed., pp. 3–14.
[3] *Lettre de M. Bergasse aux Commettans au Sujet de sa Protestation contre les Assignats-Monnaie,* pp. 5–6.
[4] *Réponse de M. Bergasse au Mémoire de M. de Montesquiou sur les Assignats,* pp. 3–6.
[5] *Ibid.,* pp. 31–37.
[6] *Réplique de M. Bergasse à M. de Montesquiou;* A. P. Montesquiou, *Réponse à M. Bergasse, Maury,* etc.; A. P. Montesquiou, *Réponse à la Réplique de M. Bergasse.*

municates a passive existence, a changing value. . . . Picture the clergy crying to the buyers, 'Do not buy these lands; you will be anti-clerical and stupid; your acquisitions will not be legitimate, nor solid; scorn the Assignats as some false and criminal bills.' "[1] Montlosier and many others emphasized the inalienability of the Church's possessions.[2]

Writers frequently referred to the larger per capita circulation in England. An Englishman, however, warned the French not to generalize from English experience; business was thriving there, and the circulation of bank notes was not forced.[3] A member of the Society of 1789 prophesied that the construction of forty-three ships would cause a further depreciation of the Assignats because heavy foreign expenditures were involved.[4]

A citizen of Lille questioned the possibility of ever redeeming the Assignat. Confidence was lacking with an issue of but four hundred million livres; the people in the Provinces were still wary of paper money in any form. He declared further that the law which made the Assignat equivalent to gold and silver was vicious because it was retroactive.[5]

During the controversy of 1790 a number of pamphlets appeared in which the authors opposed the extension of the use of the Assignats to the payment of debt. One writer wished to confine their employment to the replacing of revenues hitherto received through taxation; and he feared that the increased issues made necessary by the reduction of debt would result in increased prices and, hence, in increased public expenditures.[6] Even Montesquiou saw the necessity of rigidly limiting the "dette exigible" if the confidence in the Assignats were to be maintained.[7] Condorcet made a masterly attack on the Assignats. He deemed a forced paper an unnecessary adjunct in the payment of debt through the sale of lands, so long as the nation was willing to

---

[1] M. Cerutti, *Idées Simples et Précises sur le Papier-Monnaie*, pp. 15–16, 20–21.
[2] Montlosier, *Observations sur les Assignats*, pp. 8–13.
[3] *Lettre d'un Anglais à un François. Qu'est-ce que le Papier-Monnaie*, pp. 9–11.
[4] *Assignats. Discours Prononcé le 3 Septembre 1790 à la Société de 1789*, pp. 9–11.
[5] *Opinion sur les Assignats et Proposition d'une autre Mode de Libération*, pp. 5–11.
[6] *Observations sur les Assignats par un Membre de la Société de 1789*, p. 8.
[7] M. de Montesquiou, *Mémoires sur les Assignats ou Supplément aux Mémoires sur les Finances du Royaume.*

accept free paper. Condorcet contended that forced paper depreciates because it is not the equivalent of the quantity of money of which it expresses the value; because it cannot be employed abroad; and that the privilege of being tenderable in payment for land would not guarantee either the time of the redemption, nor the maintenance of its value.[1] Lavoisier was not so uncompromising: he attributed any loss that the Assignat had suffered at this early stage to the disproportionate issues of large denominations, and to the unusual condition of the silver market.[2]

Probably the keenest of the early critics of the Assignat was Boislandry. In 1789, he supported a plan for the creation of interest-bearing notes, which were to circulate freely, and which were to be used for the reimbursement of the debt.[3] He found in the excessive issue the most important cause of the early depreciation; but he added that a money without weight or title is at the mercy of public opinion. Boislandry realized that a large proportion of the total monetary stock was normally in hoards; and he concluded, therefore, that depreciation was likely to begin before most people anticipated. Paper circulates twice as rapidly as gold and silver even before depreciation begins; but as depreciation advances, the rate of circulation increases even more rapidly.[4]

Boislandry, at this early stage, found twelve possible reasons for the lack of confidence in the Assignat:[5] (1) slow collection of taxes and insufficiency in case of war; (2) uncertainty as to the real situation of the finances; (3) denunciations and declarations against the executive power; (4) lack of consistency and order in the deliberations of the Assembly; (5) critical situation of the Colonies; (6) certain league of all powers of Europe against France; (7) successive and considerable creations of Assignats ahead of reimbursement; (8) fear of counterfeiting, lately increas-

---

[1] Condorcet, *Nouvelles Réflexions sur le Projet de Payer la Dette Exigible en Papier Forcé*, pp. 1–6.
[2] A. L. Lavoisier, *De l'État des Finances de France au Premier Janvier 1792*, pp. 64–66.
[3] L. Boislandry, *Observations sur les Dangers du Papier Monnaie*.
[4] L. Boislandry, *Considération sur le Discrédit des Assignats*, p. 62.
[5] *Ibid.*, pp. 7–12.

ing; (9) fear that the Clergy might regain their lands; (10) fear that the prolongation of the war might lead to issues beyond the value of the lands; (11) excessive issues of Billets de Confiance; (12) excess of small Assignats — much beyond the quantity of 24, 12 and 6 sou pieces in circulation before the Revolution.[1]

Several writers expressed disapproval of the Assignats by suggesting possible alternatives. Odet favored an interest-bearing note.[2] Lucadore proposed the formation of a patriotic organization to collect a quantity of gold and silver which would enable the Government to make the Assignat redeemable in gold: knowledge of the right to redeem would result in a general acceptance of the Assignats.[3] Caille favored the issuing of five milliards of notes by a national bank as a method of insuring immediate payments for public lands sold.[4] Maréchal proposed a somewhat similar plan, except that the notes were to be issued on the security of lands and houses.[5]

The eulogistic pamphlets were not as numerous as the critical ones. Clavière was the spokesman for the adherents to the Assignat system. Through his influence on Mirabeau, Clavière's name is to be closely linked with the history of the Assignats. Clavière found an urgent need for more money in the four main channels of circulation: the work of the field, the buying of the crude products of the soil, the preparation and distribution of these products, and finally their consumption. Moreover, he contended that for political expenditures, for hoards, and for the transfer of taxes and the purchase of luxuries, additional money was required.[6] Evidently the Assignat had not filled the gap, for in 1790 Clavière proposed the organization of a bank, which might create additional money, and he hoped the scarcity of money would be overcome.[7] Later he repeated his emphasis on the need for more money. He also recognized the desirability of balancing the

---

[1] Though this analysis takes us into 1792, somewhat beyond the scope of this chapter, this is an appropriate place to include all of Boislandry's contributions.
[2] *Extrait des Idées de M. Odet.*
[3] P. G. J. Lucadore, *Projet d'un Etablissement Patriotique.*
[4] D. Caille, *Précis du Plan d'un Etablissement.*
[5] M. R. Maréchal, *Le Triomphe des Assignats sur l'Argent.*
[6] E. Clavière, *Opinion d'un Créancier de l'État*, Vol. II, pp. 83–85.
[7] *Lettres de M. Clavière à M. Beaumez*, pp. 6–8.

budget, and was of the opinion that by issuing Assignats for the repayment of debt, the balancing would become possible.[1] Deslandres stressed the lack of a circulating medium although eighteen hundred million livres of Assignats were in circulation.[2]

5. BILLETS DE CONFIANCE

The early issues of Assignats were mostly in denominations of 1000, 500, and 200 livres. The decree of October 8, 1790 authorized the manufacture of only one hundred and forty million livres in denominations below one hundred livres, out of a total of eight hundred millions. A scarcity of small denominations was the result.[3] The central authorities occupied themselves with this problem, but, with mechanical limitations and an urgent need for revenue, the manufacture of large denominations almost exclusively was necessary. However, the local authorities and private individuals were contributing their Billets de Confiance — so-called because the issuers invited the confidence of the public. The Municipal Council of Paris in August, 1790 rejected a proposal for the creation of a local bank for the purpose of issuing small notes[4]; a second proposal came in April, 1791 when the écu (three and six livres) was at a premium of from 6 to 7 per cent, and the Assignat of fifty livres was at a premium of 3 per cent.[5] Lyons, Tours and Orleans had already introduced Billets de Confiance.[6] In May, Anson and Montesquiou, in behalf of the Committee of Finances, approved the creation of Billets de Confiance, in which they pretended to find a means of both preventing depreciation and of overcoming the lack of numéraire.[7] The National As-

---

[1] E. Clavière, *Lettres Écrites à M. Cerutti*, pp. 9–10, 100–101, 123–124; see also for a similar treatment, *Observations nécessaires sur Necker*, pp. 14–15, and *Lettres à M. Desmeuniers*, pp. 1–8.

[2] G. Deslandres, *Du Crédit Public en France, ou au Moyens de Réunion*, pp. 15–18.

[3] M. Schwinkowski gives a succinct history and a good bibliography of Notgeld, "Ueber Kriegs-und Notgeld in alter und neuer Zeit," *Jahrbücher für National-ökonomie*, Vol. CVIII, pp. 628–638.

[4] *Actes de Commune*, 1st series, Vol. VI, p. 668.

[5] *Ibid.*, 2d series, Vol. IV, pp. 306–307.

[6] "Opinion de M. Dallarde sur la Fabrication des Assignats de 5 Livres," P.V., Vol. LIV, p. 3.

[7] *Moniteur*, Vol. VIII, p. 442.

sembly thereupon announced that agencies issuing local notes could demand the support of the Government.[1]

The dangers of these issues were soon apparent. The Society of Monopolies criticised these organizations in September, 1791 for creating excessive quantities of money and usurping a sovereign power. The officials of Paris carried this protest to the National Assembly. They advised that body of the many dangers involved, and emphasized that there was a widespread misconception that the municipalities were responsible for and were supervising issues of private organizations.[2] The Section of Tuileries petitioned the Paris officials in October to scrutinize the accounts of the Patriotic Bank, the largest private organization issuing Billets de Confiance. Beugnot, soon after, estimated the Billets de Confiance in the Provinces at one hundred million livres, and in Paris at forty millions.[3]

Although Cambon ostensibly believed that the depreciation of the Assignat and of the exchanges was caused by the excessive issues of Billets de Confiance, he disclaimed (February, 1792) any right of the Government to interfere with their manufacture; for he was of the opinion that any citizen might ask for the confidence of his fellow-citizens.[4] The Patriotic Bank, the most notorious of these institutions, had a reserve in April, 1792, of but five millions in Assignats against seventeen and one-half millions of notes outstanding.[5] In spite of public pressure, the local Institutions continued their activities during 1792; the Government was forced to be conciliatory because of the retardation in the manufacture of small notes for which it had begun to make some provisions.[6]

Authors have written disparagingly of the Billets de Confiance. The early depreciation of the Assignats has often been attributed to their excessive issues. During a period of over eighteen months, however, the Government thus met the urgent need for small denominations; and in filling that need, they probably did much to

[1] "Report of May 17 by M. Montesquiou," P. V., Vol. LV, 653, pp. 11–12.
[2] Actes de Commune, 2d series, Vol. VI, pp. 265–267; Vol. VII, pp. 442–443.
[3] Moniteur, Vol. X, pp. 702–703.
[4] Ibid., Vol. XI, pp. 475–476.
[5] Ibid., Vol. XII, p. 114.
[6] Ibid., Vol. XIV, p. 33. A. Colson, "Tableaux des Billets de Confiance Emis dans les 83 Departements," Revue Numismatique, 1852, pp. 349–354.

prevent the Assignat from depreciating further, for a relative excess of large denominations would have resulted in a diminution of confidence in the Assignat. An investigation undertaken by the Government, the results of which have recently been reprinted, revealed but three instances of abuse in forty departments. The issues were moderate and covered by Assignats in all other cases; the total issues were considerably less than one hundred million livres.[1]

Rabaut introduced a motion for the manufacture of five livre notes in April, 1791. The lowest denomination in circulation at the time was the fifty livre note.[2] Beaumez opposed the suggestion mainly on the grounds of the disastrous effects of small notes on the workers; for the poor held small denominations almost exclusively. Dallard demonstrated that the creation of small Assignats was incompatible with the principle of retirement through land purchases.[3] The law of May 6 (enacted after a long debate) authorized the issue of one hundred million livres of five livre notes.[4]

In December, 1791, when the Assignats of smaller denominations were at a relatively high value, and the public was losing confidence in the Billet de Confiance, the cry for smaller denominations of Assignats was raised.[5] The Assembly approved an issue of 300 million livres of notes of 50, 25, 15, and 10 sous, on December 23.[6] By August, 31 millions of 10 sous notes and 42 millions·of 15 sous notes had been distributed.[7] The Government had overcome all deficiencies in small denominations before the end of 1792.

6. NUMÉRAIRE

The market for gold and silver during the early years of the Revolution was in an abnormal state: a large proportion of the numéraire had seemingly disappeared. The demand for the met-

[1] C. Block, *La Vérification des Caisses Patriotiques, Commission de Recherche,* 1910, pp. 149–97.
[2] "Motion de Rabaut," P. V., Vol. LIII, 632.
[3] "Opinion de M. Dallarde," P. V., Vol. LIV, 635.
[4] *Moniteur,* Vol. VIII, pp. 327–328.
[5] Arch. Parl., Vol. XXXVI, p. 54.
[6] *Moniteur,* Vol. X, pp. 702–703.
[7] Arch. Parl., Vol. XLVIII, p. 683.

als, especially for public uses, was unusually great with the result that the premium on gold and silver tended to increase. In 1792 Raboul recommended the demonetization of gold and silver on grounds of their instability.[1]

Several contemporaries were aware that the greater premium on the exchanges than on gold and silver made the exportation of gold and silver profitable.[2] But more than any other single factor, hoardings probably accounted for the scarcity.[3] The recoinage of 1785 made the importation of gold profitable and the importation of silver unprofitable. The effect on the monetary supplies was adverse because gold was more acceptable for hoards on account of its greater value in proportion to its bulk. Solignac recognized this fact, and, therefore, recommended a return to the former ratio of 14.5 to 1.[4] Moreover, the Government required large supplies of gold and silver for military purposes, for the use of certain institutions, and also for coinage.[5] The depreciated exchanges made the purchases abroad — the most fruitful source of supply — a costly procedure. Other explanations of the scarcity of the precious metals were made: Custine, for example, explained the scarcity by the heavy exportations during the last war[6]; Brissot attributed it to the Caisse d'Escompte's suspension of payments.[7]

[1] Arch. Parl., Vol. XLV, pp. 88–89.
[2] Cussy demonstrated in 1791 that it required 887 livres in exchange, 768 livres in gold, and 729 livres in silver to remit approximately 30 £ sterling to England. "Opinion Prononcé par M. Cussy," P. V., Vol. LIV.
[3] See Article by A. M. in Moniteur, Vol. VIII, p. 250.
[4] Solignac, Essai sur la Proportion, pp. 1–9; Mirabeau attacked this suggestion as a repudiation of debt. Mirabeau, Relativement à l'Essai de Solignac.
[5] The Government coined 90.9 million livres of gold and silver from January 1, 1791 to September, 1792. Arch. Parl., Vol. LIX, p. 201. The expenditure for military wages was over 100 millions in 1791, a considerable portion of which had to be met in numéralre, P. V., Vol. LXIX, "Report of September 9, 1791."
[6] Réflexions du Comte de Custine sur la Proposition du Premier Ministre des Finances, pp. 14–16.
[7] J. P. Brissot, Discours sur la Rareté du Numéruire, pp. 4–11.

CHAPTER II

TAXATION VERSUS ASSIGNATS

1. INTRODUCTION

THE deplorable condition of the finances brought about the convocation of the Estates General. Necker announced a deficit of fifty-six million livres when it convened. Stourm states that the real deficit was three times as large, and the testimony presented supports his contention.[1] The system of taxation was especially iniquitous because it exploited the lower classes; and uneconomical because the Government did not receive all that was exacted from the taxpayer on account of a vicious system of collection.

In the early months of the Revolution, some fruitless attempts were made to escape from the financial difficulties. Because Necker thought increased taxation inexpedient, he presented, in August, 1789, a plan for a loan to yield 5 per cent.[2] Within one month, Necker was forced to admit the failure of the loan. The inexperienced Assembly had erred in reducing the interest to 4½ per cent. The Government then concentrated its attention upon the Patriotic Contribution, a forced loan.[3] In October, 1789, the Finance Minister suggested possible economies of 53 million livres.[4] A second loan of 80 million livres was the next proposal.[5] Although subscribers to the loan might subscribe in rentes, which were quoted at approximately one-half of their par value, the public did not rally to this loan. Every measure had failed.

That the Revolution was financed by Assignats, requisitions, exploitation, and not by taxation, is a belief almost universally held. Most writers either fail to consider taxation as a source of

[1] R. Stourm, Les Finances de l'Ancien Régime et de la Révolution, Vol. II, pp. 273-274.
[2] Choix de Rapports, Vol. I, pp. 417, 425.
[3] P. V., Vol. II, pp. 215-218.
[4] Ibid., p. 215.
[5] Choix de Rapports, Vol. I, p. 426.

revenue, or concern themselves merely with the failure to collect taxes. My purpose in writing this chapter is not to go over the ground already traversed by Gomel, Levasseur, Stourm, and Marion. They have dealt with the slow collection of taxes, with the suicidal abandonment of the more lucrative taxes, and with the weaknesses of the Government. Some of their conclusions are founded on most painstaking researches. But other sorts of inquiries are needed. Whenever possible, therefore, I have compiled the actual receipts from taxation and from other sources. Some of the results are significant. I have also attempted to collect some reliable information on the debt (in particular on the "dette exigible"), and on the amount of debt actually reimbursed. For the history of the Assignats, the debt question is of paramount importance, both because of its relation to the growth of the "Assignat idea," and because of the employment of large amounts of Assignats for the payment of debt. I have estimated also the monthly deficits. On no subject pertaining to Revolutionary Finance, has there been more confusion of thought, or more unsatisfactory results. The study of monthly deficits has enabled me to construct monthly figures for emissions. Reliance must otherwise have been placed exclusively on the random financial reports.

I have also checked the monthly reports of deficits with the emissions of Assignats as officially announced. For the period of the Reign of Terror an inconsistency — an overstatement of the emissions by approximately one billion livres — became evident. This failure to tally made a close scrutiny of the statistics of emissions and deficits necessary.

2. DEBT PAYMENTS

The National Assembly agreed to the principle of reimbursing the "dette non-constituée" by the employment of Assignats.[1] The "dette non-constituée" consisted at the time (September, 1790) of a heterogeneous mass of non-feudal dues; of payments due on account of suspended reimbursements of debts; of debts

[1] P. V., Vol. XXXII, "Décret, Septembre 29, 1790."

due to office holders whose rights had been suppressed; of repayments that were due for bonds furnished by the farmers of taxes; of the arrears of departments of the Government; and of debts of the royal family.[1] A campaign waged by Cambon,[2] Clavière, and Brissot[3] against the reduction of the debt, was not actually successful until April, 1792, when it was agreed to limit payments for debt to six million livres monthly.[4]

The financial authorities generally referred to three categories of debt; namely, "dette perpetuelle, dette viagère, and dette exigible." The "dette perpetuelle" is analogous to the permanent annuity of today. The "dette viagère" was composed, probably exclusively, of life annuities. The supporters of the law of September 29, 1790, requiring the reimbursement of debt by the creation of Assignats, concerned themselves primarily with the "dette exigible," the conglomeration of debts described above as the "dette non-constituée." Term debts, a species of debt of recent origin, were sometimes classified as "dette exigible." What we might today designate as floating debt composed the major part of the "dette exigible." A large proportion of it was created by the suppression of the financial and administrative practices of the Ancient Régime. A small proportion was contracted as far back as the seventeenth century.

The attempt to define and determine the "dette exigible" caused much trouble. Estimates varied considerably. Necker calculated the "dette exigible" as low as 300 million livres in 1790[5]; Montesquiou estimated it as high as 2300 million livres in 1791.[6] Lavoisier, the chemist, discussed the subject superbly. He appreciated the difficulties of classification and the relativity of the term "exigible." Lavoisier graded the "dette exigible" in order of maturities and demonstrated forcibly that the debt, payable on demand, was considerably less than had been commonly sup-

---

[1] Arch. Parl., Vol. XXXV, pp. 681–690.
[2] *Moniteur*, Vol. XII, pp. 48–49.
[3] *Discours sur la Nécessité de Suspendre le Paiement des Liquidations*, Novembre 24, 1791.
[4] *Moniteur*, Vol. XII, pp. 399–401.
[5] "Lettre de M. Necker," P. V., Vol. XXX.
[6] "Mémoire de M. Montesquiou," P. V., Vol. LXIX, p. 69.

posed. He subdivided the debt commonly classified as "exigible" into (1) paper payable to bearer; (2) debt payable after a definite period; (3) obligations due on designated days; (4) debts of an indefinite maturity; and (5) debts still to be liquidated.[1] Lavoisier did not consider the last two as payable on demand. He also excluded 353 million livres of term debts, payable in the course of twenty-eight years. The debt payable on demand (exigible) was estimated at 1100 million livres.[2]

Young, writing in 1790, estimated the total debt at 5587 million livres, 1879 million livres of which were designated "dette exigible."[3] Calonne estimated the total at 4760 million livres and the "dette exigible" at 2208 millions.[4] Both Young and Calonne had to be satisfied with inadequate sources of information because the liquidation of the newly acquired Revolutionary debt had not begun.

Montesquiou, in August, 1790, found the "dette exigible" to be 1900 million livres. A few months later, although he included an item of 600 million livres for term debts, he reduced the total of "dette exigible" to 1469 million livres.[5] At successive intervals of a few months, Montesquiou then obtained estimates of 1287 and 2300 million livres.[6] The extreme variations in his estimates were due in some part to his failure to exclude term debts consistently. But the state of knowledge of the magnitude of the debt was in a continuous state of flux because of the liquidations that were occurring. His estimates were of an official nature, it is to be remembered.

Cambon estimated the "dette exigible" at 1548 million livres in April, 1792.[7] If an allowance is made for the 500 million livres that had been paid off by April, 1792, it will be evident that in this computation he agreed with Montesquiou's latest estimate closely Cambon estimated in April, 1792, that the annual charge

---

[1] Lavoisier, *De l'État de France*, pp. 24–25.
[2] *Ibid.*, pp. 26–33.
[3] A. Young, *op. cit.*, Vol. I, p. 578.
[4] C. A. Calonne, *De l'État de France*.
[5] "Rapport de Octobre 29, 1790," P. V., Vol. XXXV, pp. 10–13.
[6] "Rapport Février 6, 1791," P. V., Vol. XLV, Table, p. 22; and Arch. Parl., Vol. XXXIV, p. 582.
[7] *Moniteur*, Vol. XII, p. 48.

for the "dette perpetuelle et viagère" was 261 million livres.[1] In August, Cambon estimated these same annual charges at 89.9 million livres; he put the "dette exigible" at 25.7 millions, and the "dette à terme" at 416 million livres — a unique classification.[2] To follow such kaleidoscopic changes in debt classification is not easy. It now becomes necessary to add together the "dette à terme," the "dette exigible" repaid since April, and the "dette exigible" as given, to attain Cambon's earlier estimates of the "dette exigible." Perhaps a recent decision to limit reimbursements rigidly, explains Cambon's attempt to distinguish term debts from the "dette exigible." Because the more permanent annual charges were thus materially reduced, it is also possible (but not probable) that Cambon now for the first time excluded the payments on the "dette à terme" from the annual charges.

The lack of agreement in the various reports is to be attributed largely to the failure to agree on classifications; and in less degree, to the securing of more reliable information by later estimators. Montesquiou and Cambon exaggerated the debt payable on demand by including term and other debts not subject to payment for many years. Although the Government had obligated itself to pay off all the "dette exigible," and although the debt payable on demand might technically have included term debts, floating debts which could not be liquidated for years, and other such debts, nevertheless, for practical purposes, the debt payable within one or two years should have received special consideration. The procedure of Lavoisier is especially commendable here.

My estimate of the amount of debt is as follows (1791–92):

	Millions of livres
"Dette perpetuelle"	1,200
"Dette viagère"	1,000
"Dette exigible" (payable on demand)	1,200
"Exigible" after January 1, 1793	600
	4,000

The Government subscribed to a difficult undertaking when it agreed to reduce its indebtedness by from one to two milliard livres. The Treasury had made noteworthy progress when the

[1] *Moniteur*, Vol. XII, pp. 177–180.
[2] *Ibid.*, Vol. XVII, pp. 407–408, 780–782.

outbreak of the war in 1792 called a virtual halt to the proceedings. The reduction of the debt by one milliard livres within a period of thirty months had been an achievement. (This estimate includes anticipations reduced and arrears on rentes paid — see the discussion below.) The amount involved was the equivalent of two years of ordinary expenditures. This rapid payment of the debt should not be overlooked in any study of Revolutionary finances. The influence of this courageous attempt to meet national obligations cannot have failed to create some degree of confidence in the Revolutionary paper money. The large expenditures for this purpose exhausted a large proportion of the Assignats issued by the Government in 1791 and 1792.

One may contend with some justice that the issuing of paper money for the repayment of debt is not sound finance. However, the notion that issues were to be restricted to the values of the domains was held in these early years; and that a large proportion of these limited issues was devoted to the repayment of debt, was probably advantageous. Had these Assignats been used to meet the ordinary needs of the Government, the effect on prices would have been much more marked. The rentiers hoarded some of the money received in payment of public debt. Probably the failure of prices to advance more rapidly in the early years is in part attributable to the extensive employment of Assignats for this purpose.

The reimbursements (cumulative) of debt at various times, according to official reports, were as follows: (In millions of livres.)

1791	July 1	346.4
	August 1	396.8
	December 1	472
1792	April 1	579.2
1794	March 21	1017

The last figure is Cambon's. Were the payments for debt from April 1, 1792 to March, 1794 as large as is here indicated? According to Cambon's statement, 45 millions of livres of Assignats were utilized for the repayment of debt, from April 1 to May 15, 1792. For the remainder of the period under consideration, 5 million livres monthly, the legal maximum, would be a liberal allowance;

for monthly debt payments after May, 1792 were but 6 million livres.[1] The total up to March, 1794 would scarcely come to 700 million livres. I can explain the discrepancy of approximately 300 million livres only by assuming that Cambon included the reductions of the anticipations of the pre-Revolutionary period, and the arrears on rentes paid (omitted in the previous estimate). Necker reported that the anticipations had fallen 85 million livres by May, 1790.[2] (Finance ministers in the pre-Revolutionary days frequently increased the national debt by borrowing on the security of future revenues. Such debts were referred to as anticipations.) Montesquiou asserted that the amount of anticipations reduced by April, 1790 was 147 million livres, and by December, 1790, 210 million livres. He estimated that 114 million livres of Assignats had been employed in 1789–91 to reduce the arrears of interest payments on rentes. The inclusion of these items by Cambon in the total of the debt repaid, is not consistent with the practices of his predecessors. However, there is much to be said for the inclusion of these arrears in the debt payable on demand.

3. Deficits

Although Marion is aware that a number of the important payments were diverted to the Caisse de l'Extraordinaire — an institution attentive to extraordinary receipts and expenditures — he often quotes as the deficit the difference between the ordinary receipts and expenditures. Gomel also slips, for he almost invariably refers to the ordinary deficits and ignores most of the disbursements of the Caisse de l'Extraordinaire.[3] The payments made in 1791 for the "culte," for the arrears of rentes, and for the expenses of 1789 and 1790 — disbursements covered by the As-

---

[1] Monthly deficits in 1793 included the following payments for "dette exigible" (Arch. Parl.):

	Millions of livres		Millions of livres
January	(2.9)	May	4.9
February		June	4.-
March	7.7	July	4.2
April	7.6	August	1.6

[2] " Lettre de M. Necker," P. V., Vol. XXX.

[3] C. Gomel, *Histoire Financière de la Législative et de la Convention*, Vol. I, Introd., p. vi.

signats — should be considered in arriving at an estimate of deficits. The payments for debt purposes contributed much to the exhaustion of the Caisse de l'Extraordinaire and one can hardly deny that such expenditures should be included in the monthly deficits. Consider the nature of some of the payments. One of the results of the Revolution had been a suppression of certain privileges that possessed a monetary value. The Government now had to face the onerous task of repaying the capital value of these sinecures. Moreover, since the system of farming of the revenues had been renounced, the Government was now forced to return the monetary security furnished by the farmers-general. This earmarked money had long been squandered. Also, the public authorities had promised compensation for the non-feudal dues suppressed. Even if an amelioration of conditions was expected through the lighter taxation which the lower interest charges would make possible, the part of the deficit due to debt payments was nevertheless genuine.

Gomel puts the deficits of the last three months of 1794 at 41, 32, and 36 million livres. These deficits include only those computed from expected monthly receipts and expenditures (ordinary) of 48 million livres, together with a category of expenses labelled "expenses particulières de 1791." Some deficits, as we have seen, are not included in Gomel's figures. Only a small proportion of the disbursements of the Caisse de l'Extraordinaire are taken into account. The Caisse de l'Extraordinaire was the medium through which the Government received extraordinary receipts (Assignats in particular), and disbursed extraordinary payments. However, the Treasury continued to make some of the extraordinary payments, and gradually displaced the Caisse de l'Extraordinaire in 1792.

For the last three months of 1792 and the first three months of 1793, Gomel puts the deficits at 116, 83, 165, 137, 198, and 233 millions.[1] This series of deficits has little value either for comparison with the earlier series, or on its own account. Debt payments had virtually ceased; the exclusion of payments for debt from "deficit" figures does little to invalidate this later series, and much to in-

[1] C. Gomel, *op. cit.*, p. xvi.

validate the series of 1791. Also, in the later period, the deficits of the nation had become largely the deficits of the Treasury. The suppression of the Caisse de l'Extraordinaire in January, 1793 completed that change. That suppression, in itself, makes the series just quoted lack homogeneity, for with the displacement of the Caisse, virtually all deficits were included. The Treasury then made all disbursements.

Marion's treatment of this particular subject is not free from confusion.[1] He first notes that a decree of March 12, 1790 burdened the Caisse de l'Extraordinaire with the responsibility for 60 million livres of new payments. He then refers to the act of April 17 which directed the Caisse de l'Extraordinaire to expend approximately 228 million livres for the "culte," for the salaries of the Clergy, for the arrears before 1791, and for the substitution of funds for any deficits in the expected monthly receipts of 48 million livres. He adds that the deficit for April was 55 million livres; for May, 28.7 million livres; for June, 24.6 million livres; for July, 29.4 million livres; for August, 30.5 or 43.0 million livres. Finally, he refers to a number of extraordinary expenses, 76.6 millions in all, authorized by the decree of February 18, 1791. What then are these enumerated deficits? Clearly, they are not the deficits of ordinary revenues, for the deficit given for April is 55 million livres, while the budget called for ordinary revenues and expenditures of but 48 million livres.[2] On the other hand these figures cannot include the reimbursements for "dette exigible" of which Marion says not a word here. For the repayment of "dette exigible," in itself, about 60 million livres monthly were expended. It appears that Marion collected a heterogeneous number of monthly deficits which include varying proportions of the actual deficits. The estimate presented for April is probably one for the total deficit in Marion's opinion — it is obvious that this reported deficit for April is too large for the ordinary deficit, and too small to include debt and other extraordinary deficit payments. The deficits estimated by Marion from May to July inclusive are the

[1] M. Marion, *Histoire Financière*, Vol. II, pp. 266–267.
[2] The deficit of ordinary receipts for April was 24.3 million livres. Arch. Parl., Vol. XXVI, p. 312.

differences between the actual ordinary receipts and the 48 million livres of monthly ordinary receipts that were expected. The alternative estimate for August includes both the ordinary deficit and the extraordinary deficits which were designated "expenses particulières de 1791." Marion presents these deficits as the actual deficits. Perhaps he intended to include ordinary and extraordinary deficits with the exception of the payments authorized by the act of February 18, 1791 (mentioned by him after the enumeration of the deficits). The payments for debt, however, are neglected.[1]

A study of the deficits from October, 1790 to January, 1792 is beset with many perplexities. Until October 1, 1790, the receipts of the Treasury from the Caisse d'Escompte give no cause for confusion, for up to that date, the Caisse d'Escompte supplied the Treasury with the extraordinary funds. The flow of funds changed in October; the Treasury now began to take cash from the Caisse de l'Extraordinaire, borrowing from the Caisse d'Escompte having ceased. The estimated expenditures and receipts for the period October–December, 1790 (Lebrun's estimate for the Committee of Finances, October 13, 1790) as well as the actual deficits follow.[2]

MILLIONS OF LIVRES

	Receipts	Expenditures	Expected Deficits	Actual Deficits
October	42.3	82.3	40.0	41.0
November	23.0	75.4	52.4	48.0
December	21.0	70.0	49.0	45.0

The forecast was satisfactorily close.

The year 1791 was one of very heavy payments for debt incurred in 1789 and 1790, and for other extraordinary purposes. I have compiled the deficits for 1791 in tabular form with an accompanying table of detailed notes. The details for the year 1791 illustrate the difficulties inherent in the inquiry.[3] In a sim-

---

[1] In March, 1791, Lebrun announced that the payments for which the Caisse de l'Extraordinaire was to be responsible were to be made by the Treasury, but the Treasury was not to mention these transactions in its accounts. Such procedure probably accounts for some of the confusion. Arch. Parl., Vol. XXIV, p. 43.

[2] Arch. Parl., Vol. XIX, pp. 585–588.

[3] Note at end of chapter.

ilar way I have compiled figures for the deficits through 1795, and have compared the deficits, which are in truth emission figures, with the emission figures given by the random financial reports. The two series move harmoniously until August, 1793. A

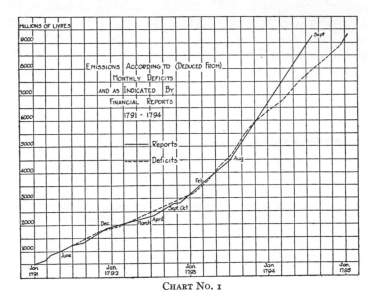

CHART No. 1

discrepancy of upwards of one milliard livres emerges in the next thirteen months. Had the emissions of the Government consciously been exaggerated? Had the deficits been understated? Or is there some other explanation?

Frécine, on June 7, 1793, recommended legislation for improving the mechanical features of the Assignats. A bill was soon approved; the notes in circulation were to be withdrawn and burnt; and improved notes were to be manufactured and substituted. The fact that the new notes were to be "exchanged and not emitted," calls for special comment.[1] A manufacture of 2 milliards of notes, ordered on September 28, 1793, had as one of its avowed purposes the replacement of old notes. The Treasury was not permitted to put these notes into circulation without an

[1] Arch. Parl., Vol. LXVI, pp. 137–139.

act of the Convention.[1] Notes might be exchanged without an act of the legislature; but an exchange was not considered an emission. Now let us turn to some other evidence.

A report of May, 1794 divided the notes that had been destroyed into two classes: first, notes received from the proceeds of sales of domains; second, notes exchanged. The amounts of these two classes of notes burnt were given as 1153 million livres and 879 million livres respectively.[2] A year later, Vernier referred to the second class again in reporting that 989 million livres of "exchanged and mutilated" notes had been destroyed.[3] The possibility is at once suggested that, perhaps, the emission of notes had been exaggerated, and that this exaggeration had been caused by including, as emitted notes, notes that had been issued for exchange purposes. Several considerations count against this hypothesis. In the first place, exchanged notes had not previously been considered as emitted notes. Several issues for exchange purposes — largely to get more convenient denominations into circulation — had been decreed before September, 1793, and these had never been considered as notes emitted. Nor were the notes that were withdrawn from circulation for exchange purposes and burnt, included in the totals of notes burnt. In the second place, the inclusion of these notes as notes emitted was not in accordance with the laws of June 7 and September 28. We shall return to this hypothesis later, however.

Cambon announced officially in March, 1794, that the burnings of Assignats had been erroneously reported.[4] The reported burnings, according to Cambon, by that time lacked 791 million livres of equalling the actual burnings. (Compare this estimate with the estimate of 879 millions of exchanged notes burnt up to May, 1794.) The report in the Moniteur was brief and offered no explanation. Gomel accepts Cambon's statement.[5] The Journal des Débats et Décrets gave a more complete version of Cambon's

---

[1] Arch. Parl., Vol. LXXV, pp. 299-300.
[2] J. Déb et Déc., Vol. LIX, pp. 378-379. (Journal des Débats et Décrets, an important journal of the period which gave condensed versions of the Parliamentary debates.)
[3] Moniteur, Vol. XIX, p. 600.
[4] Ibid.
[5] C. Gomel, op. cit., Vol. II, p. 97.

announcement; and, in that version, Cambon says, "cette erreur s'est propagée depuis l'Assemblée Constituante."[1] (The Assemblée Constituante was in session from 1789 to the fall of 1791.) The important law authorizing the exchange of notes became effective in September, 1793. That is not conclusive evidence that the forgotten quantum of incinerated notes was not the notes exchanged under the provisions of the laws of June and September, 1793. To one familiar with Cambon's tactics, the phrase quoted above might be taken as proof that the item of 791 million livres was the total of notes exchanged. My provisional conclusion is that Cambon was aware that 791 million livres had been exchanged against notes in circulation under the provisions of the acts of June 7, 1793, and of September 28, 1793. It is possible, also, that some of the notes exchanged under the earlier decrees in order to get more convenient denominations were included in the 791 million livres. Cambon was aware, moreover, that it was inconsistent with previous practice to consider notes withdrawn from circulation for exchange purposes as notes burnt. Besides, it was deceitful, if, as he pretended, the error was of long standing; because the notes emitted to replace notes withdrawn from circulation for exchange purposes before 1793 had not been counted as notes emitted. A subtraction of the burnings from the emissions, therefore, would not give the correct quantity in circulation.

The difficulty has not yet been solved, for between August, 1793 and September, 1794 the reported emissions outstripped the deficits. Probably the acts of May and September, 1793 are of significance here. Is not the excess of emissions to be attributed to the classification of notes issued for exchange purposes as notes emitted? Including these notes with notes emitted was, of course, contrary to the law and a complete reversal of policy: the notes issued in exchange for the notes of larger denominations had not, before September, 1793, been included as notes emitted. Cambon either included with the notes burnt the notes exchanged before 1793 or gave a misleading notion of what this doubtful item was. (For he said that the error was first committed in 1791.) Since the notes issued for exchange purposes in 1793 and 1794 were

[1] *J. Déb. et Déc.*, Vol. LVII, p. 148.

included as notes emitted, Cambon was justified in subtracting notes withdrawn for exchange purposes in 1793 and 1794. So far as the figures for emissions included notes emitted for exchange purposes, a series based on emissions exaggerates the deficits.

One cannot be sure that the excess of emissions over deficits was due to the inclusion of notes issued for exchange purposes in the total of notes emitted. But since the discrepancies between notes emitted and deficits first emerged in a period in which a quantity of notes approximately equal to the above discrepancy was emitted for exchange purposes, it is not unreasonable to take the above view. If the additional notes emitted for exchange purposes were included in notes emitted, and the notes withdrawn for similar purposes were included in the notes burnt, then the notes in circulation were correctly given. But one might infer from Cambon's remark that a proportion—probably not large—of the "exchanged" notes included as notes burnt had not been previously included as notes emitted.

4. TAXATION

On June 17, 1789, a singular decree, declaring all taxes illegal, but consenting to them provisionally, was passed by the National Assembly. A few months later, amidst the general disorder of the day of August 4, the dime was suppressed. Thus a violent agitation against taxation was begun, which most of the leaders were later to regret. The issuing of the Assignat in December, 1789 made it possible to dispense with taxation to a large extent.

Montesquiou, on February 26, 1790, called upon the nation to end the régime initiated by the decree of June 17.[1] March witnessed the suppression of the Gabelle and some proposals for substitute taxes.[2] Hope was expressed that improved administration might hasten the collection of taxes.[3] Dupont, the Physiocrat, found it necessary to warn the Assembly of its prejudice against indirect taxes: he invoked the law of necessity as a reason for saving some of the indirect taxes.[4] Necker was held responsible

[1] "Rapport du Comité de Finances," Feb. 26, 1790, P. V., Vol. XIV, pp. 4–5.
[2] Ibid., March 4, 1790, P. V., Vol. XIV.
[3] Ibid.
[4] P. V., Vol. XXXV, 488, pp. 4–5.

for the increasing arrears of taxes.[1] The Contribution Foncière, the corner stone of the new system of taxation, was not voted until November 20–3, 1790.[2]

The reaction against taxation persisted through 1791. The reports of February 10 sealed the fate of the unpopular "droits à l'entrée." The leaders of the Assembly presented a strong theoretical case against the "Aides"; and Dupont and five others endorsed a report which declared indirect taxation and liberty incompatible.[3] The assessments for the "Contributions Mobilière et Foncière" for 1791 were not determined until March, 1791.[4] The Government received 140,000 livres from these taxes in September, and the munificent total of 13 million livres for all taxes for the month of August.[5] (This compared with a normal collection of 40 or 50 millions monthly.)

The administrative improvement, though daily promised, seemed as far off as ever early in 1792. Gomel rightly condemns a system of taxation that burdened the local governments with the responsibilities of collection and yet did not give them any interest in efficient collection. Cambon had a distressing tale to tell the French people in May, 1792.[6] The new taxes, introduced to supplant the suppressed taxes of 1790, which, it had been expected, would yield 50 million livres, yielded but 300,000 livres up to April 1, 1792. The Contributions Foncière and Mobilière of 1791 had yielded 40 million livres up to January 1, 1792, and 60 million livres by April 1, 1792, as against expected receipts of 300 millions. Clavière reported in May, 1792 that only 21,000 of the 40,000 municipalities had completed their rolls for the Contributions Foncière and Mobilière for 1791.[7] Five thousand municipalities had not completed their rolls in October, 1792 — and these were due in 1791.[8]

[1] P. V., Vol. XXXV, 495, pp. 7–8.
[2] Ibid., Vol. XXXVII, Déc. et Instructions, p. 2.
[3] "Report on the Taxes commonly called Entry taxes," P. V., Vol. XLVI.
[4] "Third Report made in the name of the Committee of Public Contributions," P. V., Vol. XLIX.
[5] Moniteur, Vol. IX, p. 718.
[6] Arch. Parl., Vol. XLIII, pp. 673–674.
[7] Ibid., Vol. XLIII, p. 220.
[8] Ibid., Vol. LII, p. 346.

Some improvement was evident early in 1792, in spite of these unfavorable signs; but the bettering of conditions was more noticeable in the second half of 1792.[1] One hundred and twenty million livres of the Contributions Foncière and Mobilière were in the coffers of the Treasury by October 1, and 154 million livres by November 1, 1792.[2] But 6 million livres of the assessment of 15 millions of the Patente tax for 1791, had been received by November. In addition, an appreciable proportion of the custom and stamp duties had been collected.[3]

Clavière presented an optimistic report of the proceeds expected from the public contributions for the year 1793.[4] He anticipated from a number of payments due since 1790 and previous years, together with the proceeds from the sale of salt and tobacco in 1793, receipts of 176 millions. Clavière estimated yields of 476 million livres from the direct taxes for 1791 and 1792, and from the Patente tax for 1793. The indirect taxes of 1793 were expected to yield 143 million livres. In 1793, the aforementioned revenues, as well as the yield of the "Poste," lotteries and a few miscellaneous revenues, would enrich the Treasury, in Clavière's opinion, by 850 million livres.

He was much too sanguine. Vernier, soon after, made a report for the Committee of Finances (March 21, 1793), in which he attributed the poor collection of taxes to ignorance — and to the lack of zeal on the part of municipalities.[5] The Contribution Foncière for 1793 was voted on August 1, 1793.[6] The unsatisfactory returns from taxation, the increased depreciation of the Assignat, and the extension of hostilities with Holland, Spain, and England, forced the authorities to adopt more radical measures. A member of the Jacobin Society had proposed a contribution on incomes in February, 1793.[7] Cambon submitted a plan in May

---

[1] Arch. Parl., Vol. LIII, p. 419.
[2] A report of November 15, 1792 gave 180 million livres as recovered up to October 1, but only 146 millions received. *Moniteur*, Vol. XIV, p. 482.
[3] *Ibid.*
[4] *Ibid.*, Vol. XV, p. 417.
[5] Arch. Parl., Vol. LX, pp. 371–383.
[6] *Ibid.*, Vol. LXX, pp. 176, *et seq.*
[7] *La Société des Jacobins*, Collection de Documents Relatifs à l'Histoire de Paris, Vol. V, pp. 42–43.

After the Terror the rate of depreciation increased rapidly. The emphasis was now shifted from the collection of taxes to the problem of collecting them in a stable currency or "au cours."[1] Many measures were broached; their discussion will be of greater significance in the chapters on depreciation. The verbose debates were of little practical importance. Confidence in the Assignat might increase with the suggestion of new plans; but confidence was destroyed during the sessions of the Convention by the ineptitude of the Convention, and during the Directorate rule by the lack of harmony between the Directorate and the Legislature, or between the Conventionalists and Constitutionalists in the Legislature, or, finally, between the two chambers.

The only plan of practical significance was one for a forced loan of 600 millions suggested in November, 1795. The Government concentrated its efforts on this futile measure.[2] Dupont, in a masterly discourse, indicated some reasons for its failure. Adversely affected by the disorganization accompanying the Revolution, the net income of the country had fallen from 1500 million livres in 1788 to 800 million livres in 1795. Nor was much capital free. It was unavailable because of Cambon's vigorous measures, the sales of land, and the civil wars. Dupont demonstrated that another obstacle was the dearth of circulating media. The Government, nevertheless, proposed to raise 600 million livres within 45 days from the "upper fourth."[3] In the police reports of Paris Schmidt describes many arbitrary assessments.[4]

The Government, however, did not admit failure. Most of the numerous financial bills proposed during the disastrous month of Vêntose 4 (February–March, 1796) included some suggestions for the enforcement of the collection of the forced loan. The Council of 500 resolved in February, 1797 to give the delinquent subscribers the privilege of paying nineteen twentieths in "inscriptions,

[1] When a paper money depreciates rapidly, the Government finds it difficult to increase tax assessments rapidly enough to overcome the losses due to the receipt of taxes in a depreciating currency. Hence comes the proposal to accept the paper money "au cours," i.e., at its depreciated, not nominal value.

[2] *Réaction Thermidorienne*, Documents Relatifs à l'Histoire de Paris, Vol. II, pp. 480, 490.

[3] *Moniteur*, Vol. XXVI, pp. 681–683.

[4] A. Schmidt, *Tableaux de la Révolution Française*, Vol. III, p. 54.

ordonnances," and other securities.[1] Later in the same month the Legislature, in offering relief to the victims of heavy assessments, virtually conceded the failure of the forced loan.[2] Faipoult, the first Minister of Finance under the Directorate, described the deplorable financial condition inherited by the Directorate, as follows: "In four lines, here is the situation of the public treasury. It has a liability of 74 million livres in numéraire and has but twenty million livres of bills on Spain available.[3] One hundred million livres of Assignats per day do not suffice for a third of our needs."[4] Ramel, during the last days of the Assignat, rendered a report in behalf of the Committee of Finances that revealed, in a few words, the extent of the non-collection of taxes during the Revolution. Fifteen thousand seven hundred and twenty-five million livres had been assessed from 1791 to September, 1795; 13,-118 millions remained uncollected in February, 1796.[5]

Here is a summary of the finances of the Revolution. From 1790 to 1793 the administration of taxes was deficient but it tended to improve. From May, 1793 to December, 1794, the Maximum Period, the Assignat remained the chief source of revenue, the administration of taxes continued to be inadequate, and the Government enforced a vigorous system of maximum prices and requisitions. In the final period ending December, 1795, taxation suffered because of the rapid depreciation. However, the amounts collected increased rapidly and, therefore, were of some importance. Frantic employment of a rapidly depreciating paper money, some reliance on requisitions, a bankrupt policy of payments, and many other makeshift arrangements were employed.

5. TAXATION VERSUS ASSIGNATS

Marion frequently comments on the persistent non-recovery of taxes; in his opinion, the collection of taxes was uniformly bad.[6] Gomel's conclusions are similar. The writers on Revolutionary

[1] J. Déb. et Déc., Vol. XVII, p. 348.
[2] Ibid., Vol. XVIII, pp. 72–73.
[3] A loan from a banking house.
[4] Quoted in Guyot, Le Directoire et le Paix, p. 62.
[5] J. Déb. et Déc., Vol. LXXX, p. 174.
[6] M. Marion, op. cit., Vol. I, pp. 321–322, 385–386; Vol. II, pp. 140–145.

finances are obscure as to the taxes collected and as to the purchasing power obtained from the issuing of paper money. What information can be of greater value to the historians of the finances of the Revolution? There is a paucity of data on the monthly deficits, taxes, and other receipts. No writer has analysed adequately the annual expenditures and receipts.

I have collected figures for receipts from taxation and other sources of revenue for monthly and annual periods during the years 1789–94. Although the Government was more secretive in 1795, I believe that my results are reasonably accurate for that year. For the first twenty-eight months of the Revolution, I relied primarily on two reports, the first by Necker (May 29, 1790, Procès-Verbal, vol. xxi), and the second by Montesquiou (September 9, 1791, Procès-Verbal, vol. lxix). For a few years after 1791 the Treasury, in publishing the monthly deficit (a deficit from the expected ordinary receipts of 48.6 million livres), revealed the receipts from taxation. It is necessary to reduce the

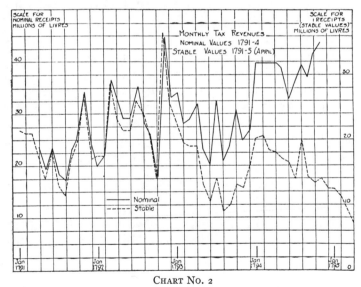

CHART No. 2

receipts from taxation thus obtained by five million livres to allow for the outlay of the Caisse de l'Extraordinaire and the Treasury for the expenditures of the "culte" (provided for by Assignats).[1] The net receipts from the sale of salt and tobacco were equivalent to a tax on the consumer, and hence may be considered as additional taxes. The only other questionable item, the receipts from the sale of silver, constituted a sale of a capital asset. The receipts from sales of copper were of minor importance. (Cambon admitted in 1795 that these sales had been unprofitable to the Treasury.) The Assignats received from the rents of public lands and from the proceeds of sales, are indistinguishable. Both were burnt.[2] Neither item was included in the ordinary receipts.

A graph of the monthly receipts from taxation is significant. The most important generalization is that the receipts from tax-

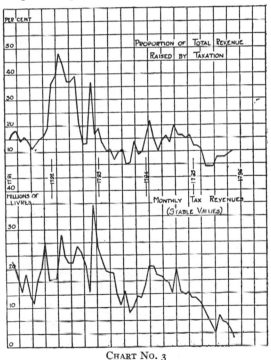

CHART NO. 3

[1] The original expenses of the "culte" were considerably reduced by the laws of September 18, 1793, August 16, 1794, and September 17, 1794. *Moniteur*, Vol. XXI, pp. 789–792.

[2] *Ibid.*, Vol. XV, p. 105.

ation tended to increase, although with the progress of depreciation, each Assignat received had less purchasing power. The receipts from taxation were at a minimum in 1790 and 1791. Gomel contends that the people's anticipation of depreciation is the explanation of the slow collection of taxes. But depreciation had scarcely begun by 1791. It is true, however, that large tax payments were made in 1795, a year of rapid depreciation. The payments of arrears in 1795 does not necessarily signify that the public awaited this opportune time to pay their over-due taxes. Rather, when the real cost of payment became negligible, people were willing to become law-abiding. The postponement of payment was due in the early years almost exclusively to poor administration, rather than to hopes of future depreciation. However, some planned postponements were made, no doubt, in 1793 and 1794.

The table that follows summarizes the results of my statistical study of the finances of the Revolution. I have reduced the nominal receipts to stable values by employing an index based on the average value of the Assignat according to the local tables of depreciation. By stable value is connoted the value in terms of Assignats of 1790. *Real* and *stable* will be used interchangeably. That there were decided improvements during some periods of the paper money regime, improvements of the greatest importance for the finances and for the Assignats, is evident from this table. A remarkable increase in tax receipts (both nominal and real) and in the proportion of tax receipts to total receipts occurred in 1792. These favorable conditions were maintained in 1793, and were improved further in 1794. Unhappily, as a result of the growing war expenditures, the improvement was relatively unimportant in 1793-94. Unfortunately, France's fiscal system consisted mainly of taxes that required long and costly surveys. The system was not, therefore, suitable in a period of depreciation. It is astonishing, therefore, that the real (or stable) value of tax receipts increased in 1791 and 1792. This table reveals that all assumptions of a persistent non-recovery of direct taxes are ill-founded.

MONTHLY AVERAGES

	Taxes		(Millions of livres) Other Sources (Assignats, etc.)		Per Cent Proportion of taxes to
Date	Nominal	Gold	Nominal	Gold	all revenue
May 1–Dec. 31, 1789	33	33	36	36	48
Jan. –Dec. 1790	16	16	38	38	30
Jan. –Dec. 1791	19½	17½	103	93	16
Jan. –Dec. 1792	30½	23	90½	67½	25
Jan. –Dec. 1793	28	15	266	35	9½
Jan. –Dec. 1794	41	16½	214	90½	15
Jan. –Nov. 1795	118	6½	1334	75½	8 [1]

The three charts that follow represent (1) the monthly receipts from taxes; (2) the percentage of total receipts to be credited to taxation; (3) the monthly stable (or real) receipts. Note in particular the rapid decline of real receipts beginning late in 1794, the initial period of rapid depreciation.

A summary of the annual amounts of expenditure follows:

MILLIONS OF LIVRES

Year	Nominal	Stable
May 1–Dec. 21, 1789	656	656
1790	657	657
1791	1571	1451
1792	1450	1085
1793	3532 [2]	1801
1794	3180	1284
1795 [3]	16380	981

The annual figures are a summary of the monthly data; the stable expenditures equal the nominal expenditures reduced monthly by a table of depreciation. The expenditures should be considered with the extent of the yearly depreciation in mind.

[1] The data for 1795 are unsatisfactory. Of the 3,000 millions collected by taxation to the end of 1795, the amount received from 1789 to 1794 was deducted. I compiled the figures for the taxation receipts from four reports, the first of which was issued on December 22, 1794, and thereafter at intervals of three months. I assumed that until July, 1795, taxes remained approximately at the level of 1794. In July the Government passed a law ordering (1) the payment of arrears within a month with a penalty of "au cours" payments for non-payment, and (2) the collection of the Contribution Foncière "au cours."

[2] Cambon estimated the expenditures from 1789 to September 1, 1793 at 6554 million livres. My estimate of expenditure (above) gives 4330 million livres (1789–92) plus 2300 million livres from January 1 to September 1, or 6630 million livres in all.

[3] Through November 15 only.

The heavy expenditures of 1789 were largely for the payment of debt to the Caisse d'Escompte and the reduction of large amounts of anticipations and arrears on rentes. The marked increase for 1791 may be explained by both the heavy reimbursements for debt and the preparations for war. In 1793 and 1794 with armies on every frontier and civil war within, the expenditures were unprecedented.

A study of the stable values reveals that for 1794 the Government received a stable revenue only 67 per cent as large as that received in 1793. That the Government was able, nevertheless, to maintain undiminished vigor in the warfare of 1794 and 1795 is to be attributed, in my opinion, to the success of the policy of maximum prices and requisitions, which enabled it to obtain its war necessities at preposterously low prices. This is a concrete measure of the happy results of maximum prices during war times. We often invoke the canon of fiscal necessity as the first law of taxation. Does not that canon justify taxation through requisition at maximum prices without which success in the campaigns of 1794 would probably have been impossible?

The inadequacy of the measure of depreciation used in reducing the nominal revenues to stable revenues requires comment here. Even the department tables did not give to commodity prices their proper weight; and, therefore, the actual depreciation was less, and the stable receipts more than is here indicated.

The Government obtained from taxation 16 per cent of all the revenues for the years 1790–94, 9 per cent for the year 1795, and 13 per cent for the entire period.[1] Taxation was not a negligible factor during the French Revolution. Too much has been said of the unsatisfactory collection of taxes, and too little of the actual yield. The results were neither uniformly good nor uniformly bad. However, the power of the Assignat is not to be denied. The evil results of a fiat paper money are well known. The contributions of the Assignats are not recognized adequately. In six years the

[1] Falkner compares the total emission of 45 milliards with the total taxes of 3 milliards for the years 1790–1795, and concludes that but 7 per cent of the total revenues were raised by taxation. Such statistics for an extended period of depreciation employed without a consideration of the changing value of money, are misleading. S. V. Falkner, *op. cit.*, p. 111.

Government realized over 7 milliards (stable value) by means of them, an amount equal to fourteen years of normal revenue.[1] Well may we agree with the inflationists of the Revolution, and with Blanc and Jaurès, that the Assignat supported fourteen armies. One quotation — and that from a speech in January, 1796, when the Assignat had already been discredited — will suffice here. Ramel eulogized the Assignats in January, 1796, as follows: "They have led to the destruction of class and of privilege; they have destroyed the monarchy and established the Republic. They have armed and equipped these formidable columns which have carried the tricolors beyond the Alps and the Pyrenees."[2]

6. EMISSIONS

This chapter would be incomplete without some discussion of the statistics of circulation, emissions, burnings, and exchange of Assignats. The Assignats were primarily a financial tool; hence the exigencies of finance largely governed the emissions.

The official statistics are inadequate and often inconsistent. The issues decreed were not made public after April, 1795. The notes decreed should be distinguished from those emitted, because a legislative order was necessary for a transference from the Caisse de l'Extraordinaire to the Treasury; and Assignats emitted should be distinguished from those in circulation. Notes burnt and demonetised should be subtracted from notes emitted to obtain the figures for the notes in circulation. Errors in interpretation have resulted from the practice begun late in 1791 of ordering notes to be manufactured even before they were decreed. Issues were also decreed which were to be used for exchange purposes only. A few decrees were provisional; the notes decreed were to be issued as

---

[1] Falkner estimates that the stable value of the receipts from paper money was 6 milliards. Since I used a measure (the average of the local values) which gives a higher value for the Assignat than the measure based on the price of gold and silver used by Falkner, the higher total reached in this study is to be expected. Falkner also uses the dubious method of calculating the stable value of the Assignat by yearly instead of monthly periods. Reducing monthly emissions by monthly values for the Assignat, is more accurate. S. V. Falkner, *Das Papiergeld der französischen Revolution*, pp. 108-109. J. Hirsch criticises the Dawes Committee for making a similar error. *Die deutsche Währungsfrage*, pp. 17-18.

[2] *Moniteur*, Vol. XXVII, p. 351.

the notes received from the proceeds of land sales were burnt. The opportunities for confusion and error are apparent.

Much of the statistical information on this subject is taken from a study by Ramel.[1] After the Committee of Finances obtained full control of the emission of Assignats in 1795, facts were often concealed; but the irregular financial reports contained some information.

The decrees of December 19, 1789, April 17, 1790, and October 8, 1790, authorized emissions of 400, 400 and 800 million livres respectively. The second and third of these decrees authorized the creation of notes which were to be exchanged for the Billets de Caisse and Promesses d'Assignats received from the Caisse d'Escompte.

In June, 1791, the Legislature approved an issue for 600 millions. With this legislation a fundamental change was introduced. This decree limited notes issued under this law to the replacement of notes received in payment for land purchased. Since but 160 million livres had been received for the payment of land and had been taken out of circulation, the privilege of issuing only 160 million livres at once was granted by the law of June 19.[2] Regardless of the deficits of the Treasury, they were not to be issued more rapidly than the incoming notes received in payment for land were burnt. This rather significant change has escaped the attention of writers on the subject. The decree of June 19 limited emissions to 1360 millions plus notes substituted for those incinerated. It was an easy transition to limit emissions to 1400, 1600 millions, or to any other total.

It was voted on November 1, 1791, "to put into circulation 100 million livres additional so that the maximum amount of notes put into circulation would equal 1400 million livres."[3] Fifteen hundred and sixty million livres (including notes destroyed) had already been authorized. Did the Government now interpret "to

---

[1] *Des Finances de la République Française en l'An IX.* Levasseur, Stourm, Falkner, and Gomel avail themselves of Ramel's results. Gomel did some independent research. Unfortunately, I have been unable to obtain Ramel's report. although from the authors quoted, I learnt of his results.

[2] Arch. Parl., Vol. XXVII, p. 336.

[3] *Ibid.*, Vol. XXXIV, p. 567.

put into circulation" as "remain in circulation"? A law of April 4, 1792 provided for an increase of the notes "à mettre en circulation" from 1600 to 1650 million livres. A change in the wording came with the law of June 13, 1792; it has never attracted a word of comment. Cailhasson, the reporter of the bill, had asked that the notes "en circulation" be increased from 1650 to 1700 million livres.[1] In the final reading of the bill the new phraseology was more clearly put: "The Administrator of the Caisse de l'Extraordinaire is authorized to emit the quantity of Assignats necessary to pay for the expenses and payments decreed by the National Assembly until the circulation shall rise to 1800 million livres."[2] Thus the Government violated the law by interpreting "to put into circulation" as "remain in circulation" and then legalized it by a clever change in the wording of the law. A change that legalized an increase of circulation of 500 million livres in June, 1792 — the amount of notes which had been burnt and, therefore, the difference between the notes put into circulation, and the notes remaining in circulation — has passed unchallenged and unnoticed.

Stourm and Levasseur, relying largely on Ramel, assert that the National Assembly was responsible for issues of 1800 million livres of Assignats. They make no distinction between decrees of emission, of creation, or of circulation. This summary is inaccurate, for it charges the National Assembly with the responsibility for an unrestricted issue of 600 million livres for June, 1791. The amount actually decreed for creation and emission to September, 1791 was, in millions of livres:

400	December 19, 1789.
400	April 17, 1790.
100	September 28, 1790.
400	October 8, 1790.
250	Burnt to the end of the session of the National Assembly. (Decree of June, 1791.)
1550	

Stourm, Levasseur, and Gomel say that the Legislative Assembly "created" 900 million livres of Assignats.[3] This estimate

---

[1] Arch. Parl., Vol. XLII, p. 533.

[2] Ibid., Vol. XLV, p. 172.

[3] R. Stourm, op. cit., Vol. II, p. 306; E. Levasseur, Histoire des Classes Ouvrières, Vol. I, p. 230; C. Gomel, op. cit., Introd., p. iv.

probably takes into account two decrees (April 30, and July 31, 1792) which authorized issues of 300 million livres each, and an additional issue of 300 million livres, which will be discussed later. Yet it is significant that the circulatory limit was increased by only 700 million livres during this period. The law of December 17, 1791 was not limited, as Gomel supposes, to providing for the replacement of notes burnt, but also authorized the issuing of notes for fiscal purposes.[1] Their emphasis on decrees of creation suggests that Levasseur, Stourm, and Gomel do not realize the greater importance of decrees of emission and of those limiting the total circulation. Decrees of creation were significant only when the privilege of raising the limit of notes in circulation was granted; and even this was of no practical importance until the legislature legalized the transference of the Assignats from the Caisse de l'Extraordinaire to the Treasury. The decrees of November 24, and December 17, 1791, authorized emissions of 300 million livres in all, but the notes were to be taken from the unused portion of the creation of June, 1791. Evidently some duplication resulted here, since the authors named had included the entire creation of June, 1791 in the total attributed to the National Assembly. The "creation" of July 31, 1792 was for the most part not emitted until the Convention period.[2]

Decrees were more numerous under the Convention. The decrees that I have been able to find follow:

MILLIONS OF LIVRES

October 24, 1792	400
February 1, 1793	800
May 7, 1793	1200
June 18, 1794	1205
April 15, 1795	3200
Total	6805

Ramel gave a summary figure of notes emitted by decree under the Convention in excess of seven milliards. The procedure con-

---

[1] C. Gomel, op. cit., Vol. I, p. 63.

[2] Cambon spoke of a creation of 300 million livres voted on November 1, 1791. (Arch. Parl., Vol. XXIV, pp. 563–564; Moniteur, Vol. X, pp. 645–655.) I have been unable to find a record of this creation.

sisted, as a rule, of an anticipatory order of manufacture followed within a few months by a decree of creation. The Treasury received Assignats to the extent of its monthly deficit on the condition, at first, of not exceeding the circulatory limit, and later, of not exceeding the limit set by the decree of creation. The decree of February 1, 1793, which limited the Assignats in circulation to 3100 million livres, was the last decree of this nature.[1] The whole process was thereafter hastened by the omission of one step;.for the decrees of "creation" and of "circulation" were merged.

The remaining decrees of the Convention period were secret; they are to be accredited to the Committee of Finances. Ramel asserted that in the six months after April, 1795, the authorities decreed issues of 19,450 million livres. Stourm erroneously attributes the 35½ milliards emitted without publicity entirely to the Directorate.[2] The danger of concentrating attention on the decrees of creation is apparent from the secret report read to the Conseil of 500 in November, 1795, which revealed that 5 milliards of the notes decreed by the Convention Government remained unmanufactured as late as November 13, 1795 — more than two weeks after the termination of that Government.[3]

The Directorate, using the printing press with remarkable success, issued 21,000 million livres in three months. Five milliard livres remained from the creations of the previous Government; issues of 4 milliards were authorized on October 30, December 27, 1795, and January 10, 1796; a final vote of 1150 million livres was taken on January 28. I can find no record of 3 milliards supposedly issued during this period. A decree of December 21 allowed the manufacture of 16,326 million of livres necessary to attain a circulation of 40 milliards.[4] The decree of January 28, 1796 revealed that almost 39 milliards were in circulation.[5] Evidently

---

[1] The two creations that follow the decree of February, 1793, carry no suggestion as to a change in the circulatory limit. *Moniteur*, Vol. XXI, p. 14.
[2] R. Stourm, *op. cit.*, Vol. II, p. 306.
[3] *Moniteur*, Vol. XXVI, pp. 499–504.
[4] *Actes du Directoire Exécutif*, Vol. I, pp. 623–624.
[5] On February 17, 1796, the Minister of Finance acknowledged that over 16 milliards had been put into circulation since December 21, 1795. *J. Déb. et Déc.*, Vol. LXXXI, pp. 223–224.

from December 21, 1795 to January 28, 1796 more than 15 milliards of Assignats had been put into circulation.

A thorough compilation of Treasury deficits should be made and used in conjunction with the decrees of emission and limitations of circulation in order to obtain monthly figures for notes emitted. To obtain the figures for notes in circulation, deduct from the notes emitted all notes burnt and demonetised. These tables of emissions, burnings, and circulation are often checks on one another.

The notes destroyed were received, in the early years, mostly from the sale of lands; they yielded 464 millions of a total of 505 millions burnt by May, 1792. The remainder was received in large part in payment of the Patriotic Contribution.[1] It is necessary to deduct notes demonetised in 1793–94 from the emissions in order to obtain the series for notes in circulation. The Government, in true Republican spirit, had demonetised all Assignats created during the Royalist Period. Deductions are not made for demonetised notes received for taxes and other public dues, nor for the small "royal notes" replaced by other notes. For notes received in payment of taxes were reissued; and no decrease resulted from the withdrawal of the small "royal notes," as others were substituted.[2] The Convention on December 4, 1793, ordered the Treasury to manufacture 500 million livres of Assignats to replace royal notes of 5 livres, rather than those above 100 livres, as Gomel says.[3] Obviously, only a deduction of notes demonetised in the hands of the people is required. Where notes issued for exchange purposes were included as notes emitted, the corresponding Assignats withdrawn are included as notes burnt. That is necessary in order to obtain the net circulation.

Several issues were decreed for exchange purposes only and were substituted for less convenient denominations. I have omitted them in the compilations of notes emitted — with the exceptions already noted. The authorities, in some instances, borrowed quantities of these notes when the manufacture of notes was too slow.

---

[1] See "La Situation de la Contribution Patriotique," P. V., Vol. XLII.
[2] *Moniteur*, Vol. XVI, p. 599.
[3] C. Gomel, *op. cit.*, Vol. II, p. 210; Arch. Parl., Vol. LXXXI, p. 67.

The laws that authorized a manufacture of notes were generally promulgated in anticipation of decrees of creation or emission. The mechanical processes at first were too slow to satisfy the precarious needs of the Treasury.[1] By introducing "manufacturing" decrees relatively early the Treasury overcame that obstacle; when the Government authorized a creation of 1200 million livres on May 7, 1793, 500 million livres had already been manufactured. With time the decrees of manufacture, creation and of emission became almost indistinguishable. Writers often confuse decrees of manufacture with decrees of emission. Gomel interprets the decree of December 23, 1791, which was an order for the manufacture of more notes, as though it were a decree of emission.[2]

7. Summary

This chapter emphasizes the necessity of including a study of the finances in a paper on the Assignats. The Assignat was primarily a financial tool: recourse to paper money followed upon the relative failure of other sources of revenue.[3] As other methods of raising revenue improved or became less dependable, the necessity of resorting to the Assignat became less or more urgent. I have presented a statistical study of taxation, in which the thesis is maintained, that although taxation was sub-normal during the Revolution, it was not uniformly bad. The varying success in the collection of taxes is especially important in a study of paper money.

The Assignat was the Revolutionary paper money employed to meet the extraordinary expenses of the Revolution. A study of the finances of the Revolution should include a discussion of the periodic deficits. Thus the extent of the reliance on the Assignats

---

[1] The manufacture of the first 180 million livres of Assignats was not completed until October 5, 1790. "Etat de la Situation de la Caisse de l'Extraordinaire," P. V., Vol. XXXIII, 435.

At one time because of the slowness of the manufacture of notes, the Government issued larger denominations than were convenient. Arch. Parl., Vol. XLIX, pp. 140–141.

[2] Gomel, *op. cit.*, Vol. I, p. 63; Arch. Parl., Vol. XXXVI, p. 325.

[3] Keynes has a brilliant discussion of the possibilities of raising revenues through the creation of paper money. J. M. Keynes, *Tract on Monetary Reform*, pp. 46–49.

can be comprehended. Deficits and emissions of Assignats were virtually identical.

In the section on emissions, I have pointed out that care must be taken if confusion is to be averted. Decrees of creation, emission, circulation, manufacture, and exchange are to be differentiated. The statistics of deficits and emissions did not check in every instance. At least one important inconsistency required investigation.

8. NOTE ON DEFICITS OF 1791
MILLIONS OF LIVRES, 1791

Month	(1) Extraordinary Deficit		(2) Ordinary Deficit	(3) Repayment of Debt	
January........	60 ⎫ (A)		(B)	55	(C)
February.......	72 ⎬		67	55	
March.........	55 ⎭			55	
April..........			24.3 (E)	60	
May...........			28.5	60	
June..........		(17.6) (F)	24.6	60	
July..........		(6.4)	29.4	50	
August........		(12.5)	30.5	56	(K)
September......		99 (H)	24	0	
October........	(19.7)	91.2	21.7	10.5	
November......	(18.5)	130.2	13.3	10.5	
December......	(12.1)	28.1 (I)	23.9	27	
Totals.......		572.0	287.2 (G)	499.0	
Grand Total, 1358.2 (J)					

NOTES TO TABLE

(A) The estimated deficits for January–March, 1791 (estimated by Lebrun on January 14, 1791) were 60, 70, and 73 million livres, a very close forecast indeed. *Moniteur*, VII, pp. 126–128.

(B) The Caisse de l'Extraordinaire in April transferred 75.6 million livres to the Treasury to cover deficits for the first three months of 1791. This help was rendered on the presumption of monthly expenditures of 48.6 million livres. Since the actual expenditures for the period were less than expected, the Treasury returned 8 million livres to the Caisse. (Arch. Parl., Vol. XXVII, p. 340.)

(C) The monthly estimates of debt payments are based on data furnished by Montesquiou on September 9, 1791 (P. V., Vol. LXIX, p. 27); by Dufrèsne on December 9, 1791 (Arch. Parl., XXXV, pp. 681–690); by Cambon in April, 1792 (*Moniteur*, Vol. XII, pp. 177–180).

(E) Instead of the anticipated expenditures (ordinary) of 291 million livres from January to June, but 241 million livres were so consumed. Therefore the ordinary deficits were 50 million livres less than is here indicated. I have referred to an order for the transfer of 8 millions for the period from January to March, but have found no record of a transfer to the Caisse of the remaining 42 million livres. Perhaps the Treasury appropriated this money for meeting some extraordinary expenditures during the year.

(F) The figures in parenthesis give the totals for a category of extraordinary expenses labelled "expenses particulères de 1791." Where two figures are given in this column, the second always includes the "expenses particulères."

(G) The monthly deficits tabulated in this column are the differences between the *actual* "ordinary" receipts and 48.6 million livres, the *theoretical* "ordinary" receipts.

(H) The three estimates (99, 91.2, 130.2) that follow in this column (for September–November) were obtained by subtracting from the aggregate monthly deficit the corresponding amounts in columns two and three. (Arch. Parl., Vol. XXXIV, p. 563; *Ibid.*, Vol. XXXV, pp. 324–325.)

(I) This is the most unsatisfactory estimate of the year. It was obtained from a public report, but an omission of some of the extraordinary deficits is possible nevertheless; this deficiency is probably not of major importance because of the reduction of war expenditures for the winter.

(J) By February 26, 1792, the Treasury had emitted 1924 million livres. On January 1, 1791, the total of emissions was 524 million livres. The net increase of emissions during this period was, therefore, 1400 million livres. The total deficits for 1791 (according to these calculations) were 1358.2 million livres. A transfer to the Treasury from the Caisse de l'Extraordinaire of 5 million livres monthly, or 60 million livres yearly, was made for the expenses of the "culte." Because of the wording of the decree responsible for that transfer, a *probability* that this monthly expense for the "culte" was included in the published deficits, is precluded; for expenditures for the "culte" were included in "ordinary expenses" although provided for by the Caisse de l'Extraordinaire. The deficit for January, 1792, was 71 million livres; and the deficit for February need not be considered, as it was not covered until March. The results are then:

(millions of livres)

Increased emissions, 1400. Deficits, 1489.

The correspondence would be closer if the questionable item of ordinary deficits of more than 40 million livres was excluded from the total for deficits. And although I am inclined to give the expenditures for the "culte" additional consideration in the computation of the deficits, I have been unable to convince myself with certainty on the point.

(K) Marion, for the period from October, 1790 to August, 1791, asserts that 600 million livres of Assignats were consumed in meeting "deficit" payments. I put that aggregate at approximately 1,000 million livres.

CHAPTER III

LAND AND THE ASSIGNAT

1. LAND VERSUS ASSIGNAT

IN the words of the accepted report of the Committee of the National Assembly, "to pay off the public debt, animate agriculture and industry and have the lands better administered," the church lands were to be alienated.[1] The paper received in payment for the lands was to be burnt.[2] Was the land a "gage" (security) for the Assignats only incidentally? Were the lands really disposed of to pay the debt? Was the Assignat merely an organ of the land agent?

In its origin, I am inclined to believe that the Assignat was not a land paper in the sense that it was issued to make the sale of land possible. Rather, it might be designated a revenue paper, a substitute for the previous borrowing from the Caisse d'Escompte.[3] Because an immediate resource was needed, the paper money became the most important care of the Government. To assure confidence in the paper money, the Government, presenting a proposal for the creation of 400 millions of notes, announced a sale of an amount of land of equal value.[4] The idea became generally accepted that increased issues of Assignats were necessarily balanced by increased lands put on sale. Thus on July 31, 1792, the Committee of Finance and Domaines, in proposing a new issue of 300 millions, recommended that more forests, episcopal palaces, and religious houses be put on sale, for 2400 millions of notes ordered to be created were now balanced by 2444 millions of domaines on

---

[1] P. V., Vol. XXII, 308.
[2] *Ibid.*, p. 7.
[3] See Chapter II for the evolution of plans that finally culminated in the Assignat. Necker's report of November 14, 1789, and the Plan of Commissioners of December 19, 1789 were important. P. V., Vols. VII and X.
[4] Arch. Parl., Vol. X, p. 681.

sale.[1] It was considered necessary that the land should be placed on sale as more Assignats were issued.[2]

Much has been written about the availability of these new resources of land and about the pressure of the excessive debt; and it has been contended that the problem was to find an intermediary for stimulating the sale of lands and reducing the debt.[3] Such an interpretation of the origin of the Assignat seems to neglect its historical evolution, and in particular, the close continuity of development from Necker's advocacy of a loan from the Caisse d'Escompte to the final vote for the Assignat. The successful plan, favored because of the antipathy for both the Caisse and Necker, borrowed much from the latter. The origin of the Assignat is to be attributed to the urgent need of an immediate resource, rather than to an appreciation of the possibility of the beneficial effects of additional issues of paper money upon the sale of lands. Gomel condemns the resolution in the first decree dealing with the Assignat, which urged the necessity of repaying the public debt.[4] The resolution, however, was not taken seriously then.[5] It is true that the problem of debt payment arose in August and September, 1790. The point of contention was whether the Assignat or a non-circulating paper (Quittance de Finance) was to be the intermediary for debt payments.[6] The most spirited debates on paper money were held during this period. Evidently the writers who contend that the Assignat was created to repay the public debt rely largely on the history of these two months. But the question at issue in the fall of 1790 was not one of creating the

[1] *Moniteur*, Vol. XIII, pp. 293-295.

[2] Johannot contended that land was an ideal security because it increased in value with increased issues of paper money. *J. Déb. et Déc.*, Vol. LVII, pp. 63-65.

[3] E. Levasseur, "Les Finances de la France," Acad. des Sci. Mor., Vol. XXX, pp. 112, 192. M. Marion, *op. cit.*, Vol. II, p. 51. J. Jaurès, *Histoire Socialiste de la Révolution Française*, Vol. II, p. 93.

[4] C. Gomel, *Histoire Financière de l'Assemblée Constituante*, Vol. I, pp. 515-516.

[5] Arch. Parl., Vol. X, p. 681. "The products of the Caisse de l'Extraordinaire shall be used to pay the 'créances exigible' and 'arrières' and to repay all debts of which the National Assembly shall have decreed the extinction."

[6] The issue was between Talleyrand who fought for the Quittance de Finance (P. V., Vol. XXX and XXXI, September 18 and September 24) and Mirabeau who fought staunchly for the Assignat (P. V., Vol. XXXI, September 27). As early as October 10, 1789, Talleyrand had anticipated this problem. *Choix de Rapports*, Vol. I, p. 97.

Assignat, but rather its relation to the payment of debts. The Assignat had already been employed extensively to meet current obligations. Whether there should or should not be Assignats was a question scarcely touched upon during the whole weary month of debates.

It was during the same period that attention was emphatically drawn to the use of Assignats for promoting the sale of land. Mirabeau in September, 1790 attributed to the paper money the power to convert dead land into circulating wealth.[1] Montesquiou, a week earlier, had said that the sale of land would be hampered by the scarcity of numéraire.[2] Even Calonne, an unflinching opponent of the Revolutionary money, estimated that half of the circulation of 1200 millions was necessary for the purchase of land.[3] Time left that particular justification of the Assignat in the background; little was heard of it after 1790. All of the long list of financial reports from the first days of Cambon in 1792 to the days of Eschassériaux in 1795 proclaimed the supremacy of the Assignat and the subsidiary position of the land. But that is not necessarily inconsistent with the contention that the Assignats made the sale of lands possible.

Issued as a financial tool, the Assignat in 1791 and 1792 began to assume a new function with which its character was completely altered. Its defenders were soon emphasizing its contribution in filling the void left in the circulation as the metals were increasingly hoarded. Smaller denominations were deemed necessary. If the Assignats were to fill the ordinary channels of circulation, certainly they would not all be redeemed by the sales of land. To sustain the value of the paper money became the most important task of the Government. Increased aggregates in circulation induced depreciation. Depreciation might be averted by increasing the sales of lands and thus reducing the circulation, and by inspir-

---

[1] P. V., Vol. XXXI, September 27, 1790. See also L. Blanc, *Histoire de la Révolution Française*, Vol. I, p. 446.

[2] P. V., Vol. XXX, *Déb. et Déc.*, 436, pp. 9–10.

[3] C. A. Calonne, *De l'État de France*, pp. 88–89. Deslandoes (*Société des Jacobins*, Vol. I, p. 208) assumed a similar position. Roederer (*Oeuvres*, Vol. VI, p. 3) said that the Assignat would make it possible for capitalists and creditors to acquire public domains.

ing confidence by making known the adequacy of the national resources. Issued in large denominations and with "free course," and accepted on favorable terms in the purchase of lands, the Assignat might have been primed to act as the complement of the land agent; but issued in small denominations, with a "forced course,"[1] it drew the land agent into the paper money ranks.

2. LAND, A GENERAL SECURITY VERSUS LAND, A SPECIAL SECURITY

Each Assignat contained some such printed words as "Domaines Nationaux."[2] Any holder of Assignats could buy lands; but any holder could, if he chose, buy anything else; and, moreover, the possessor of gold or certain kinds of script could also buy lands. Thus no particular significance can be attached to this feature of the fiat money. To support the notes issued, either for the purpose of redemption or for a psychological reason, the Treasury maintained the nominal values of the resources on sale more than equivalent to the notes issued. At first this was not an easy task. Many sales, difficult to consummate, were scheduled.[3] By exaggerating the value of the resources, by seizing the Émigrés' possessions and by making numerous condemnations during the Reign of Terror, the authorities overcame this difficulty.[4]

As the circulation increased, each Assignat became the equivalent of a smaller parcel of land. As increased issues were unaccompanied by increased amounts of land put on sale, the value of each Assignat in terms of land should have fallen. But large blocks of lands were placed on sale which were not easily sold; and hence the value of each unit of money might well have increased in terms of land. Consistently with the policy of the Government, it might be expected that the lands on sale would maintain an

---

[1] A creditor might not refuse an offer of payment in a money that had a forced course (cours forcé). Subercaseaux says that the concept is similar to the term "legal course" (legal tender). *Le Papier-Monnaie*, pp. 89–90.

[2] *Moniteur*, Vol. IV, p. 512.

[3] *Ibid.*, Vol. XXIV, p. 484. G. Lecarpentier (*La Vente des Biens Ecclésiastiques pendant la Révolution Française*, pp. 60–61) gives a complete list; Barnave (*Oeuvres*, Vol. II, pp. 3–11) commented at the time on the impossibility of selling colleges, biens de Malte, etc.

[4] Condemnations in Paris from April to July, 1794 totalled 2158. Cambon pretended that the wars could be financed with the guillotine. P. H. Wallon, *Histoire de Tribunal Révolutionnaire*, Vol. V, p. 270.

aggregate stable value not much larger than that of the Assignats. (To obtain the stable value of the Assignats, reduce the value of the total Assignats in circulation by the value of the Assignat as given by the local tables of depreciation; similarly, reduce the aggregate nominal value of the lands.) The contrary was the case. Beginning in the latter months of 1794, the stable value of the paper dropped far below that of the land. By November, 1795 the stable value of the Assignat had fallen to perhaps one-fifth of the estimated stable value of the lands on sale. Concomitant with the rapid depreciation of the Assignats in terms of land, of gold, and of commodities, the bulwark of the Assignats, land, became disentangled from the Assignat and maintained a fairly constant stable value. The value was not in fact constant throughout the period, for the authorities were not equally reliable in their estimates, and they considered a changing quantum of lands.

In May, 1795 Balland advised the Convention to give the Assignat a fixed value in land. Competition had reduced the "land" value of the money. Bourdon and Balland were responsible for the law of 10 Prairial 3 (May 29, 1795) which gave practical effect to the idea of attaching each Assignat to a particular period of land.[1] The possessor of an Assignat could purchase any parcel of land by agreeing to pay seventy-five times its net revenue in 1789. Thus competitive bids were to be eliminated; for they were responsible for the reduction of the "land" value of the Revolutionary money, and hence (they reasoned) the general value of the paper. They realized that lands were selling at a much higher price; but the essence of the plan was to give the Assignat a fixed security, and a more valuable one than its current market value warranted. With the great rush of bargain hunters came the realization that the land was being squandered, and Balland, himself, suggested a few days later that the presence of two or more competitors for the same tract was an indication of a fictitiously low estimated revenue for 1790. He suggested competitive bids in such cases. Rewbell, Dubois-Crancé, Vernier, and Cambacères all savagely attacked the act, and its suspension followed on June ninth.[2]

[1] *Moniteur*, Vol. XXIV, pp. 578–580.
[2] *Ibid.*

From the idea that the price of land should be fixed, it was an easy transition to the idea that the Assignat would appreciate if it were tied to individual parcels of land.[1] Dubois-Crancé sponsored an issue of Assignats stamped to indicate that they were tied to special parcels of land.[2] The Cédules d'Hypothèque (mortgage notes) were based on the same principle, a special hypothecation of lands.[3] A proposed decree (March 8, 1796) authorized the creation of 600 millions of Mandats, and the non-competitive selling of 1800 millions of lands.[4] The law of March 18 divided the land to be sold into two parts; the larger part, 1200 millions, was to be sold in a non-competitive manner at 22 times the appraised annual revenue. The Mandats were to be secured by the remaining 600 millions of land in a concrete manner by apportioning the Mandats among the departments. Only holders of Mandats were to have the privilege of purchasing the special security at 22 times the annual revenue. The plan was never given a fair trial because of the excessive issues of Mandats, the low appraisal of the annual revenue, and the administrative laxness displayed in setting aside specific parcels of land. Non-competitive purchases proved to be a method of exploiting the Government. The plan for a "special" security of the Mandat was never really put into practice.[5]

Had the policy of tying each Assignat or Mandat to a definite tract of land been faithfully executed, and had competitive bids been dispensed with, I cannot agree with Levasseur that this special security would have been similar to the general security.[6] As depreciation proceeded, the sales of land would have become a greater source of employment for the circulating medium. Further depreciation would have been prevented by increased sales. The depreciation in terms of gold and commodities would have been reduced by a relative appreciation in terms of land, and the land

---

[1] "Paris pendant la Réaction Thermidorienne et sous la Directoire," Collection de Documents Relatifs à l'Histoire de Paris, Vol. II, p. 200.

[2] J. Déb. et Déc., Vol. LXXXI, pp. 22–24.

[3] Moniteur, Vol. XXIV, pp. 291, 543–545, 622–623.

[4] Ibid., Vol. XXVII, pp. 642–644.

[5] Recueil des Actes du Directoire Exécutif, Vol. I, pp. 841–842.

[6] E. Levasseur, Histoire des Classes Ouvrières et de l'Industrie en France de 1789 à 1870, 2d ed., Vol. I, pp. 166–167.

would have been completely disposed of.[1] Rousseau in describing the Mandat expressed the theoretical possibilities well.[2] "The new money rendered realisable at will according to an evaluation that is fixed and constant, is not at all like the Assignat, the ideal representation of a fugitive and indeterminate value; it is money the title and the value of which are as invariable as the object that it represents."

Sales at competitive prices may have yielded more revenue; but at fixed prices, all the lands would have been sold, and the Government would no longer have been able to keep up its pretense of issuing a "land paper." It is unfortunate for the development of monetary theory that the Government failed to follow a policy of fixed prices for lands; but the Government probably followed a course consistent with its own interests.

3. LAND AND THE VALUE OF THE ASSIGNAT

There is almost an unanimity of opinion among writers, that the land security did not contribute to sustain the value of the paper money. Mill,[3] Levasseur,[4] Senior,[5] and Hawtrey[6] so express themselves. Gomel, Marion, and Stourm do not grapple with the problem. Thornton, alone, sees in the possible purchase of land an alternative employment for the Assignat that might make possible a reduction of the quantity in circulation, and hence sustain its value.[7]

The Cahiers offer convincing proof that the consternation caused by Law's blunders was not forgotten at the outbreak of the Revolution.[8] Something had to be done to imbue the people with

[1] Wickell points out that the sale of lands at a fixed price would have been a barrier to extreme depreciation. K. Wicksell, *Vorlesungen*, Vol. II, pp. 173–174.
[2] *Moniteur*, Vol. XXVIII, p. 151.
[3] J. S. Mill, *Political Economy*, 6th ed., Vol. II, pp. 81–83.
[4] E. Levasseur, *Histoire des Classes*, Oeuvrières, Vol. I, pp. 166–167.
[5] N. W. Senior, *Three Lectures on Cost of Obtaining Money*, pp. 78–79.
[6] R. G. Hawtrey, *Currency and Credit*, p. 260.
[7] F. H. Thornton, *An Enquiry into the Nature and Effects of the Paper Credit of Great Britain*, p. 260.
[8] The first two references are in the Collection de Documents Relatifs à l'Histoire de Paris. *L'État de Paris*, p. 48; *Cahiers de Paris*, Vol. III, p. 175; Arch. Parl., Vol. V, p. 727; Vol. VI, pp. 34, 40; "Protestation de M. Bergasse contre les Assignats-Monnaie"; "Lettre de Mirabeau à Cerutti, January 5, 1789."

confidence in paper money. The availability of the land offered the opportunity. One has but to believe that confidence is a factor in the value of paper money to believe that the land security contributed to sustain the value of the Assignats. The parliamentary debates and the newspapers of the day are proof beyond dispute that the land security had an important influence on public opinion. The contemporary discussions of or writings on the Assignats without some strong emphasis on their relationship to the land were rare indeed. Regardless of whether the confidence in the land was justified, its presence must have been instrumental in sustaining the value of the Assignat.[1]

The display of the balance between the Assignats on the one hand and the lands on sale on the other was an important factor in determining the degree of confidence with which the paper money was regarded. The scrupulous care with which these figures were exhibited, and the pertinacity with which all finance ministers uncovered new "gage," attest to the demands of the French people for an adequate security. On February 1, 1793 Cambon sponsored a new issue of 800 millions. The security of 3100 millions then just equalled the notes emitted. Cambon unearthed new resources of 4400 millions, 3400 millions of which were to be put on sale immediately.[2]

The early depreciation — much exaggerated — which Levasseur and Hawtrey attribute almost exclusively to the large denominations, was probably partially caused by some misgivings as to the new security. The "culte" (a charge on the revenue from the land) was not provided for; the Church was hostile; the church lands were heavily mortgaged; and finally dissensions and lack of organization were delaying sales.[3] Such doubts about the security led people to rid themselves of the paper money quickly, and resort to the more reliable gold and silver for hoarding. I doubt

[1] Bailleul, a financial authority of the period, was at a loss to explain a depreciation of the Assignat of over 99 per cent when the price of the land had only increased 40 times. *J. Déb. et Déc.*, Vol. LXXXI, pp. 9-10.

[2] *Moniteur*, Vol. XV, pp. 340-346.

[3] P. V., Vol. XV, *Déb. et Déc.*, 210; P. V., "Finance Report," Vol. XV, pp. 18-19; Actes de Commune, Vol. VI, pp. 98-100; "Les Provinces à l'Assemblée Nationale, 1790"; also, "Opinion de l'Evêque de Nancy."

whether an appreciable depreciation occurred before 1792; if it did, I am prone to put more stress on the impaired confidence in the land security than in the successive issues of large denominations. However, although a minority doubted whether the expropriation of the Church was final, a general confidence in the land security existed.

Although more will be said on this subject in Chapters VII and VIII, a few instances in which the presence of the land security appreciably affected the value of the Assignat are presented below. The upward reaction of the Assignat in the second half of 1792 is explained by Hawtrey as a reaction from a speculative excess. May it not also be attributed in part to the new confidence instilled by the confiscation of the Émigrés' possessions? In December, 1794, rumors of peace and of the restoration of confiscated lands brought about a further depreciation of the Assignats.[1] In February, 1795, suggestions of Vernier, Thuriot and others that the wealth of individuals be added to the public security supporting the Assignats, resulted in a rise.[2] Lack of faith, inherited from the Assignat régime, doubtlessly contributed to the precipitate fall of the Mandat. But the lax and inefficient administration of the land sales under the Act of 28 Ventôse is relevant. A number of keen observers believed that the dissipation of the security was the explanation of the increasing distrust of the Mandat.[3]

Perhaps Levasseur is correct in contending that the wage payer did not concern himself with the land security. The emphasis, however, should not be placed on the attitude of the disburser of wages, but of the general public. A general belief in the security of the Assignats made possible their acceptance. The danger of a minority of doubters would be very evident, however. The gospel of distrust spreads easily.

If this faith in the security existed, Levasseur errs in insisting that a nominal pledge of ultimate redemption through the sale of land, would not help to sustain the value of the money. It is an error to assume with him that redemption was of the nature of a

[1] *Thermidorienne Réaction*, Vol. I, p. 351.
[2] *Ibid.*, p. 646; and *Moniteur*, Vol. XXIII, p. 575.
[3] F. D. Ivnerois, *Histoire de l'Administration des Finances de la République Française pendant l'Année 1796*, 2d ed., pp. 62–63.

"say so" redemption.[1] The graph that follows indicates the importance of mechanical redemption. Redemption through land sales was of vital significance from 1791 to 1793; and it was during this period that the Assignats burnt came almost exclusively from the sales of land. In addition, hoarding of notes for the later

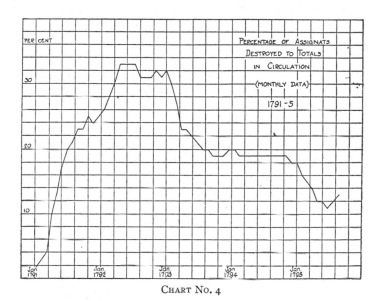

CHART NO. 4

installments of payments was of vital importance. Beginning late in 1793, receipts from sources other than land sales (mainly notes exchanged) began to contribute an appreciable proportion of the notes to be destroyed — thus in November, 1795, this item equalled 25 per cent of the total (1051 out of 3665 millions). To offset this, however, we should consider an item of 4461 million livres received from the sales of lands, but not burnt. These receipts came almost exclusively in the latter part of 1793, in 1794 and 1795.[2]

Undoubtedly, the land security might have had a much more

---

[1] E. Levasseur, "Les Finances de la France," Acad. des Sci. Mor. Vol. XXX, p. 299.
[2] From Ramel's report. See S. V. Falkner, *op. cit.*, p. 110.

material effect in bolstering up the value of the Assignats.[1] Maximum prices below the market price, discussions of agrarian laws — the expropriation of private owners for example — the general insecurity of property,[2] the Reign of Terror and its wholesale condemnations of the rich, the alternative attractiveness of tenant farming with its nominal rents paid in a depreciated currency, all detracted seriously from the lucrativeness of land purchases.[3] The depreciation of the paper money was unfortunate, because the value of later installments on lands purchased were reduced to nominal sums, and thus the land was deprived of some of its potential value for the support of the Assignat. More will be said presently as to how far sales were dependent on an anticipation of such relief. Perhaps the land policy of the Government was partly responsible for the period of most rapid depreciation (June, 1795 to March, 1796) when land sales were practically suspended.

Especially during the maximum period, when the usual channels of circulation were partially closed, were the possibilities of land sales wasted.[4] Some of the local documentary studies afford some information about the sales during the Reign of Terror, i.e., the maximum period. In the Department of Yonne, 2.7 million livres of land were sold within a period of twenty-six months before the establishment of the maximum. These figures are in terms of prices estimated on the basis of the revenue of 1790, so that there is a basis of comparison. This monthly average óf 105,-000 livres is to be compared with an average of 33,000 livres for the twenty months of the maximum period and 192,000 livres for the following fourteen months. The decline is not so marked for the Districts of Bain and Rennes in the Department of Ille-et-Vilaine, where the figures for the 3 periods were 71,000, 41,000 and

---

[1] Mathieu, on January 10, 1793, perceived the possibilities. He advocated: A. A system of education planned to show the necessity of land sales; for higher prices for lands would result in lower prices for commodities. B. Policing and security to encourage sales. *Moniteur*, Vol. XV, pp. 103–104.

[2] Cambon on February 28, 1793 warned the Convention that the pilfering from lands was curtailing the sales of lands. *Ibid.*, Vol. XV, p. 588.

[3] M. Marion, *La Vente des Biens Nationaux pendant la Révolution*, pp. 136–137, 145, 155, 157–165; Arch. Parl., Vol. LIV, p. 686. The latter contains an informing discourse of Creuse-Latouché on the relation of price fixing and the sales of land.

[4] Mallarmé realised that the system of maximum prices should encourage investments in land. Arch. Parl., Vol. LXVI, p. 70.

68,000, respectively. Sales fell during the maximum period although the Émigré lands were then put on sale, and a large amount of purchasing power became available for capital investments upon the introduction of stringent maximum and hoarding laws. Maximum prices below market prices, accompanied by rationing and drastic laws against the hoarding of commodities, left the public with a surplus of purchasing power. That the depression of prices resulting from price fixing, was not a decisive factor is evidenced by the large increase in the number of self-sufficing farmers. The importance of procuring subsistence from one's own farm in a time of threatened famine, is apparent. The personal and financial dangers involved in becoming a land-owner, appears to have been an effective deterrent to land buying. A Government with no scruples about property rights, a Government that made the visible evidence of wealth a grave personal danger, could not be a very successful land agent.

4. THE WASTE OF THE NATIONAL RESOURCES

There remains the question whether the Government, in directing the sales, made the most of its opportunities, and whether, therefore, the sales gave the Assignats the maximum possible degree of support. A difference of opinion obtains as to this particular problem. Marion and Benzacar jointly hold that because of the continued depreciation of the Assignat the state received almost nothing.[1] Marion, on his sole responsibility, reiterates that view.[2] Another opinion is that the original sales were made at prices which were ridiculously low, because the revenues for the year 1790 had been underestimated.[3] The minimum sales price (the "prix d'estimation") was based upon a multiple (twenty-two) of the estimated revenues of 1790. A more moderate con-

---

[1] M. Marion et J. Benzacar, *Ventes, Gironde,* Collection de Documents Inédits sur l'Histoire Economique de la Révolution Française, Introd., pp. xxii-xxiii; also M. Anglade, *De la Sécularisation des Biens du Clergé,* p. 150.

[2] M. Marion, *La Vente des Biens Nationaux,* p. 116, and *Histoire Financière,* Vol. II, p. 220.

[3] The references to sales in this chapter are all in the series of Collection de Documents Inédits sur l'Histoire Economique de la Révolution Française, unless otherwise specified. P. Moulin, *Ventes, Bouches-de-Rhône,* Introd., p. xxix. C. Porée, *Ventes, Yonne,* Introd., p. clxviii.

clusion is that of LeCarpentier, who estimates that the proceeds
from the sales of the church lands were 830 millions (stable values),
or about one-third of what should have been received.[1] For the
Department of Vosges, the authorities find profitable sales up to
the year II (1793–94); and for the District of Epinal, to which the
study is largely confined, the revenue was about 50 per cent of the
estimated value, both being stated in stable values.[2] In the District of Toulouse of the Department of Haute-Garonne, the total
value of property sold was over 15 millions, and the stable value of
the receipts 5 millions.[3]

The problem of the relationship of the "prix d'estimation" to
the sales price is of great significance here. Porée, who made a

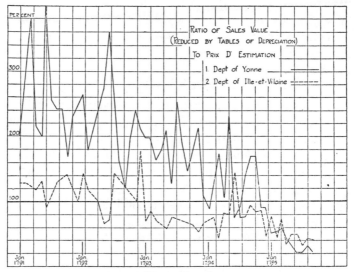

CHART NO. 4A

brilliant and thorough study of the land sales of the Department
of Yonne, says that the sale prices were consistently higher than
the "prix d'estimation," even allowing for the depreciation and
the expectations of depreciation at the date of sale. He attributes

---

[1] G. LeCarpentier, *La Vente des Biens Ecclésiastiques pendant la Révolution
Française*, p. 114. (Not in the series of documents.)
[2] L. Schwab, *Ventes, Vosges*, Introd. lxi.
[3] H. Martin, *Ventes, Haute-Garonne, District de Toulouse*, Introd., pp. lvii-lviii.

the excess to the high rate of capitalization which resulted in a low "prix d'estimation." Porée estimates that the lands actually sold at approximately 33 years purchase instead of the 22 years provided by the law. The chart that follows was constructed by taking monthly figures for the "prix d'estimation" and for sales,

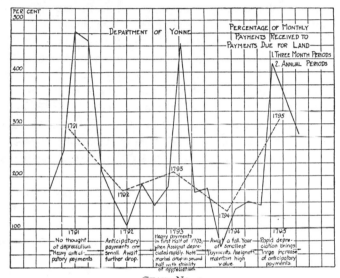

CHART NO. 5

reducing the latter by the appropriate local table of depreciation and calculating the ratio of the series thus obtained to the "prix d'estimation." Evidently for the Department of Yonne, Porée was correct in his generalization respecting the relatively high level of sale prices. But a similar curve for the Department of Ille-et-Vilaine points to no such conclusion. The sales price reduced to stable values scarcely equals the "prix d'estimation." Perhaps the estimate of the annual revenue was low in Yonne or high in Ille-et-Vilaine; or perhaps land was selling at a greater number of years purchase in Yonne. A number of other possibilities are suggested; but in any case the dangers of generalization are apparent.

For the determination of the profitableness of the sales, a familiarity with the value of the resources in stable currency is requisite.

Calonne,[1] Talleyrand,[2] Montesquiou,[3] and Lavoisier,[4] all estimated that the value of the church possessions was about two milliards. Necker's estimate of one milliard seems clearly out of line.[5] All these estimates were made before depreciation had really begun.

A number of difficulties soon appeared. In the majority of sales consummated in 1791, the selling price was considerably higher than the "prix d'estimation." In many instances, doubtlessly, this was due to the alertness of the bargain hunters, quick to discover lands underestimated by the experts. With the passing of time and the waning of enthusiasm, the excess of the sales price over the "prix d'estimation" was made possible by the depreciation of the Assignat.[6] Financial ministers evaluated the unsold lands according to the prices received for lands already sold. In these optimistic evaluations, the possibility of reaching the saturation point in sales was not considered; and no allowances were made for the fact that the more desirable lands had been purchased first. In so far as these high valuations were only a reflection of future depreciation, they were only too well justified, for sale prices were likely to go up with depreciation. The downward trend of the curves measuring the ratio of the stable value of the sale price to the "prix d'estimation", is significant. During the year 1791, it appears, further depreciation of the Assignat was not discounted by purchasers. From 1792 to 1794 expectations of further depreciation might have made possible sales in stable values at prices relatively higher (as compared to the "prix d'estimation") than prevailed in 1791. That the curve descends in-

---

[1] C. A. Calonne, *op. cit.*, p. 88. Income of 60 millions capitalized at 30 times.
[2] *Choix de Rapports*, Vol. I, p. 97. Income of 70 millions capitalized at 30 times.
[3] "Report of Committee of Finance," P. V., Vol. XXVIII, p. 15.
[4] M. Lavoisier, *Réflexions sur les Assignats*, Oeuvres, Vol. VI, pp. 365–367.
[5] J. Necker, *Treatise on the Administration of the Finances of France*, Vol. III, p. 407. An income of 25 millions was capitalized at 40 times.
[6] Nothing can be more misleading than the statements of Marion and Schmidt to the effect that the Government received the Assignat at par for land and paid it out at its depreciated value. M. Marion, *Histoire Financière*, Vol. II, p. 173; C. Schmidt, *Paris pendant la Révolution*, Vol. II, p. 136. Also see L. Schwab, "La Valeur et le Paiement des Biens Nationaux dans Les Vosges," *Bulletin d'Histoire Economique de la Révolution*, 1913, pp. 346–351, for a criticism of Marion's treatment of the subject.

stead may be attributed to the early selling of the more desirable sites, to the alertness of bargain hunters, and, finally, to the glutting of the market. The hopes of the finance ministers, evidenced in the later estimates of the value of the public land, proved to be exaggerated.

That part of the excess of the sales price over the "prix d'estimation" is explicable by the anticipation of depreciation, will be evident from what follows. Most fortunately, Porée has furnished us with the monthly receipts of the land office of the Department of Yonne. With the aid of these figures, and the monthly statements of lands sales, as well as the provisions of the laws of May 14, 1790, June 3, 1793, and 8 Nivôse 2 (December 27, 1793) regulating the time of payments, the monthly receipts "due" have been estimated. They have been compared to the actual receipts for 3 months and annual periods. The following interpretation is suggested.[1]

1791. The very heavy anticipatory payments reflect the presence of surplus savings and the absence of any thought of depreciation.

1792. The very significant fall in relative payments indicates that surplus savings had decreased, and beyond much doubt, that some speculative account was taken of future depreciation.[2]

1793. The increase in the annual figures reflects the very heavy payments made in the third quarter of the year. The payments relative to amounts due were much smaller in 1793 in the three other quarters of the year. The ranks of the "bear" speculators received large reinforcements. But the precipitate fall in the value of the Assignat in the third quarter of the year justified this lack of faith, and a precipitate rush to pay ensued.

1794. As a result of the unexpected vitality injected into the Assignat during this year the payments barely kept up with the amounts due. The only period when payments fell below the amounts due was the second quarter of this year.[3]

---

[1] I make these suggestions with great caution, for other interpretations are possible.

[2] I am considering the effects of depreciation on the payments made, not on the sales consummated. If depreciation was anticipated, payments would be postponed as much as possible, but sales would probably increase. The latter would involve partial payments upon the signing of the contract. However, the effect on payments for past contracts was of greater importance.

[3] Since payments were consistently more than the amounts due, it might be con-

1795. More surprising than the heavy payments in the spring and summer of 1795, was the very slight excess of receipts in the fall and winter of 1794–5, a period of marked depreciation; but the depreciation apparently had not progressed sufficiently to tempt the new landed interests. They anticipated a further reduction of the burden by means of increased depreciation.

The optimism of the financial authorities merits some discussion. Thus, Camus for the Committee of Finances in June, 1791, on the basis of the return of 314 of the 544 districts, evaluated the domaines at over 2400 millions.[1]

Montesquiou's estimate in September, 1791 was 3500 millions. The surplus above the "prix d'estimation" of unsold lands was put at over 500 millions. Feudal equities belonging to the nation, a very doubtful asset (later renounced by the Government), were put at 300 millions.[2]

Cambon, by April, 1792, could parade 4500 millions of resources. He did not include the future excess of the "prix d'adjudication" (sales price) over the "prix d'estimation," and initiated a policy of differentiating between the amount of resources necessary to cover notes already in circulation, and the remainder of resources available for the issuing of additional notes and other debts. This was a rather hazardous practice, for the folly of new issues was minimised.[3]

Cambon estimated the total in October, 1792 at 6000 millions. For the first time, however, the possessions of the Émigrés were included (1000 millions).[4] Cambon's aggregate was 7500 millions by February, 1793.[5] Johannot, in May, 1793, estimated the total at 7700 millions, although of the lands already sold, he included only those not paid for.

In December, 1794, Johannot based an estimate on the monthly

tended that the public were consistently "bulls." But that leaves out of account the fact that people frequently prefer to pay the entire sum at once. The attempt of the American Government to introduce installment payments for Liberty Loans, is a parallel case.

[1] *Moniteur*, Vol. VIII, p. 705.
[2] P. V., Vol. LXIX, "Mémoire," pp. 73–76.
[3] *Moniteur*, Vol. XII, pp. 179–180.
[4] *Ibid.*, Vol. XIV, pp. 229–230.
[5] *Ibid.*, Vol. XV, p. 343.

rentals received by the Government on unsold lands. By capital-
ising the latter at 40 years purchase, he obtained a total of 12 milliards, and added 2 milliards for buildings and 1 milliard for the
heritages of the Émigrés.[1] By April, 1795 Johannot's appraise-
ment was 17 milliards.[2] Éschassériaux, in November, 1795 definitely returned to a metallic basis for his estimate of 7 milliards.
Two milliards were in Belgium. The Conseil of 500 (March,
1796) estimated the possessions not alienated as approximately
8½ milliards.[3] With the exception of the last two estimates, the
authorities appraised the national resources in paper livres. However, they scrupulously avoided mention of that fact and often
pretended that their valuations were in gold livres.

What conclusions are to be drawn from these surveys of the
value of the resources? Were Talleyrand, Calonne and Montesquiou accurate? Or should more weight be given to the later
calculations of Cambon, Johannot, and Éschassériaux? Is the
rapid increase in value wholly to be attributed to the addition of
new resources? Evidently not, for resources which received no
increments, increased in value. Taking the inflated and doubtful
figures of the ministerial reports, but reducing the totals to a stable
basis with the aid of the local tables of depreciation, what results
do we obtain? Payments on lands have been deducted when not
excluded, and the stable values of all payments made up to each
particular date have been substituted. The stable values of the
national resources thus obtained are:

MILLIONS OF LIVRES

1790	2000	February, 1793	5000
June, 1791	2200	May, 1793	4800
September, 1791	2900	December, 1794	5100
April, 1792	3200	April, 1795	3400
October, 1792	4600	November, 1795	7900

[1] D'Ivnerois (*A Cursory View of the Assignats*, pp. 14–18) criticised Johannot's
estimate harshly. He demonstrated that the expectation of sales at 40 years purchase was preposterous when the market was glutted. He also pointed out that
Johannot had made no allowance for the large proportion of lands to be restored.
[2] Prunélé (*Fortunes, Publiques et Particulières*, pp. 24–25) also examined Johannot's results. Prunélé thought (1) that the estimate of monthly revenue was excessive because large sales of these possessions had occurred, and because the revenue
of lands to be restored had been included, and (2) that the rate of capitalisation was
excessive.
[3] *Actes de Directoire Exécutif*, Vol. II, p. 2.

This procedure may seem futile; but one disturbing element is removed. That the first three estimates show such a marked upward trend after the inflated element due to the declining value of the Assignat has been eliminated, is probably due to the discovery of new resources, real and mythical. The larger totals for the next four estimates result from the new lands, the "biens de seconde origine." The absence of any marked changes in 1793–94 is singular, for extensive civil confiscations occurred during this period. The decline in the spring of 1795 was even more exceptional. Both of these anomalies are probably partially explicable by the unprecedented glut in the land market. The important law of April 15, 1795, which deprived the Government of a considerable proportion of its exploitations, is relevant as regards the decline in 1795. The signal increase in the latter part of 1795, although in part attributable to new acquisitions, is in the main a reflection of the increased exaggerations of the official surveyors. Officials also were probably not quick in bolstering valuations during this initial period of rapid depreciation. All the valuations merit the criticism that the calculations were made on the supposition that only a small proportion of the resources were to be sold at any particular time.

A study of particular categories of the national resources sheds some additional light on the subject. The financial experts, in appraising the forests and the former possessions of the Émigrés, were glaringly inconsistent. Of particular significance are the more sober estimates of the less interested authorities, the registry office, and the land office. They had no incentive to exaggerate.

1. ÉMIGRÉS' POSSESSIONS — MILLIONS OF LIVRES

Date	Reporter	Evaluation (nominal)
October, 1792	Cambon	1000
February, 1793	Cambon	3000
May, 1793	Cambon	3000
June, 1793	Administration de l'Enregistrement	1200
August, 1793	Administration des Domaines Nationals	1700
April, 1795	Johannot	11900
November, 1795	Eschassériaux	2000 metallic
Current estimate	Stourm (based on indemnification of Restoration Government)	2500

2. FORESTS — MILLIONS OF LIVRES

Date	Reporter	Value of Assignat	Evaluation (nominal)
June, 1791	Camus	93	183[1]
September, 1791	Montesquiou	83	392[1]
April, 1792	Cambon	71	1100
February, 1793	Cambon	65	1200
May, 1793	Johannot	55	1200
April, 1795	Johannot	15	2000
November, 1795	Éschassériaux	..	2000 metallic
February, 1796	Camus	..	2800–2900 metallic

Stourm attempts to estimate the value of the newly acquired possessions. Relying mainly on Montesquiou's report of September, 1791 and on Cambon's report of April 3, 1792, he estimates that the value of the church and crown lands was 3 milliards.[2] That estimate appears to be too high. Some of the items included by Cambon and Montesquiou may certainly be considerably pared down, if not entirely eliminated.

Montesquiou allowed (1) 510 millions for the excess of sales price over "prix d'estimation"— a wholly unjustifiable assumption; (2) 275 millions for possessions the sale of which had been suspended, including hospitals, educational institutions, and homes for the poor — all items of low and doubtful selling value; (3) 200 millions for the domains of the crown — a figure which Cambon himself later reduced by one-half; (4) 300 millions for the sale of feudal dues on government lands — a doubtful item at the time, and a claim later relinquished by the Government; (5) 300 millions for "la vente éventuelle des tailles épars." Add these items, and one must conclude that Montesquiou's report, unamended, affords a poor basis for any estimate. M. Bergasse, a contemporary, remarked that Montesquiou was in error to estimate the value of the unsold land according to the price received for land previously sold. He feared that speculators had forced prices up, that many bought without the intention of or capacity to pay, and that the high prices paid were in part attributable to anticipation of depreciation, and hence of a reduction in the cost of later installments.[3]

---

[1] Includes only those on sale.
[2] *Finances de l'Ancien Régime et Révolution*, Vol. II, pp. 450–454.
[3] *Réplique de M. Bergasse à Montesquiou*, pp. 81–83.

Cambon falls into many of the exaggerations of Montesquiou.[1] The most important reason for discounting Cambon's estimate is that by April, 1792, the Assignat had depreciated by about a third, and the estimate reflected that shrinkage. Moreover, Cambon evaluated the colleges, factories, and other items in the same group at 248 millions, to which he added 148 millions (three-fifths) on account of the excess of sales price over the "prix d'estimation". His total estimate of 2850 millions included approximately 1000 millions attributable to the excess of sales price over the "prix d'estimation".

Stourm bases his estimates of the "biens de seconde origine" (lands of the Émigrés, and civil confiscations) largely on the indemnity proffered the victims in 1825, and arrives at a total of 2300 to 2500 millions for "biens" of this category. For sales before Prairial 3 (June, 1795), the "restitution figures" were based on the sales price reduced in accordance with the local tables of depreciation. For sales after Prairial 3, the valuation was based on the revenue of 1790, capitalized at 20 years purchase.[2] Because of the damage suffered by the Émigrés' lands between 1790 and 1793, and because Stourm capitalized the income at 3 per cent, I am inclined to believe that Stourm's figures are rather high.[3] It is noteworthy, also, that not even the imaginative ministers of finance found that the confiscations of the holdings of the Émigrés and Condemned had contributed to the stable value of the resources so large an amount.

The contention has been made that for the lands of the Émigrés the sales price did not rise sufficiently to offset the depreciation. From the charts that follow, it will be seen that no generalisation can safely be drawn as to the relation between the "prix d'estimation" and the "prix d'adjudication" (sales price). For the Department of Yonne, the "prix d'adjudication" reduced by the values of the local tables remained consistently at a higher level than the "prix d'estimation," at least until early in 1795. Com-

[1] Arch. Parl., Vol. XLI, pp. 148–150.
[2] M. DeNervo, Les Finances Françaises sous la Restauration, Vol. III, pp. 127–128.
[3] A. Young (Travels in France, 2d ed., Vol. I, pp. 352–353), after a careful study, puts the average yield in 1789 at 3¾ per cent.

pare those results with the results for the Department of Ille-et-Vilaine where the "*prix d'estimation*" was almost consistently at a higher level. (The prix d'estimation was the value of the land as estimated by the authorities from the income yielded in

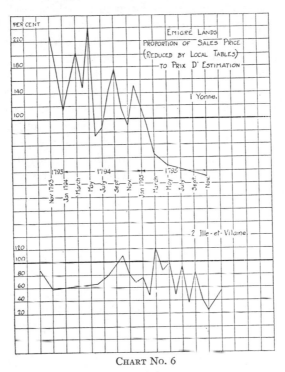

CHART No. 6

1790.) I would reduce Stourm's aggregate figure of 5½ milliards to 4 milliards as a maximum. Stourm finds Éschassériaux's report the only candid one made during the paper money period. He is aware that Éschassériaux's estimate of the resources comes very close to his. Stourm seems unaware of the fact, however, that Éschassériaux's calculations, unlike those of Cambon and Johannot, were on a metallic basis. It will be remembered that Stourm relies largely on the findings of Cambon. He also appears to be unacquainted with the fact that Éschassériaux excluded at least 1½ milliards of resources sold and paid for by November,

1795. That, in itself, would reduce Stourm's estimate by 1½ milliards. In my table of stable valuations of the national resources, Éschassériaux's figures seem distinctly at variance with all the other results. His evaluation of the forests at 2 milliards (metallic value) is just one indication of the untrustworthiness of his figures. The value of the total resources did not e..ceed 4000 millions. That was, however, what might be called a contingent saleable value; contingent on their being placed on the market gradually. In fact, first almost all the domains of the Church, and later the possessions of the Émigrés were thrown on the market at once. The excessive fall of values that ensued escaped observation only because of the depreciation, present and expected, of the circulating media, and, because of the low "prix d'estimation." Marion and others bewail the depreciation of the Assignat, and say that the depreciation made later installments of payments valueless. But they disregard the fact that many sales would never have been consummated had it not been for expectations of further depreciation. The sales of 1791, perhaps, were not aided by such unpatriotic calculations. But who will deny that later sales were appreciably increased because of the anticipated lightening of the burden of future installments of payments by reason of currency depreciation? Loutchisky has investigated the purchases of national domains in certain districts. The increasing proportion of purchasers among the urban bourgeoisie and the declining proportion of rural purchasers, is significant.[1] Attention is here drawn again to the ratio of monthly payments made to payments due for purchases of land. It will be remembered that evidence of the anticipation of depreciation was indicated as early as 1792.

Hawtrey, on the basis of the lack of support given to the loans issued by the Government, concludes that savings were not available, and that the sale of lands, therefore, could not have been successful. But is the assumption tenable that the failure of the loans of a bankrupt and tottering government, is an unmistakable indication of the absence of saving? Moreover, should allowance

[1] J. Loutchisky, La Petite Propriété en France avant la Révolution, pp. 92–95. District of Laon: Bourgeoise bought 22.1 per cent "biens de première origine," and 49.2 per cent of "biens de seconde origine."

not be made for the new investments which the reduction of the government debt would make possible? Marion takes an opposite position in assuming that the vast payments required might conceivably have been made, even if depreciation had not developed. His error lies in failing to understand, first, that a large proportion of the purchases were made on the expectation of depreciation, and, second, that maximum laws, requisitions, wars, and insecurity deprived the farmers of the ability to make full payment even when depreciation was not anticipated. The many defaults that occurred when the Government attempted to collect the last quarter "au cours" for sales under the laws of 28 Ventôse 4 and 6 Floreal 4, are not without significance here.

What was actually received? Ramel and Stourm abandon this problem in despair; Marion does not concern himself with it. It is impossible to obtain a total for the different kinds of paper received for the lands. Fortunately for the Assignat and Mandat period, that complication is not serious, and, therefore, a respectable estimate is possible. I have collected the figures for the monthly burnings of Assignats and reduced them to stable values. Allowances were made for the receipts from sources other than land. The interpolations frequently necessary in 1794 and 1795 detract somewhat from the accuracy of the figures. The results from 1791 to November, 1795 are given in the following table. The total burnings (1790 value) were 900 millions; the nominal figures were 2100 millions. From November, 1795 to March, 1796, Assignats received from the sales of lands were almost valueless because of the extreme depreciation; and the difficulty, with the meagre information available, of distinguishing between sales receipts and receipts from the forced loan, seems insurmountable.[1]

---

[1] By December, 1795 17 millions had been received for total sales of 29 millions in the Department of Yonne. From December, 1795 to March, 1796 the remaining 12 millions received were equivalent to about 60,000 livres in stable currency. *Ventes-Yonne*, I, Introd., p. clx.

THE ASSIGNATS

MILLIONS OF LIVRES

Month	1791		1792		1793		1794		1795	
	Nom-inal	Real	Nom-inal	Real	Nom-inal	Real	Nom-inal	Real	Nom-inal	Real
January...	..	..	17	14	20	13	40	20	28	7
February..	39	37	25	18	18	12	62	31	28	7
March....	..	..	37	27	21	13½	62	28	28	5½
April.....	52	49	28	21	20	12	33	14½	27	4½
May......	37	33½	34	24	23	13	50	21	27	3½
June......	39	35½	29	20½	38	18½	50	20	27	2
July......	35	31	19	13½	41	18	50	20½	100	5
August ...	29	26	19	13½	31	13½	50	19½	100	4
September	16	14½	19	13½	28	12	50	18½	100	3
October...	26	23	26	18	29	12	33	11½	95	2
November.	23	20	13	9	35	17	33	10½	95	1
December	30	25½	12	8	37	20	33	9½	..	...
Totals ..	326	295	278	200	341	175	546	225	655	45

Nominal Total = 2146. Real Total = 940.

Monthly figures for land sales are to be found in the *Moniteur* or in the Parliamentary papers for all months up to 1794, except July–September, 1792. In 1794 and 1795, reliance was placed mainly on five official reports.

The sales of lands during the Mandat period, although consummated at unfavorable terms, contributed substantially to the Government's revenues. These contributions were made possible by a series of retroactive and unconstitutional laws, culminating in the law of July 25, 1796. The Government demanded the payment of the last quarter in Mandats "au Cours," though the Mandat then was quoted at 3 per cent. The last report obtainable reveals sales of 547 millions and payments of 1586 millions up to January 23, 1797.[1] On the assumption that all these sales were finally liquidated, the "au cours" payments would total 137 millions (stable value). Sales began in Floreal and Prairial, and the first three payments were demanded in Prairial, Messidor and Thermidor. Hence the value of the earlier payments can be roughly estimated as follows:

[1] *Recueil des Actes du Directoire Exécutif*, Vol. IV, p. 712.

Sales = 547 millions of livres.
Average value of Mandat at time of payments = 5 per cent.
Stable value of these payments = 27.5 millions of livres.
Reduce by one-fourth (payment made "au cours" after the disappearance
   of the Assignats) = 6.9 millions of livres.
Net receipts = 20.6 millions of livres.

The total receipts of 158 millions should be further reduced by perhaps one-third to one-half to allow for the remaining payments ("au cours") made after the official termination of paper money in February, 1797.[1] By the Act of July, 1796, the Government required four payments over a period of 16 months for the payment of the last quarter on lands bought during the Mandat period.

During a period of insecurity, of exploitation, and of adverse public policy, the Government was able to withdraw from circulation through land sales approximately 2 milliards of Assignats, and over 1500 millions of Mandats. These withdrawals equalled well over 1 milliard at their 1790 values when received. Considering the economic conditions, the difficulty of selling large quantities of land and the chaotic forces at work, I conclude that the Government was moderately successful in disposing of its lands, and that some authors have gone altogether too far in saying that the land was practically given away. Moreover, a large proportion of these resources remained unsold when the paper money-fiasco ended; and land sales formed a not unimportant part of the budget in later years.[2]

The objection may be raised that the Government received no advantage from the sale of lands, since the Assignats thus received were burnt; but, at least, the paper money later disbursed was issued at a *relatively* higher value.

The three tables below, constructed from material in the local archives, substantiate the above conclusion.

---

[1] This reduction is made because we are interested in the effects of land sales on the value of the Assignat.

[2] The budget of 1798 included 50 millions from land revenues and 20 millions from sales. L. M. DeNervo, *Les Finances Françaises sous l'Ancien Monarchie*, etc., Vol. II, p. 287. The budget of 1806 called for 10 millions, and the budget of 1808 for 45 millions. F. N. Mollien, *Mémoires d'un Ministre*, Vol. II, pp. 80, 376. As late as 1814, 260 millions of lands remained unsold. L. M. DeNervo, *Les Finances de la Restauration*, Vol. II, pp. 72–73.

A. DEPARTMENT OF YONNE (ooo's omitted)

Law	Prix d'Adjudication (Sales Price)	Prix d'Estimation	"Real" Payment
Before 28 Ventôse 4...........	29,754	4,840	4,090
28 Ventôse 4...........	1,106	1,106	325
16 Brumaire 5.........	6,297	342	328
Vendemaire et Brumaire 7.....	1,706	1,500	1,706
Total................	38,863	7,788	6,449

Three facts are worth noting:

1. The gold value of all payments equalled 65 per cent of the estimated value in 1790 — rather low estimates, it will be remembered, in Porée's opinion.

2. Sales before the Mandat period netted one-half of the estimated value of all the resources and 80 per cent of "prix d'estimation" of these resources.

3. At least 25 per cent of the estimated values of all resources were realized after the paper money régime.

B. DEPARTMENT OF VOSGES. DISTRICT OF REMIREMONT. INTROD., p. lviii

"Biens de Première Origine" (ooo's omitted)

1 Year	2 "Prix d'Estimation"	3 "Prix d'Adjudication"	4 Price really paid (Stable Value)	4 to 2 (Per Cent)
1791..........	91.5	176.6	84.2	92
1792..........	38.4	76.5	27.6	71.8
1793..........	11.7	26.7	6.7	57
Ans II and III .	3.3	13.3	1.2	38.5
Total...	145.0	293.2	119.9	82
"Biens de Seconde Origine"				
Ans II and III.	52.9	144.1	8.7	16.6
Grand Total...	197.9	434.3	128.7	65

C. DEPARTMENT OF VOSGES. DISTRICT OF ÉPINAL. INTROD., p. lxxi

"Biens de Première Origine"

1 Year	2 "Prix d'Estimation"	3 "Prix d'Adjudication"	4 Price really paid	4 to 2 (Per Cent)
1791..........	168.7	241.3	113.3	70
1792..........	13.8	24.3	7.4	54
1793..........	19.1	55.6	15.4	81
An II.........	25.2	97.2	11.7	46
An III........	103.4	362.1	26.0	25
Total.........	330	780.3	174.3	52.8
	"Biens de Seconde Origine"			
Ans II and III.	57.1	104.2	15.7	27.4
Total.........	387.1	884.5	190.0	49.1

A comparison of the metallic value of the receipts and the "prix d'estimation" in two districts in the same department indicates, first, that there was an appreciable diversity of results even in the same department, and second, that "real" receipts for sales of church and crown possessions compared quite favorably with the "prix d'estimation" for sales until the middle of 1795. The results of the sales of the possessions of the Émigrés and Condemned were not so advantageous.

Finally, one more table is of some value. The conclusion to be drawn is that, for a constant area of land, a fairly constant amount of money of stable value was paid between 1791 and 1796, regardless of the particular time of sale. Evidently, depreciation did little harm to the revenues. A generalization on the basis of this one department would be untenable, however.

VENTES-DEPARTMENT OF HAUTE-GARONNE, PP. 578–579

Decree	Hectares sold	Money (00,000 omitted)	Nominal Price per Hectare	Real Values per Hectare
May 14, 1790..........	5,456	7.2	1,075	273
June 3, 1793 and 8 Nivôse 2.........	4,179	9.2	2,232	231
12 and 27 Prairial 3 ...	310	3.1	11,064	335
28 Ventôse 4.........	803	2.3	1,328	298

5. SUMMARY

Too much emphasis has been put on the theoretical difficulties of land sales, on the too long deferred redemption of the paper money through the sales of land, and on the alleged impossibility that a land security could help support the value of a paper money. The position taken by Senior, Mill, Levasseur, Hawtrey, and others was a natural reaction from the exaggerated hope and faith placed in the land by the adherents of the Assignat system, and by advocates of "land currency" in general. One may wonder whether the critics have not pushed their case a little too far; whether in their fight against the land fallacy, they have not fallen into slight errors of exaggeration. Their discussions of monetary principles are dissociated from the daily life of the Revolution, from the intoxication with, and the penetration of, the land idea. What did it matter to the man in the street that land-secured paper money was not in accordance with the best paper money traditions so long as a thorough system of propaganda and education made him believe that the Revolutionary paper money was not a replica of Law's paper money of unhappy memory, but was in reality "circulating land". Few would deny the relationship between confidence and the supply of money, and therefore between confidence and the value of money.[1] No careful student of the documents of the period can fail to see that much of the confidence in the Assignats originated in their land security. A reduction of the circulation resulted both from the increased confidence and from the mechanical redemption through land sales.

The importance of the land for the retirement of the paper money should not, however, be exaggerated. Even in France, where the desire to own land was intense, the market was limited.

---

[1] There is little disagreement as to the importance of confidence. In the early part of the 19th century, Thornton and others argued that an increase in confidence would be accompanied by an increase of money in circulation. Confidence was the *sine qua non* for acceptance; but contemporary writers assume that the money has been accepted. Bendixen contends that *belief* in the paper money is necessary. (F. Bendixen, *Währungspolitik und Geldtheorie*, p. 36.) Katzellenbaum is of the opinion that there are no degrees of confidence. (S. Katzellenbaum, *Russian Currency and Banking*, p. 30.) Also see the interesting discussions in L. Mises, *Die geldtheoretische und geldrechtliche Seite des Stabilisierungsproblems* (especially p. 13), Bortkiewicz's comments in the *Schriften des Vereins für Social Politik*, Vol. CLXX, pp. 267–269, and Chapter II of J. M. Keynes, *Tract on Monetary Reform*.

Sales of 4 milliards of lands in six years would have required on the average about a third of the net income of the people. Under such conditions, alienation could have been achieved only through the tapering down of later payments by depreciation. Average receipts of 200 millions (value of 1790) during the paper money régime, and unknown large hoardings for later payments, testify to the land hunger of the French and to the support given to the Assignat by actual sales.

The German Government, in the last days of the circulation of the mark, issued a new currency, the Rentenmark.[1] Secured by land in a manner somewhat similar to the Assignat, it was a bribe to the farmer without whose support the new money would not have been accepted.[2] Limited in quantity and ably managed, the Rentenmark maintained its value during the critical transitional period. Hawtrey perceives little advantage in the security behind it and attributes its success to the gold bonds in which it was denominated.[3] The security was only an eye-wash, in the opinion of Cannan.[4] Former Finance Minister Rheinhold describes the Rentenmark as "money based on trust, money based on hope".[5] Did not the Rentenmark attain the success which the Assignat would have, had it been issued in moderation?[6] Certainly, the denomination in gold bonds made little impression on Germany.

[1] See J. Hirsch, *Die deutsche Währungsfrage*, pp. 29–30.
[2] H. Schacht, *op. cit.*, pp. 83–87.
[3] Hawtrey's "Review of Schacht's Stabilisation of the Mark," *Royal Statistical Journal*, 1928, pp. 100–101.
[4] E. Cannan, *An Economist's Protest*, p. 361.
[5] P. P. Rheinhold, *The Economic, Financial, and Political State of Germany since the War*, p. 24.
[6] The public was skeptical in the early days of the Rentenmark. That is evident from the *British Overseas Report on Germany*, 1924, p. 7.

CHAPTER IV

MEASURES AND EXTENT OF DEPRECIATION

1. Previous Consideration of the Choice of a Measure

Writers on the Assignats are, in general, unconcerned about the choice of a suitable measure of depreciation; they are prone to use measures without consideration of the appropriateness of the measure.[1] Often, they shift from one measure to another without comment, even unthinkingly. Foreign exchange quotations, the price of gold and silver, and scattered price statistics are equally serviceable.

Jaurès, Bornarel, Illig, Hawtrey, and Falkner recognize the presence of a problem.[2] The consideration given to this problem by Jaurès and Bornarel, can be dismissed quickly. Jaurès recognizes that the depreciation varied with the three measures employed: commodity prices, gold and silver prices, and foreign exchange quotations.[3] Bornarel, also, is aware that the extent of depreciation was dependent on the particular measure used; it is not a matter of indifference whether the price of commodities, or the prices of gold and silver are employed for this purpose.[4]

Illig, a German of the Knapp School, dogmatically refuses to consider any measure of depreciation but the foreign exchanges. "We recognize no rate for the Assignat but a sinking exchange rate of 'valutarischen' money. It declined according to the relations which the provinces of France had with foreign countries."

[1] Levasseur, White, Stourm, and others.

[2] The authors of the "Bullion Report," confronted with an argument that the apparent depreciation of the paper was but an appreciation of gold, discussed the appropriateness of gold quotations as a measure of depreciation. Any careful reader of the "Bullion Report" will agree that the Bullionists failed to prove that the depreciation of the paper was not partially an appreciation of gold, and hence that gold quotations were a satisfactory measure of depreciation. E. Cannan, *The Paper Pound of 1797–1821*, pp. 6–16.

[3] J. Jaurès, *Histoire Socialiste de la Révolution Française*, Vol. III, pp. 325–326.

[4] F. Bornarel, "Etudie sur les Assignats," *La Révolution Française*, Vol. XVI, p. 122.

But two pages back, however, he attempts to demonstrate that the exchange rates of Hamburg on Paris moved in close sympathy with the course of the Assignat, and he employs the price quotations of gold and silver to measure the value of the Assignat.[1]

Falkner deals with the topic in a more intelligent and consistent manner than any other writer. He relies mainly on the Treasury prices for gold and silver. The foreign exchanges, according to him, do not constitute a reliable measure of depreciation because the state of the exchange of goods and of the balance of accounts, as well as the international credit situation, all reacted on the exchanges. Price statistics are the least objectionable gauge of depreciation, he thinks, if the requisite facts can be collated. Falkner, however, criticises his measure: the exchange on gold countries reacted on the price of gold; the value of gold and silver was affected by the hoarding of metals.[2]

The problem of the selection of a proper measure of depreciation receives inadequate attention from Hawtrey in his chapter on the Assignats in *Currency and Credit;* his failure to consider this problem, which detracts from the value of the chapter, is inexplicable in the light of a contribution to the subject in an earlier essay on the Restriction Period, later republished in *Currency and Credit.* The particular index to be used, as well as the relative values of the possible measures, concerns Hawtrey in the earlier paper. He deplores the use of gold as a measure of depreciation during the Restriction Period because the gold market was in an artificial state. The accuracy of the foreign exchanges as a measure, is questioned; moreover, the gold points were unstable during the Napoleonic Wars. Hawtrey even finds fault with Jevons' price indices; the commodities considered are of a limited range; price increases of an inflationary character are indistinguishable from those caused by scarcity; nor do the indices distinguish paper from gold depreciation.[3] Compare this acute summary of the difficulties to be encountered in the choice of an adequate measure — as given in his contribution to the *Economic Journal* — with his

[1] H. Illig, *Das Geldwesen Frankreichs*, pp. 71–73.
[2] S. V. Falkner, *op. cit.*, pp. 33–34.
[3] R. G. Hawtrey, "The Bank Restriction of 1797," *Economic Journal*, Vol. XXVIII, pp. 62–63.

failure to remind us of the presence of a problem in his chapter on the Assignats.[1]

He jumps from one measure of depreciation to another without comment. First, he employs the Treasury prices for gold and silver; in 1793 and 1794, he alternates between the Treasury figures and the foreign exchange quotations. Now, he fails to make an allowance for the movement of the gold points that accompanied the outbreak of the war with England. After the period of maximum prices, he shifts without warning or comment to the use of price quotations to measure the depreciation. Only a few stray suggestions remind us of the more adequate treatment in the earlier essay. Thus the increase in the value of the Assignat in the latter part of 1793 is attributed partly to the decreased value of gold. In his discussion of the depreciation of 1795, he tells us that the rise of prices was proportionate to the increase in the price of gold and silver, which is rather doubtful as we shall see. The utilisation of all three measures is not objectionable; but their indiscriminate use without a caution respecting their unequal values and the too easy movement from one measure to another, are to be criticised.[2]

Contemporary writers, in some instances, discussed this problem in an indirect manner. Lavoisier said, "If one consults the price of wheat, of meat, or of most agricultural products, of land or of daily wages, it will be seen that the increase of their prices is not nearly in proportion to what one calls the loss of the Assignats." He added that part of the loss was really a gain — an increased value — of gold and silver.[3] Condorcet, also, advised

---

[1] R. G. Hawtrey, *Currency and Credit*, pp. 243–249.

[2] Ferraris and Wagner both criticise the English for not distinguishing between *Wertminderung* and *Entwertung*. The former is measured by changes in the price level, and the latter by changes in the price of gold and silver. On the basis of Wagner's study of Russian paper money, Angell criticises him for not reconciling both measures. However, even in 1868, Wagner already recognised that the agio was a poor index of the changes in the price level; and, in his later study, he clearly shows the relationship of the two measures. C. F. Ferraris, *Moneta e Corso Forzoso*, p. 63. Also A. Wagner, *Die russische Papierwährung*, pp. v, 80–82, 112–116; *Theoretische Sozialökonomie*, Part II, Vol. II, pp. 696–702. Also J. W. Angell, *Theory of International Prices*, pp. 336–339.

[3] A. L. Lavoisier, *De l'État des Finances de France au Premier Janvier, 1792*, Oeuvres, Vol. VI, pp. 501–502.

that price quotations be used as a measure because the prices of gold and silver were subject to special influences.[1]

2. An Analysis of the Possible Measures

A. The price of gold and silver: the Treasury tables.

The prices of gold and silver, most commonly employed as a measure of depreciation of the Assignats, constitute the least desirable measure.[2] The indispensable attribute of an acceptable measure should be relative uniformity. As the Revolution proceeded, the metals were used less and less as an internal medium of exchange, and more and more for hoards and for remittances abroad for the absolute necessities of life. The Government was successful in its campaign against the use of gold and silver as money, only at intervals — notably for an extended period during the Reign of Terror. But the variable success of the Government, and the frequent changes in the functions of gold and silver, detract from the trustworthiness of their Treasury values as a measure of depreciation. The needs of the Government for gold and silver continued to increase from 1791 through 1792, largely as a result of the requirements for military payments (including payments for subsistence and wages) at home and abroad. Since the supplies of the metals brought to the market — at the danger of one's life frequently — were strictly limited, this inelastic demand on the part of the Government bolstered their prices perceptibly.

Hawtrey explains the apparent revival of the value of the Assignat in the latter part of 1792 as a fall in the world-wide value of gold. Was there a world market for gold? Hawtrey observes the sustained bounty on the exportation of gold and silver from France to England in the early years of the Revolution, which can be measured by comparing the premium on the London exchanges

---

[1] *J. Déb. et Déc.*, Vol. XLI, pp. 261–264, also Condorcet, *Discourse sur les Finances*, Oeuvres, Vol. XII, p. 73.

[2] In the course of the debates on the selection of a suitable measure of depreciation for the construction of the local tables, Lebrun proposed in behalf of a Committee of the Conseil d'Anciens to reject the use of the Treasury prices of gold and silver because the Treasury's willingness to buy gold and silver at any price had resulted in an increase in their value.

with the prices of gold and silver in Paris, and he refers to the greater depreciation of the Assignat in terms of gold and silver in 1795–96 that should have made necessary gold shipments from London to Paris. The existence of an appreciable premium on gold over the gold exchanges for any length of time belies the existence of a world market. Gold in England was one thing; in France it was another.[1] In one country, it remained a medium of exchange primarily; in the other, it became an instrument of speculation, a means of storing value and of remitting abroad. A change in the value of the metals in England might or might not have been accompanied by a parallel movement in France. Gold for hoarding was stored almost irrespective of its market value; in fact, market values were of significance in France only for the small proportion of the total supply that was on the market, or likely to reach it soon. Gold should have moved from England to France in 1795–96 until the bounty disappeared if a world market really existed; but France did not possess the means to purchase the supply of metals necessary to obliterate the bounty. For the bounty would have continued in spite of heavy shipments until the monetary hunger resulting from the demonetisation of paper (juristic or practical) was satiated. The varying impediments put upon international movements of gold sufficed to destroy the world market.

Speculation diverted much gold and silver from more necessary employments; and speculation had great vogue at certain epochs of the Revolution. The legal position of gold and silver changed frequently.

Writers often maintain that the premium on gold is an excellent measure of depreciation because changes in the value of gold are soon reflected in the price level. My answer is — as far as the Assignats are concerned at least — that too many factors influenced the price of gold and silver without necessarily affecting the

---

[1] The condition of the gold market in Russia from 1918 to 1922 was strikingly similar to the condition in France during a large part of the Revolution. The authorities attributed the very high value of gold in Russia before the introduction of the Chervonetz to Russia's economic isolation. The value of gold was determined by its use as an insurance fund against depreciation. *The State Bank of the U. S. S. R.*, 1921–1926, pp. 26–28.

price level in the same manner: speculation,[1] government purchases, hoarding, and legal changes in the position of the metallic money.[2] In my chapter on local depreciation I point out that the depreciation was more marked in Paris than in the Provinces; does that not furnish an additional reason for avoiding the use of Treasury (Paris) prices of gold and silver?[3]

B. Foreign exchange quotations.[4]

Although Illig alone proposes to place exclusive reliance on the foreign exchange quotations as a measure, many writers use them as a measure, supplementary to the Treasury figures. Chapter X is devoted to the foreign exchanges during the Revolution; here I consider only the appropriateness of the exchanges as an index of depreciation.

For the more normal economic conditions before the Revolution the use of foreign exchange quotations would have been satisfactory. The movement of capital in and out of France had been negligible. Since the so-called invisible items may affect the foreign exchanges independently, i.e., without a corresponding effect on price levels, a large proportion of such invisible items may invalidate the use of the exchanges as a measure. The de-

[1] Mallarmé discounted the value of gold and silver quotations, because the speculators were subject to moral pressure and personal danger. Arch. Parl., Vol. LXVI, p. 72. One department refused to use the Treasury figures for gold and silver after March, 1795, on the ground that the price of gold was determined by speculative influences. P. Caron, *Tableaux*, p. 65.

[2] W. Lotz observes that in the recent war, neither prices nor rents, nor wages reflected the depreciation of the mark adequately, for the Government held prices down. Gold would have been an acceptable measure if the Government had not interfered with the gold market. *Die deutsche Staatsfinanzwirtschaft im Kriege*, pp. 29–30.

[3] Schmidt errs in his statement that the Treasury quotations for gold and silver were based on transactions — sales of land, and the like — between individuals. (The basis of the Treasury tables is analysed in this and in the next chapter.) A. Schmidt, *Paris pendant la Révolution*, Vol. II, p. 229.

[4] Ricardo was not satisfied with the foreign exchanges on all occasions: "I do not mean to contend that a convulsed state of the exchange such as would be caused by a subsidy granted to a foreign power, would accurately measure the value of a currency because a demand for bills arising from such a cause would not be in consequence of the natural commerce of the country." *Letters to Malthus* (VII). Several contemporary writers deprecate the use of the foreign exchanges as a measure of depreciation during war times. M. Fanno, *Inflazione Monetaria e Corso dei Cambi*, p. 101.

crease of foreign trade, accompanied by an increased exportation of capital, which resulted both from the harsh policy toward the Emigrés, and from the lack of confidence in the Revolution, resulted in an increase of the relative importance of the invisible items and detracted from the usefulness of the exchanges as a measure of depreciation.[1]

The danger of famine in France necessitated heavy purchases of food abroad. These purchases have been exaggerated; but they did, nevertheless, have a disastrous effect on the exchanges: Even with relatively unimportant purchases the exchanges depreciated. It was difficult to procure foreign exchange in Paris at a time when French exchange could serve no useful purpose.[2] High prices are generally accompanied by reduced consumption; but the Government resold the subsistence at prices much below the high level required by the depreciated exchanges. Even rationing did not bring an adequate curtailment of consumption.

The demand for French commodities suffered from the disorganisation of industry that resulted from the wars and the Revolution; but the demand for French exchange and commodities was still further reduced — practically destroyed — by the system of maximum prices below market prices, and the restrictions on exports which this made necessary. A free export system under such conditions would have deprived France of most of her supplies, already scarce. The corrupt policy of the Terrorists toward foreign creditors also contributed to the depreciation of the exchanges. The presence of these forces that exerted a peculiar influence on the exchanges with little or no repercussion on the price levels, makes me doubt the advisability of employing the foreign exchange quotations for the purpose in hand.[3]

---

[1] These and other points in this chapter are elaborated further in Chapter X.

[2] Boissy d'Anglas told the Convention in January, 1795 that the Government had been able to buy only 2 million quintals of wheat (about 30 million livres in metallic value) in the previous 23 months. *J. Déb. et Déc.*, Vol. LXVII, pp. 220–222.

[3] Wagner is critical of the employment of the prices of either the precious metals of the foreign exchanges as measures of depreciation. He refers to the premium on either as an agio, although he is aware that differences may emerge. Of special significance is his contention that the supply and demand for the precious metals in large part determines the agio. A. Wagner, *Die russische Papierwährung*, pp. 85–90, 112–116.

C. Price indices and price quotations.

Although an index number of prices for the French Revolution does not exist, the material for the construction of such an index can probably be found in the archives of France. A few writers have employed random price quotations as an indication of the extent of depreciation.

Of how much value are the price statistics of the French Revolution? The system of weights and measures was complicated and confusing and has many pitfalls for the unsuspecting. Price quotations varied widely not only in different departments, but in different markets in the same department, and even in the same district. Changes in quality, as is to be expected in a period of economic disorganisation, were so great from year to year that a consideration of certain commodities in 1790 as the same commodities in 1795, is scarcely justifiable. Market prices were often fictitious. Sales were often consummated at the homes of the farmers at prices considerably higher than market prices.

This is an appropriate place to point out a frequent error made by writers on this subject. Falkner, for example, in attempting to account for the formidable increase in the price of bread in Paris in the post-maximum period, contends that the people of France, faced with a decrease in the supplies of the more important commodities and a reduction of real wages, had to readjust their budgets and to spend a larger proportion of their incomes on bread.[1] (I dwell in Chapter VI on the nation-wide scarcity of all products in 1795.) Falkner is not justified in generalizing from conditions in Paris, for the people in the Provinces consumed less bread than ever. Paris consumed more bread in 1795 by virtue of the generosity of the National Government; the Provinces consumed less bread, because they received no such generous subsidies. But the main point is, however, that from the abrogation of the maximum laws in 1794 until early in 1796, the Government purchased provisions for Paris (bread, in particular), and the prices quoted by Falkner, Levasseur, and others are the prices of the market, i.e., the prices of the surplus remaining after each inhabitant had received his daily pittance of one-half, one, or one and one-half pounds

[1] S. V. Falkner, *op. cit.*, pp. 53–56.

of bread from the Government at close to maximum prices. The relatively high market prices were therefore of secondary importance. This difficulty indicates another obstacle to be faced in the construction of index numbers. If it is remembered that the market price of bread pertained to but one-third of the total sales, and that the remainder sold at prices little above the former maximum prices, the increase in its price will not seem so alarming.

During a period of controlled prices — and control extended beyond the eighteen months of the so-called maximum period — the value of index numbers is doubtful. The consumer was forced to readjust his budget, with a resulting diminution of satisfaction. The inclusion of prices reduced by the maximum system results in a low price index; and this result is misleading because the total purchasing power of the citizen's money income was reduced by the compulsory hoarding of part of it that ensued.[1] The increased purchasing power of the Assignat was a reality for the Government but fictitious for the consumer in so far as the system of rationing resulted in the forced hoarding of Assignats.

One might insist that by the value of money we mean the value of each unit. Hence if the price level falls, the value of money has increased, regardless of whether the public is now prevented from disbursing all its money. I do not object to this usage, but merely insist that the significance of changes in value would be distinctly limited. An increase in the value of monetary units that are disbursed when disbursements are hampered by peculiar economic conditions and especially by official interference, should be considered in conjunction with the number of units disbursed. If the average individual profited from the reduction of prices in 1793–94, he also was deprived of the advantage of disbursing his money as rapidly as he wished, and in the difficult period of 1793–94, the loss was much greater than the gain. I would prefer to say that the value of money fell.

Many other perplexities arise. An index number fails to distinguish between the increase in prices due to increased issues of paper

---

[1] Terhalle, in a recent study, says that maximum prices are not prices in the usual sense, for there is no "Ausgleich" of supply and demand. F. Terhalle, *Freie oder Gebundene Preisbildung*, p. 83.

money and that due to decreased production. This is a problem of capital importance in the present case because of the unparalleled disorganization of the normal economic processes.[1] A readjustment of private budgets accompanied by a reduction of the consumer's total satisfaction ensues; and this may not be registered by an index number. (If the index number is based on weights that are changed with changes in consumption, it will not fully measure the reduction of satisfaction. If the weights are not changed, the increase in prices is exaggerated. There were acrimonious debates on this subject during the recent war.)

There are more of these miscellaneous difficulties. The use of the Assignat for the payment of taxes, a field of employment in which the Assignat passed at its nominal value practically throughout the Revolution, is not considered in the construction of an index number. The increase in tax assessments lagged far behind that in the price level. Nor does a general index number include a consideration of the relatively lucrative employment of Assignats for rent payments.

All measures have serious shortcomings. Although the price indices and price quotations have many theoretical and practical deficiencies, they indicate in a tolerably accurate manner that the Assignat bought more or less of some designated commodities. We are primarily interested in what money will buy. The necessity of hoarding paper as a result of control is a practical objection that does detract from the value of price indices and price quotations especially during the period of the maximum proper; and changes in the quality of the commodities is another practical objection. The change in the character and quantity of production is of significance only when we attempt to explain the depreciation. Since the French expended so large a proportion of their incomes on bread, the price quotations of bread or wheat may furnish a tolerable substitute for the more comprehensive study of prices, made difficult by the dearth of statistics.

The prices of gold and silver or the exchanges constitute measures of doubtful validity because, being subject to independent

[1] In Chapters VII and VIII, below, I consider the problem of the supplies of commodities and the more comprehensive subject of the demand for money.

forces, they move independently of the price levels. The sympathetic movement of the prices of gold and silver and of commodities was not striking; and the same observation holds for commodities and foreign exchanges. Although the exchanges and the prices of gold and silver, as well as the prices of commodities, were affected by the issues of Assignats, the former were also subject to independent influences that would make a substitution of either of them for the prices of commodities undesirable.

3. Extent of Depreciation

Although the foreign exchanges were noticeably depreciated in 1790–91, and an appreciable premium on gold reflected an apparent depreciation of paper money, little evidence is available that prices moved upward perceptibly during these two years. The failure of prices to increase gives signal proof of the inappropriateness of the exchanges or the prices of metals as measures of depreciation.[1] When money in terms of commodities maintains its full value but depreciates on the less important gold and foreign exchange markets, there has been no true depreciation of money in my opinion. One might insist that the value of money is an average of its value in all its uses; but he would find only an inappreciable depreciation in 1790–91.

Whereas complaints of high prices were infrequent during this period, emphatic protests were entered in 1792–93, years of increasing prices. The populace had not yet learned to take its price increases as a matter of course. Evidence of the stability of prices in 1790–91 is available. The price of subsistence in Chaumont remained unchanged throughout 1791.[2] The consumers of fuel in Paris paid the same prices throughout 1791–92.[3] The wood merchants, in fact, had to contend with a concerted movement for the reduction of the price of fuel.[4] Public and market sales of grains were at a lower price in 1791 than in 1790.[5]

[1] Jaurès points out that prices began to increase in 1792. J. Jaurès, *Histoire Socialiste*, Vol. II, p. 259.
[2] *Les Subsistances en Céréales dans le District de Chaumont*, Collection de Documents Inédits, Vol. I, p. 301.
[3] G. Bienaymé, "Le Coût de la Vie à Paris à diverses Epoques," *Journal de la Société de Statistique de Paris*, Vol. XXXVII, p. 389.
[4] Actes de la Commune de Paris, 2d series, Vol. II, pp. 53–56, 627, 727–728.
[5] *Ibid.*, Vol. VI, pp. 454–463.

The price increases of 1792 were caused by the decreased deliveries to the markets and the anxiety to buy large quantities when unmistakable signs of war appeared.[1] Parliamentary debaters now began to concern themselves with the problems of subsistence and high prices. The high prices of colonial products in the early months of 1792 occasioned some dangerous outbreaks. Without doubt the ferment in the Colonies contributed to the scarcity of Colonial products.[2] Raw materials, in particular, suffered excessive price increases in the first few months of 1792. The price of a quintal of raw cotton rose from 120 to 490 livres.[3] There were large increases in the price of wheat, both in Meulon[4] and in Chaumont.[5] The price of wheat varied from 7⅓ livres to 18¾ livres in different sections in the year 1790; normal conditions had not been reestablished in 1790. Hence the abnormal increase in 1792 is not fully reflected by a comparison with 1790. In December, 1792 the price of wheat ranged from 26 to 98 livres.[6] The price of eggs doubled in the northern sections of France.[7]

Prices continued to increase through the first half of 1793; the signs of depreciation were unmistakable. A grave outbreak in Paris in the latter part of February was brought about by the high prices of spices and other commodities.[8] A coat estimated to be worth 90 livres in 1790, was on sale for 180 livres in 1793; and the market price of a measure of cloth that cost but 36 livres in 1790, was 180 livres in 1793.[9] The price of bread had increased from the normal level of 3 sous to from 6 to 12 sous in May, 1793, and a pound of meat was 3⅓ times as costly as in 1790.[10] In May the

[1] Thus the authorities of the Section of Lombard in Paris commented on excessive purchases in the first three months of 1792. Actes de la Commune de Paris, ad series, Vol. VIII, p. 105.
[2] Arch. Parl., Vol. XXXVII, p. 614.
[3] *Ibid.*, Vol. XXXVIII, pp. 678–679; Gower, the British Ambassador, commented on the increased prices for raw wool. O. Browning, *The Dispatches of Earl Gower*, p. 144.
[4] P. Caron et L. Raulet, *Le Comité des Subsistances de Meulan et l'Approvisionement de Paris, Commission de Recherche*, 1907, p. 63.
[5] *Les Subsistances en Céréales dans le District de Chaumont*, Vol. I, p. 309.
[6] *Moniteur*, Vol. XV, pp. 294–295, L. Biollay, *Les Prix en 1790*, pp. 86–101.
[7] L. Biollay, *op. cit.*, p. 176.
[8] E. Biré, *Journal d'un Bourgeoise*, Vol. II, pp. 64–72.
[9] E. Biré, *Paris pendant la Terreur*, p. 61.
[10] H. A. Taine, *The French Revolution* (Translation by John Durand), Vol. III, pp. 365–368.

Government undertook an investigation of the high prices and scarcity of meat.[1] F. Dianyère, an agent of the Minister of Interior, reported the following prices for June, 1793:

DEPARTMENT OF ALLIER

	Prices in 1789	Prices in 1793
Bread	2.3 s.	5 s.
Wine	40 l.	130 l.
Meat	6.7 s.	15 s.
Candles	13 s.	20 s.
Wool	20 s.	65 s.
Eggs	9½s.	18 s.

The average increase was 214 per cent.

A survey undertaken by police agents revealed that the price of wine — an important item in every Frenchman's budget — had increased from 35 to 64 sous within the first 5 months of 1793.[2] A municipal decree guaranteed the Parisian bakers against any losses incurred in the sales of bread at controlled prices. Perrière, an agent of the Minister of Interior, attributed the increase in the price of flour from 90 to 140–150 livres to that imprudent policy.[3] In September, 1793 Rolin announced prices for Paris as follows:[4]

	Prices in 1789–90 [5]	Prices in September, 1793
Butter (salted)	13½ s.	28 s.
Butter (fresh)	14 s.	35⅓ s.
Meat	8 s.	19 s.
Veal	6 s.	24½ s.
Tobacco	?	48, 60, 80 s.
Sugar	?	5 l., 10 s.
Coffee	1 l., 14 s.	4 l., 15 s.
Eggs	15 s.	2 l., 10 s.
Oil	?	3 l., 5 s.
Candles	?	2 l., 4 s.

The agents of the Committee of Public Safety informed that Committee of increases of 80 per cent from May to September in Gers and Landes.[6]

[1] *Procès-Verbaux des Comités d'Agriculture et de Commerce*, Collection de Documents Inédits, Vol. IV, pp. 86–87. This work will be referred to hereafter as P. V. Ag. et Com.
[2] A. Schmidt, *Tableaux de la Révolution Française*, Vol. I, p. 287.
[3] P. Caron, *Paris pendant la Térreur*, Vol. I, pp. 8–11.
[4] *Ibid.*, p. 60.
[5] I have collected prices for 1789–1790 whenever possible from Biollay, Young (*Travels*) and d'Avenal (*Histoire Economique*, etc.).
[6] *Recueil des Actes du Comité de Salut Public*, Vol. VI, pp. 435–436. This reference will be given as C. P. S. hereafter.

The unparalleled price increases of 1792 and 1793 were in large part the cause of the introduction of a maximum for grains in May, 1793, and of a general maximum, as well as an improved maximum for grains in September, 1793. The maximum prices, which had been constructed on the basis of prices in 1790 with an increase in general of one-third over the prices in 1790, endured with some modifications and many violations until December, 1794. In Chapter VI this period is considered in detail. As might be expected, commodities not subject to the maximum suffered a disproportionate increase in prices.[1] The surplus of purchasing power made available by the system of price control and rationing had few other outlets. Land purchases were inadvisable in a period of terrorism and insecurity, and hence a potential employment for the Assignats was lost.

Because I have been unable to procure the material with which to construct an index number of prices for the Revolution, I have to be content with irregular price statistics and a more regular series of grain prices for the District of Bergues. The material for the price of wheat in the District of Bergues (Département du Nord) was taken from the reprint of the documents pertaining to subsistence for the District of Bergues.[2] In Chart 1A, I compare the price of wheat in Bergues with the value of the Assignat according to the local tables of depreciation of the Département du Nord and with the Treasury values of gold and silver. The price of wheat did not increase nearly as rapidly as a consideration of the local tables or the Treasury table alone might lead one to expect. Even for 1792 and 1793, the curve representing the price of wheat did not ascend as rapidly as the other two curves. One should keep in mind the preponderant importance of bread in the French budget. Does not the higher apparent depreciation exhibited by the Treasury tables once more warn us of the fictitiousness of the depreciation reflected by the prices of gold and silver? The low prices for subsistence represented at the lower left of the chart resulted of course from the maximum, and are misleading

[1] C. A. Dauban, *Paris en 1794 et en 1795*, pp. 138–139; P. Caron, *Paris pendant la Térreur*, Vol. II, p. 310.
[2] *Les Subsistances dans le District de Bergues pendant la Révolution*, Collection de Documents Inédits.

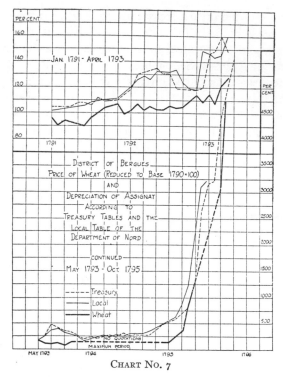

CHART No. 7

without a consideration of the rationing that accompanied the low maximum prices. The few quotations of the post-maximum period also reflect a considerable lag in the upward movement of the price of subsistence.

Prices after the maximum period soared more rapidly. In the next chapter, I discuss in more detail a comprehensive survey of prices undertaken by the agents of the Committee of Public Safety in March–April, 1795; here I present merely a summary of my analysis of the survey.[1]

COMPARED TO 1790

Relative value of all prices in 33 departments........ 758 per cent
Relative value of the prices of food................. 819 per cent
Relative value of the prices of raw materials........ 770 per cent
Relative value of the prices of clothing............. 640 per cent

[1] *Une Enquête sur les Prix après la Suppression du Maximum, Commission de Recherche*, 1910, pp. 1–134, 303–412.

Price statistics are more easily obtainable for the period after the maximum; in particular, the police reports of Paris, edited by Aulard, Schmidt and Caron, the documents pertaining to subsistence for the Department of Eure and the District of Versailles, and a few miscellaneous works contain some information. An index number for this period, however, can be at best only patchwork. Quotations for some commodities are only sporadic; we can collect a relatively complete series for a few commodities. A difficulty already referred to — the presence in Paris of a free market for a small proportion of the bread supply, coexistent with controlled prices and rationing for the major part — is not easily dismissed. Almost universally, the police and the editors of documents quote market prices only; but at least for bread, the municipal price is of greater significance. A solution of this problem is to weigh according to the proportions of the total supplies contributed by the Government and by the market. The Government probably contributed two-thirds of the total bread supplies at three sous a pound.[1] An estimate is more difficult for meat because the Government was less solicitous about providing it. (A promise of one-half pound of meat every five days for each person had been made, but its faithful execution is doubtful; the army was consuming most of it.) Only an uncertain surplus was available for Paris.[2] Because of the needs of the army and the disorders in the West, the importance of meat in the Parisian's budget had been materially reduced. A rough estimate of equal sales by the Government and by private dealers is assumed here. Each of the commodities used, namely, eggs, potatoes, soap, fuel, butter, meat (beef, veal, and pork), and bread, were given a weight of one except that bread was given a weight of three, and the three varieties of meat a combined weight of one. The results are given below. The price system was relatively unstable for a few months after the repeal of the maximum laws; the first reaction to freedom was a spectacular rise of prices.

[1] The Government was contributing 1300 sacs daily, about two-thirds of the total sales. *J. Déb. et Déc.*, Vol. LXXX, pp. 364–365.

[2] Fermon told the Council of 500 early in 1796 that the Government was buying 500 oxen (weighing 150 pounds), 450 lambs, and 115 cows daily for Paris. *J. Déb. et Déc.*, Vol. LXXX, pp. 364–365.

BASE OF 1790

		Index number	Monthly Price of gold (Average of daily quotations from Bailleul)
1795	January	580	555
	February	510	588
	March	720	714
	April	900	866
	May	Inadequate data	1,333
	June	1,310	2,575
	July	2,180	3,150
	August	2,710	3,237
	September	3,100	4,420
	October	Inadequate data	5,616
	November	5,340	12,025
	December	12,990	16,475
1796	January	11,320	24,060
	February	19,100	......
	March	38,850	......

Commodity prices increased at a more rapid rate than the prices of gold and silver. My study of the survey of the Committee of Public Safety in the next chapter verifies this point. After an initial period of dislocation, however, the gold market began to set the pace once more. The lag in the upward swing of gold and silver in the first few months of 1795 is not as apparent here as in the data presented in the next chapter. The doles of the Government to Parisians kept down prices in Paris.

Because the local tables of depreciation were not constructed independently of the prices of commodities, they give a more adequate picture of depreciation. In the next chapter, devoted to an analysis of the local tables, I compare their values with those of the Treasury tables; and, as is to be expected, the Treasury tables reflect a more rapid depreciation. The local tables moved more sluggishly because the prices of commodities were included.

4. NOTE ON TREASURY TABLES

In what manner were the Treasury tables constructed? They have been the most commonly used measure of depreciation — Levasseur, Gomel, Caron, and Hawtrey avail themselves of them — and yet nowhere has an attempt been made to analyse them. In some instances, writers assume that the Treasury figures are price quotations for gold and silver. The tables are prefaced by a note inserted by the Government which sheds some light on the question.

"These quotations are established from August, 1789 to June, 1791 according to private notes; from July, 1791 to December, 1792 according to purchases of numéraire on the part of the Treasury; from January, 1793 to February, 1794 according to negotiations of paper made at the Treasury; from March, 1794 to May, 1795 according to private notes; from May, 1795 to October, 1795 according to the quotations given by the bankers named by the Committee of Public Safety; from October, 1795 to March, 1796, according to the certificates furnished by the agents of exchange named for this purpose."

Bailleul, a contemporary collector of price statistics, published a gazette that contained several price series for the period of the Revolution.[1] In the chart below, I compare the price of gold as

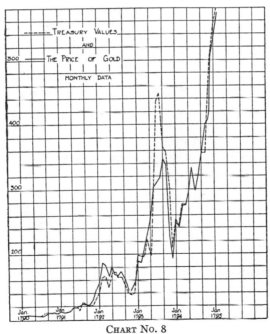

CHART No. 8

[1] A. Bailleul, *Tableau Complet de Valeur des Assignats, des Mandates, des Rescriptions, etc., etc.*, 11th ed.

given by Bailleul, with the values of the Treasury tables. The agreement of the two series is close for the first period as given above. The "private notes" referred to by the Treasury were probably the market quotations for gold. The market price of gold, according to Bailleul's figures, was higher than the Treasury values for the second period. (In this period, the Treasury figures were admittedly for public purchases of numéraire.) The reason for the discrepancy probably lies in the more advantageous terms on which the Government purchased the metals.

In the third period (January, 1793–February, 1794) the Treasury quotations fell more rapidly than those reported by Bailleul. The discrepancy was greatest in the second half of 1793. What was "paper negotiated at the Treasury"? Probably bills of exchange. The Government attempted to dispense with the use of gold and silver during this period with the result that purchases of gold and silver were curtailed and even discontinued at intervals. (See Chapter VII.) The Treasury required a medium acceptable abroad to pay for the indispensable foreign purchases. It had attempted, but unsuccessfully, to carry through a policy of economic isolation. Unfortunately, foreign exchange quotations for the Reign of Terror are scarce; but I have been able to procure the quotations on Bâle. The Treasury tables give less favorable quotations for the Assignat than do the Bâle quotations. However, the difference between the price of gold and the Treasury figures is appreciably greater than the difference between the Treasury figures and the Bâle quotations. The French exchange probably fell more disastrously in other foreign exchange markets at this time than at Bâle.

The two series give almost identical values for the last three periods. With the exception of one period when the Treasury tables were probably based on the foreign exchanges, they were apparently based on the prices of gold and silver.

CHAPTER V

LOCAL DEPRECIATION

1. INTRODUCTION

AN ANALYSIS of the department tables is of importance.[1] The Treasury figures of depreciation, based largely on the price of gold and silver in Paris, are significant and useful. An average of the department tables, however, may often be substituted with better results. An investigation of these local tables reveals an incredible degree of variation between the different departments.[2] Because the area of France was small, these variations are surprising.[3] How to account for them? They might, of course, be due to the manner in which the tables were constructed and hence be fictitious. But the value of the Assignat may actually have varied from department to department. Difficulties of transportation, actual and artificial, are probably relevant considerations. It will be necessary to test both hypotheses.

The local tables of depreciation were proposed in order to reduce the confusion and inequalities that spread into private trans-

[1] I am greatly indebted to M. Caron's recent republication of the original tables of depreciation. The French writers have not analysed these important and interesting tables. The value of my study would be considerably enhanced by a perusal of the departmental archives. They contain much information, as yet untouched, on the method of constructing these tables.

[2] An analysis of the tables, in which an attempt will be made to explain the differences in the local values of the paper money, will constitute the second part of this chapter.

[3] The British Board of Trade recently reported that the price of a loaf of bread of two pounds varied from 4d. in London to 7d. in Bradford. "First Report of Royal Commission on Food Supplies, 1925," ¶64. Pribram comments on the extreme local variations in Germany during the recent war, K. Pribram, "Zur Entwicklung Lebensmittelpreise der Kriegszeit," *Archiv für Sozialwissenschaft und Sozial Politik*, 1916, pp. 794–795. Also see a review of the United States Bureau of Labor study on "Prices in Belligerent Countries during the Early Months of the War." *Economic Journal*, 1916, pp. 126–127.

Apparently depreciation was much more advanced in 1919 in the Syrian and Arabian Provinces of Turkey than in Constantinople. "Financial Position of Turkey," *Board of Trade Journal*, March 18, 1920.

actions. In Chapter IX the origin of these tables is discussed in some detail. On the request of the Central Government, the local authorities prepared tables of monthly values of the paper money. The object was to provide a basis for reducing paper money obligations to metallic equivalents.

2. CONSTRUCTION OF THE TABLES

Each department was advised of the Treasury values of gold and silver. The officials of each department were also to collect information on the prices of land, of food, and of merchandise, and the local prices of the precious metals. These five series of price quotations were to form the materials out of which the local values of the Assignat and Mandat were to be constructed.[1] The period covered was from 1791 to 1796.

Was it advisable to include commodity prices during the maximum period? The short procès-verbal accompanying each table reveals that in at least two departments price quotations of commodities not sold on a free market were excluded.[2] The inclusion of those quotations for lands, food, and commodities which were not controlled, was advised by the Central authorities.[3] The problem of deficiencies of the different measures of depreciation is discussed in Chapter IV. Here the question whether controlled prices should be included, arises again.

A system of maximum prices and rationing induces a forced readjustment of the consumer's budget and a forced inactivity of part of his purchasing power. The inclusion of the prices of controlled commodities resulted in a somewhat mythical increase in the value of the monetary unit, and therefore one may question the value of some of the final department tables. The significant difference between the Treasury values for gold and silver and the average of the values of the 83 departments, is evident from a graph in the next section. The considerably higher depreciation reflected by the Treasury figures, as well as the imposing differ-

[1] Lois et Résolutions Completes sur les Transactions, p. 4.
[2] P. Caron, Tableaux de Dépréciation, Commission de Recherche et de Publication des Documents, pp. 64–65, 419.
[3] Lois et Résolutions Completes sur les Transactions, p. 4.

ences between departments, makes me doubt Caron's conclusion that the department tables were based very largely on the price of gold and silver in Paris.[1]

The local tables were not designed to make adjustments for the changes in the value of the paper money caused by the peculiar market conditions during the Revolution. How far controlled price quotations were used by the local authorities is problematical. Two departments confessed to their exclusion; the others remained silent on that point. The directions of the Central Government to include only commodities on a free market cannot with any certainty be interpreted to mean that the controlled ones were in fact excluded. Obedience to orders of the Central Government was often sluggish.

The price of gold was depressed appreciably by the official propaganda and violence during the Reign of Terror. The value of the Assignat in gold and silver was increased thereby. Therefore a diminution of the difference between the Treasury curve and the average local curve should have resulted from the rise of the former in 1793–94. Perhaps the failure of the curves to converge in 1793–94 can be explained by the continued inclusion of commodity prices in the construction of the local tables; for commodity prices were now depressed by the maximum (1793–94).

The inclusion of controlled prices may be criticised, but their exclusion would have resulted in a meaningless measure of depreciation. Many of the most important commodities were not sold freely during the Revolution. The failure to consider these vital commodities, therefore, would have resulted in a considerably higher depreciation, for the surplus of purchasing power was dissipated to some extent on non-controlled commodities. The controlled commodities were depressed in price and rationed. A large surplus of purchasing power was available for the uncontrolled commodities. An index constructed without consideration of the price of bread and meat, can scarcely meet the test of accuracy or adequacy. Nor was control restricted to the maximum period.

The local economists appended a short procès-verbal to each table which almost invariably was of little value. The authorities

[1] *Tableaux*, Introd., pp. lxi-lxiii.

of the departments of Somne, Hérault and Calvados alone attempted to disclose how they prepared their tables.

The prices of food and of merchandise (uncontrolled), of land, and of gold and silver, formed the materials out of which the tables of the Department of Somne were constructed. The authorities considered the prices of wheat (in its free course), of wool, wood, and meat, and of all other products habitually used.[1]

The Department of Hérault provided the Government with more complete information. The leading business men contributed the necessary information; they assembled many of the price quotations, notably those for wheat, wool, copper, sugar, draperies, cloth, and cotton. The communal authorities supplied the prices of many food products. The procès-verbal was silent on the exclusion of restricted commodities. The local officials commented on the excessive depreciation of the Assignat in food products, on the moderate depreciation in merchandise, and on the scant depreciation in land.[2]

The procès-verbal of the Department of Calvados was the most valuable. To obtain quotations for land, the investigators consulted only private sales. They objected to the use of public sales because such sales were often non-competitive, and because the conditions of the public contracts varied too much to be serviceable. Since the local quotations of gold and silver were combined with the Treasury quotations, the metallic factor received a weight of but one-fourth instead of two-fifths. They excluded quotations for wheat, barley, and rye, on the grounds that they had never been sold freely. Quotations for Colonial products were omitted because market conditions were abnormal in the Colonies. Data provided by the Treasury (the prices of gold and silver) and the rates on Bâle (foreign exchanges), sufficed for the maximum period.[3]

Another aid may be invoked here. The Committee of Public Safety, perturbed by the catastrophic increase of prices that followed the abrogation of the maximum law, ordered agents in each

---

[1] *Tableaux*, p. 419.
[2] *Ibid.*, pp. 171-175.
[3] *Ibid.*, pp. 65-67.

district to compare the prices in 1795 of a large number of commodities with those for 1790. Caron discovered in the National Archives the results of this survey for 170 districts, the equivalent of two-sevenths of all the districts. Seventy of the 86 departments were represented by 1 or more districts. Caron has rendered a great service in reprinting these documents for 50 districts in 35 departments.[1] I have attempted to analyze the returns of 1 district in each of 33 departments in the hope that such an analysis might shed further light on the local tables of depreciation.

The original survey dealt with 50 or 60 items. I have used in all 19 items. An attempt has been made to choose so that the resulting index number might be both a fair sample of the whole and representative of the objects of expenditure of the average Frenchman. Three classes of items were selected:

I. Food, etc.	II. Clothing	III. Raw Materials
1. Wheat	11. Ordinary broadcloth	14. Wood, at capital of district
2. Rye	12. Hats, ordinary	15. Coal
3. Oats	13. Shoes, strong	16. Forged iron
4. Beef		17. Steel
5. Lard		18. Glass
6. Butter		19. Raw wool
7. Soap		
8. Wax (candles)		
9. Wine, 1st class		
10. Wine, 2d class		

I computed an unweighted geometric mean (base of 1790) for each district for each of the three groups. By the choice of items, I weighted the index and then computed a simple geometric mean for all the 19 items for each district, and an arithmetic mean of the 33 geometric means (1 for each district) for all the commodities and for each of the 3 groups. The values for the Assignat for each department according to the local tables of depreciation were transcribed for the day nearest to the date of the agents' report. The local values of the Assignats had been recorded on the basis of a value of 100 per cent in 1790. It was necessary to transform these quotations to make them comparable with the index numbers of prices. A quotation of 20 per cent in the local tables was

---

[1] P. Caron, *Une Enquête sur les Prix, Commission de Recherches et de Publication des Documents*, 1910.

converted into 500 per cent to conform to a five-fold increase of prices.

Several precautions are necessary in the interpretation of these results. The national agent reported prices for days that extended over an interval of almost two months — late in February, 1795 to early in April, 1795. Prices were in a continuous flux with the general trend upward. Prices of a day in February were likely to be appreciably lower than those for a day in April. The attempt to match these price statistics with local values for the Assignat for corresponding days, cannot be completely successful since the local tables give values only by ten day periods. A more damaging deficiency results from the admitted discrepancy between market and actual prices. A large number of the agents reported that in many instances the quoted prices were market prices, and, hence, fictitious. Sales at the home of the farmer at much higher prices were common. Moreover, the price statistics related to one district and the value of the Assignat to the whole department. Thus the discrepancies between the geometric means (of all of the commodities) of the four districts of the Department of Eure, equalled 35 per cent. A minor objection results from the inability to obtain the full complement of 19 price quotations for each district. A small proportion of the local discrepancies may be explained by that particular shortcoming. Finally, let it be remembered that this study relates to a comparison of conditions for but one day in 1795 with conditions in 1790. This study, in spite of these limitations, contains valuable material for comparison with the local tables.

The results of the various computations are given below:

(Base 1790)   Per Cent
Arithmetic mean of geometric mean for the 19 items......... 719
Arithmetic mean of geometric mean for the foodstuffs........ 640
Arithmetic mean of geometric mean for the clothing......... 770
Arithmetic mean of geometric mean for the raw materials 758

The average value of the Assignat according to the local tables of depreciation for the 33 departments for corresponding days was 581 per cent (base of 1790).

The deciles both for the geometric means of all the price quotations and for the local values (reciprocals) of the Assignat are:

	Prices	Local Values
1.	972	727
2.	908	673
3.	861	659
4.	767	635
5.	740	580
6.	678	562
7.	659	520
8.	637	448
9.	583	420
10.	451	410

The standard deviation of the 33 geometric means of the 19 price quotations is 171½ per cent.

The standard deviation of the local values of the Assignat for the same departments is 110 per cent.

Some of these results warrant emphasis. The department tables indicate that it would have required 581 livres early in 1795 to do the work of 100 livres in 1790. The Committee's survey indicates that 719 livres would have been required. The dispersion was considerably wider for the price statistics than for the local values of the Assignat. This fact is confirmed both by the standard deviation and by the deciles.

What is the significance of these results for the local tables of depreciation? They reveal some of the deficiencies both of the local tables and of the Treasury tables as measures of depreciation. A measure based on price statistics exclusively would have given a more striking depreciation for the period under consideration. That is at variance with the usual experience, for the price of gold generally moves more quickly than the prices of commodities. Perhaps the more rapid relative increase in commodity prices was due to the artificial lowering of the price of gold resulting from an energetic official policy against the circulation of the precious metals. A more tolerant attitude toward dealers in metals had not yet taken effect. The reaction from the restriction of prices during the maximum period was probably a more important cause of the more rapid increase of prices. After the repeal of the maximum laws, the markets were demoralized for several months, and prices soared.

It is difficult to reconcile the more rapid depreciation in terms of commodities in the early months of 1795 with the fact that on the

basis of the local tables, the Assignats had a higher value throughout the whole paper money régime than on the basis of the Treasury values of gold and silver. The local tables were based in part
on the prices of commodities, and at least during the interim between the end of the maximum and the opening of the Bourse,
April, 1795, one would expect that they would give a lower value
for the Assignat. Instead, values of the local tables consistently
are higher than those of the Treasury tables. Apparently some
other price series made possible the higher values of the local
tables. Perhaps, the quotations for land were weighted heavily.
Did the prices of land have more weight than those of commodities, at least for the four or five months between the termination
of the maximum and the opening of the Paris Bourse? The people
were still wary of land purchases, and its price remained low.

The study of prices undertaken by the national agents included
a comparison of the price of land in 1790 with its price in 1795.
The price quotations employed were for private transactions exclusively. (In the construction of the local tables, also, the quotations for private sales were used.) Thirty of the 33 districts published the prices of an acre of average meadow land. According
to the national agents, the average value of the land in 1795 as
compared to 1790 was 439 per cent. These results are consistent
with the explanation given above for the higher values, especially
from December, 1794 to May, 1795, given by the department
tables. Perhaps land values were weighted heavily in the construction of the local tables — for the period from December, 1794 to
April, 1795, at any rate. The Treasury tables were constructed
exclusively from the quotations for gold and silver during this
period.

The remarkable diversity in the prices of commodities and of
land in the different departments helps to explain the variations
in the value of the Assignat reflected in the local tables. Of course,
even in 1790 commodities from department to department varied
in prices to an extraordinary degree.[1] The prices of 1795, here discussed, were price relatives on the base year 1790.[2]

[1] L. Biollay, Les Prix en 1790.
[2] See P. Caron, "Une Enquête sur le Récolte de 1792," Bulletin d'Histoire

The agreement between price relatives for 1795 on the base year 1790 (as compiled by the national agents) and the values of the Assignat as given by the local tables for corresponding departments, is not close. That is not conclusive evidence that the prices of commodities did not have a predominant influence in the formation of the local tables; and, of course, a higher degree of agreement would not be conclusive proof of the overwhelming weight of commodity prices in the construction of the local tables; such agreement might have been due to some other common causal factor. Within the limits of this period, the local values for the Assignat (Tables of depreciation) did not vary closely with commodity prices collected by the national agents. The correlation between the prices of gold and silver in Paris on which the local tables were in part based and of the prices of commodities reported by the national agents, might not be very close. Whatever agreement there was, is to be attributed to the inclusion of the prices of land and especially of commodities in the construction of the local tables.

Whereas the price of gold and silver in Paris, certainly, and the price of land, probably, had too much weight in the construction of the local tables, the prices of commodities and raw materials had too little weight. Because of the remarkable variations in prices of commodities, the prominent position given to the quotations of gold and silver in Paris is the more to be lamented.[1] In the light of the extreme local peculiarities, the imposition of any uniform factor on all localities was a grievous error. The reasons for not giving too much weight to land quotations have been emphasized. An acceptable index should take into account the price of gold and silver, as well as of land. However, even under the unusual market conditions of land and of the precious metals, an Assignat was much more likely to be disbursed for food or for clothes than for land or gold and silver. The related question of the appropriateness of using the price of gold and silver as a meas-

---

Economique de la Révolution, 1915, p. 138. The price of wheat varied from 11 to 45 livres a quintal. Although the average price was 19½ livres, prices in excess of 30 livres were quoted in five departments.

[1] See Discourse by Réal in March, 1797, *J. Déb. et Déc.*, Vol. XCIV, p. 445.

ure of depreciation, has already been discussed in Chapter IV. The heavy weight given to the metallic quotations was probably justified by the authorities, because they were considered a good measure of depreciation.

Little has been said of the local values of gold and silver, which were to be considered in the computation of the local tables. Few organized gold markets functioned during the Revolution. It was difficult to obtain trustworthy quotations of the prices of gold and silver. Except in Paris and a few frontier departments, the local prices of gold and silver were not considered in the construction of the final tables.[1]

3. ANALYSIS OF THE LOCAL TABLES

A comparison of changes in the average of the local values of the Assignat for the 83 departments with changes in its value according to the Treasury tables, is presented in the first chart below. The local tables on the average reflect a value for the Assignat of from 10 to 15 per cent higher than the Treasury figures. The discrepancy, as we have seen, probably results from the inclusion of commodity and land prices in the construction of the local tables. The parallelism in the movements of the two curves is probably largely due to the weight given to gold and silver quotations at Paris in both compilations. The general trend of the local curve is much more even than the trend of the Treasury curve: The Treasury curve, based almost exclusively on the speculative and flexible gold market, is more subject to wide fluctuations.

The next chart illustrates the extent of the local variations of the value of the Assignat. The local values have been arranged from high to low values for each month and then divided into deciles. The first decile is composed of the highest tenth of all the values, the second highest 10 per cent form the second decile, and so on. These deciles are represented on this chart. The uppermost curve, however, is one of highest values from month to month. The ten curves below are the curves for deciles, the lowest of which is, of course, a curve of lowest values also.

[1] Boissy expressed skepticism as to the possibility of obtaining local quotations for the price of gold and silver. *J. Déb. et Déc.*, Vol. XCVI, pp. 85–86.

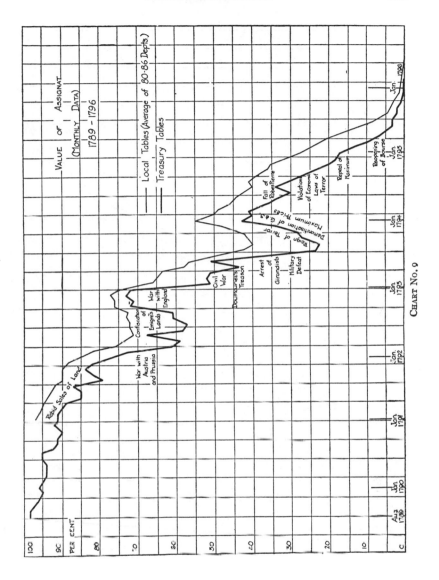

VALUE OF ASSIGNAT
(MONTHLY DATA)
1789 - 1796

— Local Tables (Average of 80-86 Depts)
— Treasury Tables

CHART No. 9

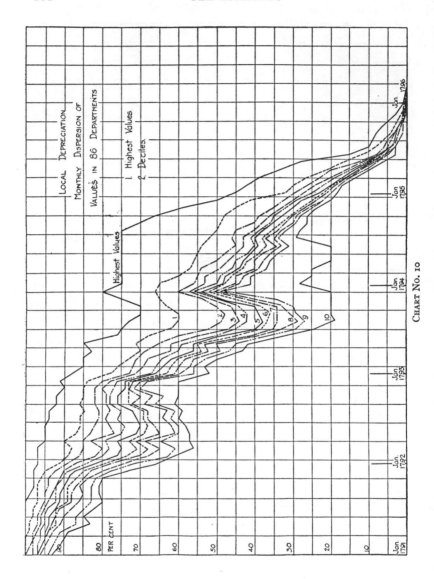

CHART No. 10

The greatest diversity of results occurs, as might be expected, when the median curve is at a value of approximately 50 per cent. In the latter part of 1793, the Assignat apparently had a value as low as 20 per cent in one department, and as high as 80 per cent in another. The variations are reduced by approximately one-half by an elimination of the first and tenth deciles:

	Variation between Highest and Lowest Values Per Cent	Variation between 1st Decile and 10th Decile Per Cent	Variation between 1st Decile and 9th Decile Per Cent
January, 1791	100–93– 7	100–93– 7	100–94– 6
January, 1792	97–66–31	91–66–25	91–72–19
January, 1793	88–52–36	78–52–26	78–56–22
January, 1794	75–18–57	65–28–37	65–41–24
January, 1795	45–18–27	32–18–14	32–20–12

I have made a territorial classification of departments, to discover whether depreciation varied with the geographical position of the departments. The chart that follows presents the monthly values of the Assignat in nine geographical areas. It reveals a significant amount of diversity according to the location of the department. In Western (Central) departments the Assignat maintained its value best, and in the Southeastern departments the Revolutionary money lost most heavily. The differences between these sections, however, were less than one-half as great as those between departments irrespective of location:

DISCREPANCIES

	A The Lowest and the Highest Department Per Cent	B Geographical Variations between Lowest and Highest Sections at each date Per Cent	C Southeast and West Per Cent
January, 1791	7	5	5
January, 1792	31	15	15
January, 1793	36	11	7
January, 1794	47	16	10
January, 1795	28	8	8

In "A," I compare the lowest and highest values of all the 86 departments; in "B" the lowest and highest among the ten sections into which France has been divided for this purpose; and in "C" the Southeast and West, the two sections most consistently lowest and highest respectively. The low values of the Assignats

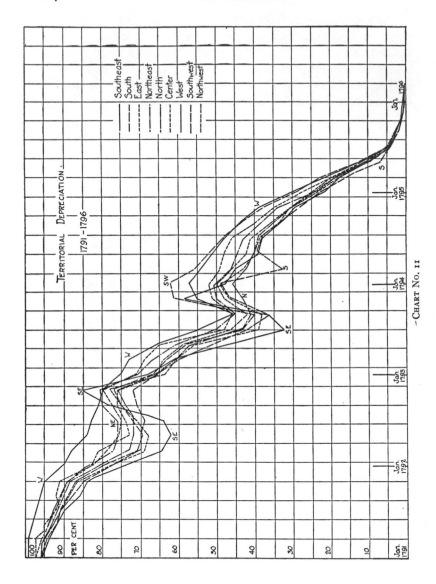

−CHART NO. II

in the Eastern departments may be explained by their proximity
to the warring frontiers, and hence to the territory in which metals
of foreign countries circulated freely. Metals circulated freely at
their full value on the warring frontiers, and thus offered serious
competition to the Assignats.[1]

A somewhat different grouping of departments is possible. (See
the two charts that follow.) In the first, I compare the depreciation of the Eastern, Central and Western departments; and in the

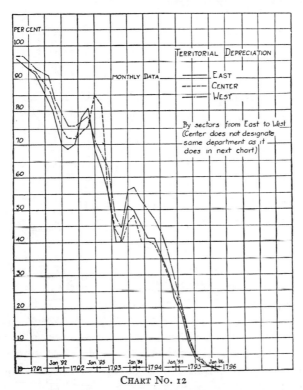

CHART No. 12

second, the depreciation of the Northern, Central, and Southern
departments. It is to be noted that Central indicates dissimilar
groups of departments in the two groupings. In one chart, Cen-

---

[1] *C.P.S.*, Vol. III, pp. 319, 340, 502. *Lettres de Ministre de l'Intérieur*, Collection
de Documents Inédits, p. 127.

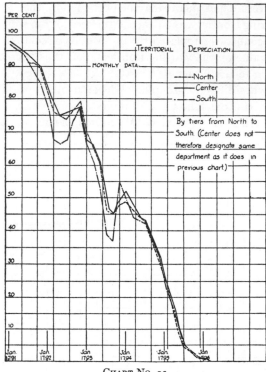

CHART NO. 13

tral designates the departments lying between the Northern and Southern departments; in the other, it designates those lying between the Eastern and Western departments. The first reveals that in the Western departments the Assignats maintained the highest values, and in the Eastern departments they suffered the greatest depreciation. According to the second chart, depreciation was greatest in the South. Although these results are consistent with the results obtained by the earlier classification, the variations between sections are not as marked. The South suffered seriously from the lack of subsistence during the entire period of the Revolution. The price of subsistence increased in the South much more than in any other section, and hence the purchasing power of the Assignat fell more rapidly there than elsewhere. The consistently high values for the Western departments — the seat of the powerful anti-Revolutionary movements — are puzzling. The accessibility to supplies and the manner of constructing the tables, are possible explanations.

Another method of analysing the subject is to compare the values of the Assignat in contiguous departments. I compare the values in Paris (Department of Seine) with those in the adjoining departments, with all the Northern departments, and finally with

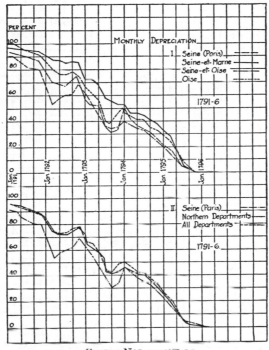

CHARTS NOS. 14 AND 15

all the departments. (The last two comparisons are made on one chart.) Why did the Assignat lose so much relatively in Paris, the center of the Revolution? Perhaps because the Assignat was disbursed first in Paris.[1] An army of public officials, rentiers, and

---

[1] Montesquiou regretted that the manufacture of notes had to be confined to one place (Paris), and that, therefore, issues were successive, and not simultaneous for the different parts of the country. Arch. Parl., Vol. XXIV, pp. 579–580.

pensioners were paid largely in Paris.[1] Secondly, the well organized and speculative markets of Paris were quick to discount the falling value of the paper money. Finally, Paris was hampered by famine conditions during a large part of the Revolution.

I present below the charts for other contiguous groups of departments. From these surveys, I conclude that there was an appre-

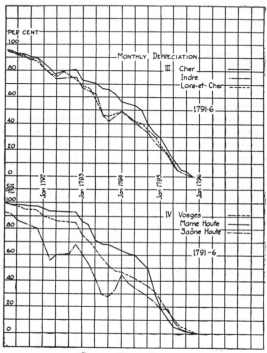

CHARTS NOS. 16 AND 17

ciable difference in the values of the Assignat in contiguous departments. It is not safe to attribute these variations to the different methods followed in the construction of the tables. If one considers the marked variations in prices in markets even in the same district, he will be convinced of the possibility of large variations

---

[1] In 1792, of 175 millions of livres disbursed for rentes, only 50 millions were disbursed outside of Paris. *Rapport sur la Suppression de Payeurs-Controleurs des Finances*, p. 13.

in the values of the Assignat for contiguous departments; and such differences may be deemed actual differences in the value of the paper money. It is surprising that in Vendée, the center of the

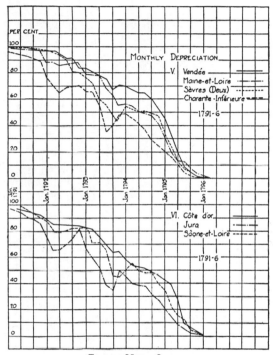

CHARTS NOS. 18 AND 19

anti-Revolutionary activities for years, the Assignat retained its value so well relatively speaking.

Caron, in the introduction to his edition of the local tables, supports his contention as to the integrity of the compilers of the tables by stating that for contiguous departments the Assignats had approximately similar values. My results indicate that Caron was mistaken on that point. Even had Caron been correct as regards the facts, that argument cannot be used as evidence of the fidelity of the compilers of the local tables. In the light of the extreme variations of prices in the markets of the same district, similar values for the Assignat for adjoining departments are not to be expected.

Caron's conviction as to the rather secondary influence of everything but the price of gold and silver in Paris, does not appear to

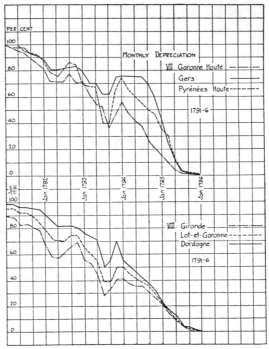

CHARTS NOS. 20 AND 21

be well founded.[1] The geographical distribution of depreciation was marked. That fact does not explain the local variations. It indicates in what sections of the country the Government had much or little success with the Assignat. The problem of why the Assignat was more depreciated in the South than in the North, is still to be explained. The extreme local variations in the prices of land and commodities explain a large proportion of the variations

---

[1] Falkner says, "The tables concerned themselves primarily with the course of paper money in metals." S. U. Falkner, *op. cit.*, p. 104.

in the local values. To some extent variations in the local tables reflected the varying conditions of the supply of commodities and also the varying confidence in the Assignat.

The brief and indefinite instructions dispatched by the Central Government allowed much discretion to the local authorities. The diversity of methods of construction may account for some part of the differences in the local values given by the tables. Here is an excerpt from the important discourse of Mollévaut on the day the local tables were decreed: "The law gives to the jury a guide and not masters; it surrounds it with materials and abandons them then to its conscience. Nothing forces the jury to stop at one of the bases, nor to adopt all. The jury shall examine which measure is the one which predominates in that territory. If all ought to influence the evaluation, if one or several ought to influence the evaluation, it shall decide according to the materials, localities, and circumstances."[1]

The fact that the elimination of the two extreme deciles reduces the extent of the variations of the local values by one half, and the fact that a close scrutiny reveals that the same departments were consistently the seats of the extreme values month by month, point to the importance of the diversity of methods of construction in explaining the differences exhibited by the tables. Why should Vendée show the highest valuation for the Assignat in almost every month of the paper money régime? That the departments with extreme values were not concentrated in one area, but rather were scattered all over France, is also of significance.

In spite of their shortcomings, the local tables of depreciation are of vital significance. They reveal at a glance the remarkable diversities in the movement of prices and in the value of paper money. As a general measure of depreciation, I believe an average of the values in the eighty or more departments is to be preferred to the Treasury quotations of the price of gold and silver in Paris. The local table includes, even if in bad proportions, the prices of commodities and of land. Moreover, a number of the unbiased errors are eliminated by utilizing an average of all the departments. I have preferred, therefore, to use it as a measure

[1] *J. Déb. et Déc.*, Vol. XCVII, p. 101.

of depreciation.[1] My general conclusion is that primarily the local variations in the value of the Assignats were due to variations in the supplies of commodities and in the confidence in the paper money; but some part of the variations — as reflected by the local tables — was not genuine, but rather due to individual idiosyncrasies in construction.[2]

[1] See discussion in Chapter IV.

[2] Wagner has an excellent discussion of a similar problem in his treatise on the paper money experiences of Russia. He points out in particular (1) that there was not a close agreement in the movements of the agio (premium on the exchanges) and the internal price level in the same locality, and (2) that the adjustment of prices to changes in the agio varied from place to place. A. Wagner, *Die russische Papierwährung*, pp. 83–85. Also see a discussion of local variations in post-war France. M. Lenoir, "Les Mouvements des Prix," *Revue d'Economie Politique*, 1924, p. 146.

CHAPTER VI

THE CONTROL OF PRICES AND SUPPLIES

LEGISLATIVE HISTORY

CONTROL of the prices and movement of grains and bread was not uncommon before the Revolution. In general, previous to 1789, the controlled price for bread had followed the market price of wheat quite closely. The poor crops of 1787 and 1788 were followed by the Revolution with its accompanying insecurity and disorganization, and hence the need for regulation was increased.[1]

The price of a 4 pound loaf of bread in Paris was 9 sous in August, 1788, and 14½ sous in February, 1789.[2] The *Parlement* of Paris investigated the causes of the high price of bread by a questionnaire method and summarized its results as follows:[3] Fully 142 answers had been received; 128 witnesses gave as one of the reasons for the high price of bread the poor crops of 1787 and 1788, and 112 — of course most of the witnesses gave several causes — practically repeated that answer in giving the excessive rain and hail as the explanation; hoardings, exportations, and sales to large cities each received from 20 to 35 votes.

The Central Government on November 23, 1788 prohibited transactions in grain outside of the market.[4] A decree of April 23, 1789 authorized the enlistment of the army for the purpose of insuring the safe conveyance of provisions to the market.[5] The Paris Assembly ordered all farmers within 25 leagues of Paris to

[1] *Les Subsistances dans le District de Bergues*, Collection de Documents Inédits, Vol. I, pp. xxix–xxx.
[2] *Les Elections et les Cahiers de Paris en 1789*, Collection de Documents Relatifs à l'Histoire de Paris pendant la Révolution Française, Vol. II, p. 497.
[3] *L'État de Paris en 1789*, Collection de Documents Relatifs à l'Histoire de Paris pendant la Révolution Française, Vol. II, p. 310.
[4] *Recueil des Principaux Textes sur le Commerce des Céréales*, Commission de Recherche, 1906, pp. 131–133.
[5] *Ibid.*, pp. 133–135.

bring a designated weight of grains to the market each day.[1] This law was not enforced.[2] The Central Government then delegated to the authorities of Paris the discretionary power of taking an inventory of the bread in bakeries and of enforcing all night baking.[3]

Although the crops of 1789 were normal again, official regulation continued through 1790 and 1791.[4] Disorders occurred less frequently, and prices fell noticeably in 1790–1791.[5] The imminent prospects of war early in 1792 had a deleterious effect on the movement of grains; transportation within France became difficult.[6] Rigorous measures were taken to guard the movements of grain in January, 1792. In March, the Minister of Interior obtained a credit of ten million livres with which to buy grains abroad.[7] The disorders accompanying attempts to transport grains attracted nation-wide attention, and the Government in March ordered the Committee of Agriculture and Commerce to investigate the causes of the interference with the free movement of grains.[8] The first three or four months of 1792 constituted the first of the periods of "famine fear" since the introduction of the Assignat. The outbreak of the war in April, strangely enough, calmed the restless spirits, and the uneasiness slowly vanished in the late spring and summer of 1792.

Continuance of the war, however, brought a renewal of the distrust of the early spring. The Committee of Agriculture and Commerce requested the farmers to provision the markets in September.[9] The grave events of August and September — the Massacres of September in particular — were accompanied by increased hoarding of food and interference with the circulation of grains. The requisition of supplies for the army further accentuated the fears of famine. The farmers, fearing a shortage, stored

---

[1] Actes de la Commune de Paris, 1st series, Vol. I, pp. 454–455.
[2] Ibid., Vol. II, pp. 145–146.
[3] Ibid., pp. 544–545.
[4] Recueil des Principaux Textes sur le Commerce des Céréales, pp. 138–140.
[5] Les Subsistances dans le District de Versailles, Collection de Documents Inédits, Vol. I, p. 41.
[6] Arch. Parl., Vol. XXXVII, pp. 107–109.
[7] Ibid., Vol. XXXIX, p. 518.
[8] P. V. Ag. et Com., Vol. II, p. 537.
[9] Ibid., p. 815; Recueil (Céréales), pp. 140–141.

their crops.[1] Prices soared rapidly during the autumn of 1792: by the end of 1792, the price of grain in the South was twice as high as in 1790 in spite of importations of two million quintals in the previous ten months.[2] The Committee of Agriculture and Commerce advised the introduction of stern measures against fifteen departments where the circulation of grains had been impeded.[3] The same committee in a report of November 3, 1792 expressed the opinion (1) that the high prices were caused by the hoarding of the farmers and the competitive bidding of public agents for grains; and (2) that the main specific should be the enforcement of free circulation.[4] Ferrand made a similar diagnosis of the troubles on November 16 except that he considered the excessive issues of paper money as a cause of the high prices.[5]

The debaters in the Convention focussed their attention increasingly on the issue of freedom versus regulation. The Physiocratic doctrine of a Natural Order, as well as Adam Smith's "laissez-faire" teachings, were prominent in the debates. The opponents of regulatory measures were strong enough to emerge victorious in the acrimonious debates of November and early December, 1792.

Fabre for the Committee of Agriculture and Commerce suggested an inventory of crops and requisitions where deficiencies were apparent.[6] Féraud, quoting Turgot and Smith, attempted to demonstrate that interference with the Natural Order had always been harmful. According to him, the high prices were caused by the competitive buying of the various governmental agencies, the unlawful interference with the cultivators, and the depreciation of the paper money. Some municipalities had already begun to "taxe" wheat, with disastrous results in his opinion.[7] (The French have a happy word which I find it convenient to use in this

---

[1] *Les Subsistances en Céréales dans le District de Chaumont*, Collection de Documents Inédits, Vol. I, pp. l–lv; C. Porée, *Les Subsistances dans l'Yonne*, *Études sur l'Histoire de la Révolution*, pp. 10–19.
[2] Arch. Parl., Vol. LIII, pp. 83–85.
[3] *Ibid.*, p. 53.
[4] *Moniteur*, Vol. XIV, pp. 377–378.
[5] *Ibid.*, p. 494.
[6] Arch. Parl., Vol. LIII, p. 433.
[7] *Ibid.*, pp. 436, 448–449.

paper: they refer to the "taxe" of commodities by which they mean the regulation of the price of the commodity. The term has not exactly the same connotation as to set maximum prices. To "taxe" is to determine the market price of a commodity; to set a maximum price is to fix a price above which a commodity cannot be sold. In actual practice, especially when maximum prices are fixed below market prices, the two concepts are similar.

Beffroy, a staunch critic of the doctrine of liberty, found sufficient justification for interference with the property rights of the farmers in an application of the principle of maximum utility; for the system of the Economists had been elaborated for the benefit of the rich. Free circulation could not be defended, he reasoned, when the administrative machinery was not efficacious in insuring subsistence for all.[1] Roland, the Girondist Minister of Interior, in a letter to the Convention received on November 19, took a more favorable view of the results of non-interference. He maintained that the functions of the Government were to prevent positive evils and to allow the fullest developments of the individual's faculties. Only the interference with this natural course of events had made possible such extreme variations in prices.[2]

Saint Just, the satellite of Robespièrre, made a very impressive discourse on November 29: Adam Smith never experienced what we are experiencing in France today. A practical system of economics can never be devised. Excessive issues of money have demoralised our grain system. The value of all the products in the State should be estimated, and an equal value of money should be manufactured to represent these products. When lands and products are both represented by paper money, then naturally prices will go up. Manufacturers produce nothing; farmers conceal their products; the Government is too weak as a result of its adherence to the system of liberty; the policy of public finance requires modification. Today one neither saves nor hoards money; every one tries to spend it quickly. But the farmer prefers to store his grain.[3]

The recommendation of the Committee of Agriculture and Com-

[1] Moniteur, Vol. XIV, p. 494; Arch. Parl., Vol. LIII; pp. 438–440.
[2] Arch. Parl., Vol. LIII, pp. 476–477.
[3] Moniteur, Vol. XIV, pp. 611–612.

merce, that the Government should superintend a "census" of crops and devise a system of requisitions, continued to meet with disapproval. Serré, in an excellent speech, opposed the inquisitorial system proposed by the Committee, because he feared that such a system would lead to apprehensions as to the sufficiency of the food supplies, and hence to hoarding and higher prices. He criticised price-fixing. The "taxe" of grains alone would obviously be unfair to the farmers. Laissez-faire has not had a fair chance because freedom of grain movements has not existed; no one dares to continue in the grain trade, and yet middlemen are indispensable.[1] Robespièrre attacked the followers of the Physiocrats as mere doctrinaires. He argued that liberty was justifiable only up to the point where cupidity begins, that the authors of the Physiocratic System had not distinguished wheat from indigo; that their vague theories could find no sane adherents in the stormy days of the Revolution; and that the first right was that of existence.[2]

Viger proposed a system of price fixing with prices set above the competitive level. "Freedom of circulation cannot exist in these troublesome days. When the enjoyment of property interferes with the exercise of the right of property by others, then society has the right to violate property rights."[3] His advocacy of a maximum above the market price was exceptional: most adherents of the "taxe" were primarily interested in arbitrarily reducing the price of grain.

Beffroy made a second attack on the Economists: Prices are not adjusted easily to their natural level, as the Economists pretend, neither to the level of wages, nor to that of paper money issues. Free trade would lead to a dependence on importations and, hence, to famine. Turgot and Smith only defend the interests of the merchant and speculator.[4] Lejeune added to the strictures against the Economists. He said that the Economists reasoned as if people were motivated only by the general interest of the

[1] Arch. Parl., Vol. LIV, pp. 36–39.
[2] *Moniteur*, Vol. XIV, pp. 636–637.
[3] Arch. Parl., Vol. LIV, p. 428.
[4] *Ibid.*, p. 670.

State. If a State has a right to a man's life, it has the right to his field.[1]

Barbaroux emphasized the necessity of encouraging importations; the public expenditure of 25 millions abroad for grain had added but 5 days of supplies; but by the loss of cultivators to the army, France was being deprived of 40 days of subsistence annually.[2]

Creuzé-Latouche, a disciple of the Physiocrats, delivered the decisive discourse on December 8: The supplies of grains are sufficient — the stability of prices for twenty-five years before the Revolution supports that contention. The interference with internal commerce has been detrimental. With arguments that are reminiscent of Adam Smith, he pointed out how indispensable the middleman was. Since 1789 freedom of commerce has not existed. The thoughtless measures enforced by Necker, together with the distrust engendered by the Revolution, account for the hoarding of supplies and the interference with the free circulation. The history of prices of the first few years of the Revolution reflect the excessive interference with the circulation; whereas the price of wheat varied from 19 to 22 livres from 1780 to 1787, the price increased to 25, 34 and 30 livres in 1788, 1789, 1790 respectively, and now varies from 25 to 60 livres. In a department situated between 2 other departments, the price of wheat may be appreciably above the price in the contiguous departments. Thus the inhabitants of Loir-Et-Cher, surrounded on either side by the departments of Sarthe and Loiret, pay 45 livres for a quintal of wheat, which is sold for 29 and 31 livres in the neighboring departments.[3]

The Convention, following Latouché's discourse, approved a law providing for a penalty of death for interference with the circulation of grain. The Girondists, defenders of the doctrines of the Physiocrats, had displayed too much power for their rising adversaries in this initial clash.[4]

The law of December 8 merely postponed the victory of the op-

[1] Arch. Parl., Vol. LIV, p. 694.
[2] Ibid., pp. 670–675.
[3] Ibid., pp. 677–687.
[4] During this period, the Committee of Agriculture and Commerce was besieged with letters demanding remedial measures. P. V. Ag. et Com., Vol. III, pp. 646–657.

ponents of freedom. Prices continued to soar and petitions to pour in upon the Committee of Agriculture and Commerce. When war with Great Britain threatened, the public became seriously concerned over the possibilities of a famine. Doumouriez's treason and the uprising in the West added to the general turmoil. Mathiez accounts for the final passage of the maximum laws by the union of the Enragés, the Commune, and the Mountain, three of the elements that were struggling for supremacy amidst the rapidly developing anarchic conditions. Mathiez's insight into the political situation is to be commended.[1] In February the so-called "Economists" could still present a bold front. Garat, the newly appointed Minister of Interior, informed the Convention that the fundamental cause of the high prices lay in the depreciation of the Assignats.[2] Creuzé-Latouche once more defended a policy of non-interference; the authority of the most profound men — it is enough to mention Adam Smith — support liberty; laws are justifiable only when necessary. No law on earth can fix the value of anything; value is the result of a complex of causes. The former "taxes" of bread and meat offer no precedent, because they merely followed the prices of wheat and of live stock.[3]

The conditions, both political and economic, had become deplorable by April, and the movement for a maximum had gained momentum. The decisive debates began in the middle of April. The representatives of the Department of Paris proposed a maximum on April 18, 1793: Let no one come to us to defend the interests of commerce — commerce is only a useful relation between members of the social corps; let no one defend the great principle of property — the right of property cannot include the right of starving your fellow-citizen. The fruits of the land, as the air, belong to everybody.[4] The petition included provisions for a maximum law, and the elimination of the middleman.

---

[1] A. Mathiez, "Le Vote du Premier Maximum," *Annales Révolutionnaires*, Vol. XI, p. 313. Mathiez in a series of brilliant articles in this journal (Volumes IX, XI, and XIII) has shed light on the many political alignments made during the course of the maximum laws.

[2] Arch. Parl., Vol. LIX, p. 192.

[3] *Ibid.*, pp. 244–253.

[4] *Ibid.*, Vol. LXII, p. 621.

A somewhat similar petition was presented to the Committee of Commerce and Agriculture on the same day. The author maintained that property is subordinate to public necessity, and that men unite for their common advantage. The influence of Rousseau is apparent here, as it is with the vast majority of the opponents of economic freedom. As a true disciple of Rousseau, the petitioner contended that the principal condition of the social contract is the assurance of existence. The high prices of grain during the last two months were explained by the high prices of other commodities, the competition of governmental agents in their capacity as buyers, the guarantee of indemnities to bakers by the municipality of Paris, and, finally, the discredit of the Assignat.[1]

Momoro used similar arguments in support of the proposed maximum laws; the Social Contract says that the production of the cultivator is destined for the subsistence of the people.[2] But Payen, Santerre and Verbeuf, in supporting price-fixing, relied in the main on economic arguments.[3]

An anonymous letter to the Committee of Agriculture and Commerce contained a proposal for a "taxe" according to the faculty of the people: It is necessary to assure the people of their subsistence; wages do not increase as rapidly as the price of bread. The exportation of 1 per cent of the annual crop results in a doubling of the price of bread.[4] On April 25 the Committee of Agriculture and Commerce presented three possible solutions. of the subsistence question. The first was a proposal for a maximum of thirty livres a setier (two hundred and forty pounds), a price considerably below the market price, and prohibition of sales outside of the market. This proposal was evidently the work of the Paris authorities, now becoming more influential in national affairs. The second was Levasseur's project to compel the declaration of supplies by the farmers. The third proposal, which the Committee favored, was Fabre's plan for "greniers d'abondance". This plan was based on the assumption that plenty of grain was available,

[1] Opinion de M. Lachevardière sur le Maximum, pp. 2–4.
[2] Arch. Parl., Vol. LXIII, p. 344.
[3] Ibid., pp. 348–351.
[4] Ibid., pp. 351–353.

but its circulation was deficient; the "greniers" were to remedy this deficiency.[1]

Beffroy presented an analysis of the arguments for and against the proposed maximum in behalf of the Committee of Agriculture and Commerce. Its partisans, he said, contended that a "taxe" alone could result in the provision of the markets, and that, without it, the price of grain would increase to two hundred livres a quintal. They were unable to explain the high prices, however, for the last three crops had been good. And, finally, these adherents of price-fixing did not believe that the "taxe" was incompatible with property rights. The opponents of public control affirmed that salaries and wages would adjust themselves to the prices of necessaries, and that the farmer would suffer if forced to accept reduced prices for grains, while other prices continued to soar. A "taxe" for all products would destroy our commerce. They alleged further that a "taxe" would be arbitrary, because conditions varied so much from place to place; and that a "taxe" reduced month by month — as was generally proposed in order to offer a bounty for the immediate provisioning of the market — would result in excessive purchases by the rich.[2]

On April 28 Creuzé-Latouche made his final appeal for liberty; but the old arguments had lost much of their force. He was now willing to make a concession to his opponents; he would offer an indemnity to the workers to offset the high price of grain.[3] Philippeaux, in supporting a maximum above the market price, joined with the opposition.[4] Ducos, also, in maintaining (1) that a maximum below costs would discourage cultivation, (2) that exchanges arc always just when left to the respective interests of buyers and sellers, (3) that the private interests forget nothing whereas the Legislature does not see all, and, finally, (4) that prices below the market prices would exhaust the supplies available, tried to delay the impending maximum.[5] Another member favored a system of insurance for the farmer at the expense of the Government. In

[1] Arch. Parl., Vol. LXIII, pp. 314–319.
[2] Ibid., pp. 332–336.
[3] Moniteur, Vol. XVI, p. 248.
[4] Ibid., p. 271.
[5] Ibid., p. 280.

that manner, he thought, the farmers might be induced to resume their normal vocation, and their fears might be dissipated.[1]

Vernier made the most brilliant defense of the existing system: France's preëminence is due to agriculture; hence agriculture should receive every possible stimulus. The "taxe" of one product will lead to the "taxe" of every other product. The enactment of an agrarian law means the enactment of a law which will only aggravate the already deplorable conditions in the subsistence markets. He advocated that wages be adjusted to the price of subsistence instead of subsistence to wages and that the paper money in circulation be reduced. He maintained that France was suffering from a dearth of grain as a result of the insecurity and the hoarding of commodities.[2]

Lecointre suggested a maximum of thirty livres a setier for fifteen departments where subsistence was inadequate. He attempted to demonstrate that the cost of production warranted a low maximum. But the price of wheat had already reached 200 livres a setier in some of the departments named by Lecointre.[3] Montgilbert proposed to combine price-fixing and communism.[4]

The debates were long and fierce on May 2. Desvars, Thuriot, Real, Genissieux, and Charles all favored the maximum. Vernier approved a maximum for bread, but not for grains. Buzot, Grandpré, and Ducos argued against public control.[5] The principle of a "decreasing" maximum was accepted.[6]

Legendre continued the fight on the following day. The animus of his argument came from Rousseau. France has seen only famine since the origin of the funereal science of economics; the right of subsistence arises with the right of toil; the duty of the Government is to assure the people their subsistence — these are the principles of the Social Contract.[7]

The Convention agreed on the details of the maximum laws on May 3 and 4. The decrees authorized requisitions on municipal-

[1] *Moniteur*, Vol. XVI, pp. 245–246.
[2] Arch. Parl., Vol. LXIII, p. 640.
[3] *Ibid.*, pp. 630–631.
[4] *Ibid.*, pp. 634–635.
[5] *Ibid.*, Vol. XVI, pp. 297–300.
[6] *Ibid.*, p. 300.
[7] Arch. Parl., Vol. LXIV, pp. 114–115.

ities and communes in favor of districts, and on individuals in favor of municipalities and communes. Henceforth only market sales were to be valid. The maximum was to be based on the average price of grain in each locality from January to April, 1793. It was to become effective on May 1. In accordance with the principle of a decreasing maximum, farmers were to receive 1/10, 1/20, 1/20, 1/40, and 1/40 less than the maximum of May on successive months.[1]

This summary of the origin of the first maximum laws is not exhaustive. I have included only the papers and discourses of practical or theoretical interest. Lack of space has made it necessary to reduce the verbose reports and discourses to the barest outlines.

The first laws encountered many obstacles of an administrative nature which will be touched upon in a later section. Within six weeks of the approval of price fixing, the Government commissioned the Minister of Interior to devise a plan for a uniform maximum.[2] The local governments, in their competition for the available supplies, had vied with one another in laxity of administration; for abundance was the reward of failure to enforce the maximum. A concerted movement for a general, rather than a local maximum, progressed rapidly in June.[3] The Convention turned to the Committee of Public Safety for counsel.[4]

By July the failure of the maximum seemed certain. The privilege of buying outside of the market that was given to public functionaries, impaired its effectiveness.[5] Public officials openly demanded the repeal of a law responsible for the starvation of France.[6] The Committee of Commerce and Provisioning was entrusted with the task of planning a substitute for the May law.[7] Raffron's renewal of the agitation to "taxe" all necessities of life — similar recommendations had been made in April — was a re-

---

[1] Arch. Parl., Vol. LXIV, pp. 56–57.
[2] *Ibid.*, Vol. LXVII, p. 21.
[3] *Ibid.*, p. 456.
[4] *Ibid.*, pp. 456, 544.
[5] *Ibid.*, Vol. LXVIII, pp. 25, 326; A. Mathiez, "Les Enragés contre la Constitution de 1793," *Annales Révolutionnaires*, Vol. XIII, pp. 297–321.
[6] *Ibid.*, Vol. LXIX, pp. 200, 536; Vol. LXX, p. 50.
[7] *C. P. S.*, Vol. XV, p. 442.

flection of the dissatisfaction with the ineffective execution of the maximum of grains. Raffron strengthened his argument with an appeal to the police power: the "taxe" of all necessaries of life is as much an expression of the police power as the regulation of weights and measures. He also bewailed the absence of competition, which might have brought about an equilibrium of prices and products.[1]

The debates on the maximum were renewed on September 3, when several members vigorously assailed the maximum laws. Thuriot, abetted by the irrepressible Danton, forcibly argued that a uniform maximum of grains was necessary. The Convention sanctioned a law on September 3 that established a uniform price of fourteen livres a quintal for wheat and twenty livres a quintal for flour.[2] The average price of wheat in 1790 for the whole of France had been twelve and two-thirds livres[3]; the increase was, therefore, between 12 and 13 per cent over the prices of 1790.

The Convention now turned its attention to the demand for a general maximum for all commodities as yet not regulated. The Committee of Subsistence reported in favor of a general maximum on September 23. Coupé, the reporter for the Committee, said that whereas formerly prices were regulated by the reciprocal interest of buyers and sellers, now they were regulated by a "conspiration générale de malveillance, de perfidie, et de fureur."[4] The Committee proposed to increase prices one-third and wages one-half above the level of 1790. A minority favored increases of one hundred per cent, and another minority (report by Lecointre) suggested the regulation of prices according to the conditions of supply: thus, since meat was scarce, the "taxe" for meat should be high. The Committee's proposals met with the approval of the Convention, and five days later the Convention embodied them in a general maximum law. In all, the law affected thirty-nine commodities, mostly necessities.[5]

Siret, a discriminating police reporter of remarkable economic

[1] Arch. Parl., Vol. LXXIII, p. 258.
[2] *Moniteur*, Vol. XVII, pp. 562–565.
[3] L. Biollay, *op. cit.*, p. 84.
[4] *Moniteur*, Vol. XVII, pp. 775–776.
[5] *Ibid.*

training, perceived the necessity of modifying the new laws in the first few months of their operation. He maintained that they were not enforceable and, hence, were demoralizing; that they were detrimental to commerce; and that they were unjust to both buyer and seller.[1] As early as February, 1794 the Government, disturbed by the many violations and the administrative difficulties, requested the Committee of Subsistence to prepare a revised law.[2] The Committee of Agriculture and Commerce concurred in the opinion that the maximum system had not fulfilled all the hopes of its proponents.[3] The Committee of Subsistence advised that the revised maximum should make allowances for the profits of the middleman and for transportation costs. Barère supported this suggestion; the great work of political economy should be to instruct the people as to their resources, as to prices, and give them other information formerly accessible to but a few. The maximum should be based on surveys and be adjusted to costs.[4] The revised maximum, which followed closely the recommendations of Barère and the Committee of Subsistence, was approved on February 12–14, 1794.[5] Barère, a great figure of the Revolution, and one whose influence on the economic policy of the Reign of Terror was great, deserves recognition for his coöperation in establishing the maximum on a more secure basis.

The rigorous system of enforcement demanded by the new laws led ultimately to a reaction. A law, voted in September, 1793, making hoarding a capital offense, was repealed in April, 1794.[6] The Committee of Subsistence and Provisioning, which had been given extensive powers for the administration of the maximum law, was shorn of much of its power.

The Government made new concessions in October, 1794. Limitless requisitions were banned; authorities thereafter had to designate the time, quality, and quantity of each shipment.[7] The legis-

---

[1] *Rapports de Grivel et Siret sur les Subsistances et le Maximum, Commission de Recherche*, 1907, pp. 106–107.
[2] *Moniteur*, Vol. XIX, p. 438.
[3] *P. V. Com. Ag. et Com.*, Vol. IV, pp. 306–308.
[4] *Moniteur*, Vol. XIX, pp. 534–536.
[5] *Ibid.*, pp. 538–540.
[6] *J. Déb. et Déc.*, Vol. LVIII, pp. 147–150.
[7] *Moniteur*, Vol. XXII, pp. 470–471.

lators now also purported to offer the cultivators an equitable return for their labor: the new maximum was to be increased to a level, two-thirds in excess of the prices of 1790.[1]

The maximum régime was collapsing rapidly, however, and no power could prevent the final repeal. Géraud made a masterly attack on the system at a session of the Committee of Agriculture and Commerce early in December, 1794. He distinguished between the general high prices caused by the excessive issues of paper money, and the high prices of particular commodities due to scarcity. He criticised the laws against hoarding, which had forced people to renounce their normal vocations; and he attacked the maximum laws, which, he asserted, had contributed to increased consumption; for increases in money wages had left the workers with a large surplus of purchasing power. Because of the losses incurred as a result of price-fixing, dealers did not replenish their stocks; and because of losses incurred as a result of the requisitions, many farmers were ruined. They could scarcely be expected to replace livestock at prices of two or three times the sales price to the Government. He concluded with a proposal for the immediate repeal of the maximum laws.[2]

Several members of the Convention opposed the repeal. Lecointre, Richaud, and Pelet anticipated violent price increases and dire scarcity with the return to economic liberty. The proponents of the regulatory system, now agreeable to a compromise, proposed indemnities for the cultivators.[3] The reaction in favor of freedom was strong, however, and the repeal was voted on December 23, 1794. All requisitions already ordered, however, were to be filled. The Committee of Commerce and Provisioning obtained the right of preëmption at market prices for all objects necessary for the army.[4] The downfall of Robespierre in August, 1794 only hastened the·repudiation of an economic policy that savored of terrorism and that was an integral part of the policy of the Terrorists.

---

[1] *J. Déb. et Déc.*, Vol. LXIV, pp. 701–704.
[2] *P. V. Ag. et Com.*, Vol. IV, pp. 608–617.
[3] *Moniteur*, Vol. XXIII, pp. 43–47; *J. Déb. et Déc.*, Vol. LXVII, pp. 22–27.
[4] *Moniteur, Ibid.*, pp. 53–54.

2. Opinions of Historians

The legislative history of the maximum laws does not lead, necessarily, to the conclusion that the maximum system was a failure. The revisions, modifications, and adjustments to the changing and complicated economic conditions merely reflect the obstacles encountered in the administration. Even the confessions of failure on the part of the authors of the system are not conclusive proof, contrary to Marion's contention. He contends, moreover, that a successful stabilization of prices at one-third above the level of 1790 was impossible without a reduction of the circulating media to one-third above 1790[1]— a rather rigid statement of the quantity theory with no consideration of the possibility of changes in balances of money and in the supply of commodities. He finds little to laud in the whole experience: "The maximum had been only a procedure to stop or rather conceal the progress of the depreciation, a procedure badly conceived, soon revealed powerless, even injurious".[2]

Du Chatelier concludes that the maximum system had disastrous effects on production.[3] Taine maintains that the system set one-half of the people of France as spies on the other half; and only the abrogation of the maximum laws, concomitant with a few other propitious events, saved the country from famine in 1795.[4] Levasseur says that price control was accompanied by a disappearance of commodities, a depreciation in the quality of goods, and the hoarding of supplies by the rich.[5] Gomel concludes that the maximum was a distinct failure: it increased prices, and resulted in a calamitous scarcity.[6] A writer who made a thoughtful study of the operation of price-fixing in the Department of Eure, finds persistent violations. Sales at the home of the farmer were frequent.[7]

A few authors defend the maximum laws. Bourne concludes

---

[1] M. Marion, op. cit., Vol. II, pp. viii, 109.
[2] Ibid., p. 255; M. Marion, Les Lois de Maximum, pp. 14-15.
[3] Du Chatelier, "Les Assignats," Acad. des Sci. Mor., Vol. CXXIII, pp. 843, 861.
[4] H. A. Taine, The French Revolution, Vol. III, pp. 377-394.
[5] E. Levasseur, Histoire des Classes Ouvrières, 2d ed., Vol. I, pp. 195-204.
[6] C. Gomel, Histoire Financière de la Législative Assemblée et de la Convention, Vol. II, pp. 70-71.
[7] F. Évrard, Les Subsistances dans le Département de l'Eure, Commission de Recherche, 1909, pp. 58-59.

that the system of control saved France when "Economic Federalism" was at its height.[1] Mathiez contends that at least for 1794, "the vigorous enforcement of laws that the Committee of Public Safety had known how to enlist for the public benefit," proved quite effective.[2] Lefèbvre, in a study of the District of Bergues, concludes that after the initial period of May to September, 1793, the maximum was in general observed, and little want was felt until after the first half of 1794. He attributes any scarcity that was prevalent to the war, and not to the maximum laws; but he concedes that central control broke down from September to December, 1794, and that clandestine commerce developed rapidly thereafter.[3]

Blanc, also, announces himself a disciple of the Jacobins. In his opinion, scarcity was caused by speculation, rather than by governmental control.[4] He concedes, however, that the shutting down of stores and factories and the hoarding of supplies was caused by the application of the maximum system.[5] But he whittles away his concession with the following conclusion: "The maximum laws gave the Assignat life, maintained them at par, and the Assignat thus supported created the prodigious resources necessary for the support of fourteen armies. The repeal of the maximum laws was a death blow to the Assignats."[6] Finally, one student ventures the statement that the maximum period was the only period when Rheims did not suffer from famine.[7]

3. RESULTS OF CONTROL

The first maximum, voted in May, 1793, provided for the fixing of the price of grain in each department on the basis of the local

[1] H. E. Bourne, "Maximum Prices in France 1793-4," *American Historical Review*, Vol. XXIII, pp. 107-113.

[2] A. Mathiez, "La Dictature Economique du Comité de Salut Public," *Annales Révolutionnaires*, Vol. XV, pp. 462-463.

[3] *Les Subsistances dans le District de Bergues*, Collection de Documents Inédits, Introd., pp. lviii-lxxiv.

[4] L. Blanc, *Histoire Socialiste de la Révolution*, Vol. II, p. 638.

[5] *Ibid.*, p. 590.

[6] *Ibid.*, pp. 590-591.

[7] M. G. Laurent, *Les Subsistances à Rheims pendant la Révolution, Commission de Recherche*, 1913, p. 472.

prices for the first four months of 1793. It did not function well. The local authorities competed for the available supplies, and often, through lax administration and the establishment of high maximum prices, obtained disproportionate supplies of grains at the expense of their neighbors.[1] Incessant protests against the non-enforcement of the maximum reached the authorities.[2] The first reaction to the maximum was a precipitate increase in the prices of the commodities not subject to control.[3] Because the authorities did not control the price of flour, the price of bread soared in spite of the control of the price of wheat.[4]

Garnier, an agent of the Minister of Interior, analyzed the situation concisely on June 26, 1793: The maximum should be repealed; the possessors of stocks refuse to sell at low prices, and those in need are unable to buy; localities exaggerate their needs, and individuals underestimate their supplies. Fifty primary assemblies in the Southern and Central parts of France, in expressing their opinions on certain constitutional questions, gave their views on the maximum system. All but one assailed the system: the maximum deprives the peasant of the fruits of his labor, as he is forced to sell at low prices and buy at high ones; he sells little, and famine follows. Only the departments near Paris, hostile to the "grande culture," favor maximum prices.[5] Ronsin informed the Executive Council (at this time responsible for the enforcement of the maximum laws) that the maximum system was the greatest single cause of the deficiency of subsistence for the French armies.[6] The Jacobins admitted in the latter part of August that

---

[1] *Les Subsistances dans le District de Bergues*, Vol. I, p. 21; *Rapports des Agents Secrètes du Ministre de l'Intérieur*, Vol. I, pp. 290–291. *C. P. S.*, Vol. VI, pp. 174–175, 451; Arch. Parl., Vol. LXX, pp. 525–526; *Correspondance Générale de Carnot*, Collection de Documents Inédits, Vol. III, p. 50. *Département de l'Orne, Recueil des Documents d'Ordre Economique*, Collection de Documents Inédits, Vol. II, pp. 106–107.

[2] *C. P. S.*, Vol. VI, pp. 315–317; *Les Subsistances dans le District de Versailles*, Vol. I, p. 336; C. Porée, *Les Subsistances dans l'Yonne, Études sur l'Histoire de la Révolution*, pp. 30–44.

[3] *Les Subsistances dans le District de Versailles*, Vol. I, p. 336; *Département de l'Orne*, Vol. I, pp. 166–167.

[4] *C. P. S.*, Vol. VI, p. 90.

[5] C. Reffatèrre, *Les Revendications Economiques et Sociales des Assemblées Primaires de Juillet, 1793, Commission de Recherche*, 1906, pp. 336–347.

[6] *Correspondance de Carnot*, Vol. III, pp. 16–17.

the subsistence problem still appeared to be insoluble.[1] The agent commissioned to buy subsistence for the Army of Tours requested permission on August 24 to buy subsistence at prices above the maximum.[2] The improved laws of September, 1793 were framed to obviate many of the difficulties revealed in the May law.

Much evidence is available of sales above the maximum prices, of unsuccessful requisitions, and of empty markets. Dealers frequently sold out their stocks and did not replenish them.[3] Farmers slaughtered their young beasts to take advantage of the high market price of animals; for, although the Government controlled the price of retailed meat, it did not regulate the price of the beast. Live stock requisitioned at maximum prices was not replaced, for replacement required an outlay of two or three times the price of sales to the Government.[4] Farmers abandoned their farms in some cases and consumed their plentiful hoards in idleness.[5] The hoarding of commodities by the rich became a frequent subject of complaint with the enactment of a general maximum in September.[6] Saint Just mercilessly assailed the rich for their excessive buying. He feared that the reduction of prices resulting from control only enabled the rich to double their purchases.[7]

Violations of the maximum law, viz. sales above the legal prices, and sales at the home of the farmer were frequently complained of.[8] We should be careful, however, not to place too much significance in these scattered reports of violation: Violation is more likely to attract comment than compliance. The more frequent reports of failure in the fall of 1794 make us reserve our decision for the previous year.[9]

[1] Arch. Parl., Vol. LXXII, pp. 474–475.
[2] C. P. S., Vol. VI, p. 93.
[3] P. Caron, Paris pendant la Térreur, Vol. I, p. 114.
[4] C. P. S., Vol. X, p. 386.
[5] Ibid., Vol. VIII, p. 247.
[6] P. Caron, op. cit., Vol. I, pp. 247–248; R. Hesden, Journal of a Spy, pp. 32–33; C. P. S., Vol. VIII, p. 36.
[7] Moniteur, Vol. XVIII, p. 108; P. Caron, op. cit., Vol. I, pp. 247–248.
[8] C. P. S., Vol. X, p. 609; Vol. XI, pp. 346, 490–491; Société des Jacobins, Collection de Documents Inédits sur l'Histoire de Paris, Vol. V, p. 650; L. S. Mercier, Le Nouveau Paris, Vol. III, pp. 80–82.
[9] See for example Le Comité des Subsistances de Toulouse, Collections de Documents Inédits, p. 173; also Les Subsistances dans le District de Chaumont, Vol. I, pp. 602–603; and Moniteur, Vol. XXI, pp. 793–798.

Technical violations were numerous, also. Dealers sold cooked rather than raw pork, because the former was not subject to the maximum.[1] Official recognition of the violation of the law was not unknown. Thus a soap corporation received permission from the Government to sell soap at prices considerably above the maximum.[2] Indemnities to public contractors for selling at the maximum were granted.[3] Relatively few of the infractions of the law were brought to the attention of the courts. Wallon only mentions a few condemnations.[4] References to judicial action are rare in documents dealing with the subsistence problem.[5] Confiscation of the commodity involved was the usual punishment in the local courts.

Clandestine trade developed in a spectacular manner. The middlemen involved (largely women) dealt in semi-luxuries, such as eggs and butter, which they bought at the maximum and resold at a profit. This trade was appreciable in the fall of 1793 and assumed added importance as opposition to the maximum waxed.[6] Sales at prices of two or three times the maximum were common.

A maximum system based on prices below the cost of production, had to be strengthened by the right to requisition. Requisitions were necessary to feed the army, Paris, and other communities without access to adequate food supplies. The Government was thus empowered to force the farmers to dispose of their products below the cost of production. Requisitions often required pressure, and failures were frequent. On many occasions departments already suffering from inadequate provisions were the victims of oppressive requisitioning.[7] The authorities often clashed, and identical supplies were frequently requisitioned for several armies.[8] The representatives "en mission" often had to acknowl-

[1] *Rapports de Grivel et Siret sur les Subsistances, Commission de Recherche,* 1907, p. 110.
[2] *Le Comité des Subsistances de Toulouse,* p. 173.
[3] *C. P. S.,* Vol. XI, p. 290.
[4] P. H. Wallon, *Histoire du Tribunal Révolutionnaire,* Vol. II, pp. 490–491; Vol. III, p. 469.
[5] See *Le Comité des Subsistances de Toulouse,* p. 163, however.
[6] R. Hesden, *op. cit.,* pp. 23–24.
[7] See for example *C. P. S.,* Vol. XI, pp. 178–179; Vol. XII, p. 736; Vol. XVIII, pp. 436, 563–564.
[8] *C. P. S.,* Vol. XI, p. 68; Vol. XII, p. 159 — at least five authorities were giving

edge their errors and moderate their demands.[1] Threats, coercion, and arrests were the lot of many local officials.[2] The Government, in its desperation, often acted unwisely. (Witness an announcement of June 26, 1794 to the effect that all of the newly harvested crops were submitted to the requisition of the Government for the use of the army and country.[3]) But in spite of all its deficiencies, the system of requisitions made possible the feeding of the army and the country.

Complaints of scarcity were frequent.[4] So long as the Government enforced sales below the cost of production the farmers preferred to hoard their supplies; and the public, encouraged by the low prices, purchased in excess of current requirements. We can only conjecture as to what extent the domestic and foreign warfare contributed to the scarcity.

The supply of products not subject to the maximum disappeared more rapidly than the controlled commodities. At a rather early stage of the maximum history, the observer, Grivel, reported that milk, a commodity not subject to the maximum, had increased in price four fold.[5]

The lack of meat, in particular, concerned the authorities; for although the Government controlled the retail price of meat, the price of the animal was not regulated. The butcher, who continued his vocation only under the relentless pressure of public opinion, encountered severe losses.[6] Grivel explained that the sale of meat at the price of 13–14 sous that cost the butcher thirty-two sous, was prejudicial to the interests of the country. Siret, Grivel's companion, explained that, whereas previously three-fifths of the

orders relating to identical supplies of subsistence; Vol. XII, p. 683. In June, 1794, the Committee of Public Safety disavowed an act of its representative who requisitioned all the grains in three departments.

[1] *C. P. S.*, Vol. XVIII, pp. 767–769; *Le Comité des Subsistances de Toulouse,* p. 332.

[2] *C.P.S.*, Vol. XI, pp. 658–659; *Le Comité des Subsistances de Toulouse,* p. 163.

[3] *Recueil, Céréales,* pp. 194–197, 207; also *C. P. S.*, Vol. XVII, pp. 51–53. In November, 1794, the Convention protested against the "limitless" requisitions of the officials.

[4] C. A. Dauban, *Paris en 1794,* pp. 59–60, 185; *C. P. S.*, Vol. XI, p. 430; C. Porée; *Les Subsistances dans l'Yonne,* pp. 63–67.

[5] *Rapports de Grivel et Siret,* pp. 160–162.

[6] A. Schmidt, *Paris pendant la Révolution,* Vol. II, pp. 222–226.

people had abstained from meat during one hundred and forty-one days annually, the people, now relieved from religious restraints, were consuming meat every day.[1] The uprising of the West, the seat of rich grazing lands, aggravated the situation. The Government in general pretended not to take notice of the many violations on the part of the butchers.[2] The Committee of Surveillance of Paris did caution the butchers, however, to discontinue sales to the rich at fabulous prices.[3] The Government had no alternative but to offer indemnities to the provisioners of meat for the army, and finally to agree to pay market prices for meat.[4] Serious proposals to enforce a "Civic Lent" were made in Parliament.[5]

The inferior quality of commodities was a common complaint. Soaps were of wretched quality and did not lather.[6] Milk was sold as cream.[7] Grivel reported a depreciation in the quality of cloth.[8] The women continually abused the butchers for selling an increasing proportion of waste with their meat.[9] The public bewailed the wretched quality of the bread.[10] Customers endured discourteous treatment in the market places, and were forced to wait in long lines for almost every purchase.[11] The "queue" became a notorious institution of the Revolution. Thus the dealers partially offset losses incurred as a result of the maximum laws, and the consumers in reality paid a higher price than a mere consideration of the prices would indicate.

A discourse rendered by Isoré before the Convention on September 18, 1794 reveals the deplorable state of affairs reached in the fall of 1794: Many middlemen and few manufacturers are thriving. The controlled price of the raw material is out of line

[1] *Rapports de Grivel et Siret*, pp. 175–181.
[2] *Ibid.*, pp. 112–113; P. Caron, *Paris pendant la Térreur*, Vol. II, pp. 260–261.
[3] B. J. B. Buchez et P. C. Roux, *Histoire Parlémentaire*, Vol. XXXII, pp. 2–4.
[4] *C. P. S.*, Vol. XII, pp. 107–108; Vol. XIII, pp. 368–369.
[5] B. J. B. Buchez et P. C. Roux, *op. cit.*, pp. 10–12.
[6] P. Caron, *Paris pendant la Térreur*, Vol. II, p. 141.
[7] *Ibid.*, pp. 260–261.
[8] *Rapports de Grivel et Siret*, pp. 124–125; also *C. P. S.*, Vol. XV, pp. 54–58.
[9] See for example C. A. Dauban, *Paris en 1794 et 1795*, p. 144; P. Caron, *op. cit.*, Vol. II, p. 109.
[10] *Les Subsistances dans le District de Versailles*, Vol. I, p. 328; Vol. II, pp. 183–188.
[11] L. S. Mercier, *Le Nouveau Paris*, Vol. III, pp. 78–80; *P. V. Ag. et Com.*, Vol. IV, pp. 454–456; P. Caron, *op. cit.*, Vol. I, p. 328.

with the price of manufactured goods, usually not controlled. Prices vary from place to place. Superfluities and deficits are the rule in neighboring localities. Sales are made fraudulently everywhere. Requisitions are excessive, and penury results. Official and unofficial buyers compete, and prices have increased. The official control of purchases has led to much corruption. The low maximum prices are responsible for the excessive purchases and inordinate violations.[1]

Favorable reports on the maximum were not numerous. Jacob Dupont informed the Convention on July 31, 1793 that the maximum had at least saved the Government large sums in the provisioning of its armies.[2] Although the people expressed much concern about their subsistence in 1794, the markets of Paris were well stocked even in the fall of 1794, as is apparent from the police reports of the period.[3] The observer, Siret, refused to condemn the maximum laws unreservedly: scarcity had been known before the introduction of price control.[4]

A system of maximum prices and rationing was likely to cause a readjustment of consumers' budgets. The public turned to the absolute necessities of life more and more when they could be obtained. Although Paris consumed 1500 sacks of flour per day in 1789,[5] the Committee of Public Safety announced that its consumption had increased to 1800–1850 sacks in 1794.[6] One reason was evident from that report. Whereas previously all of France had consumed 400,000 head of live-stock annually, now the army alone consumed that amount. The abnormal consumption of bread continued even after the maximum. Although complaints were current of pittances of a half pound of bread daily, the law allowed rations of 1 and 1½ pounds, and the daily consumption had increased to 2150 sacks by February, 1795.[7] Boissy had been successful in reducing the daily rations to 1 pound for all

[1] *Moniteur*, Vol. XXI, pp. 793–797.
[2] Arch. Parl., Vol. LXX, p. 51.
[3] *Réaction Thermidorienne*, Vol. I (numerous passages).
[4] *Rapports de Grivel et Siret*, pp. 128–129.
[5] Actes de Commune, 1st Series, Vol. II, p. 569.
[6] *C. P. S.*, Vol. XVII, pp. 176–180.
[7] *Réaction Thermidorienne*, Vol. I, pp. 601, 605, 619; *C. P. S.*, Vol. XX, pp. 206–208.

but workers.[1] The Government promised rations of but ½ pound of meat at 21 sous a pound on every fifth day. The wretched conditions in the fall of 1795 were probably unparalleled in the history of the Revolution. Even Paris had to be content with daily rations of 8 ounces of bread, and potatoes now constituted an indispensable item in the daily menu of most Parisians.[2] The larger consumption of bread in Paris is explained by the paternalistic attitude of the Government toward Paris.

Other parts of the country suffered more seriously from the deficiency of subsistence. The citizens of Versailles received but 4 ounces of bread daily in April, 1795.[3] The inhabitants of the Pyrenees obtained 3 ounces daily with difficulty in May, 1795.[4] The people of Toulouse received 8 ounces daily in the latter part of 1794.[5]

Subsistence was available for all during the maximum period; famine was absent in spite of the repeated reports of scarcity. The deficiencies of the maximum period proper were trivial compared with those of 1795. If we appraise the advantages of control, we should also consider the year 1795. I doubt whether the maximum system led to an appreciable abandonment of farms. The observant and ubiquitous representatives of the Committee of Public Safety ferreted out few offenders.[6] The discomforts and famine suffered in 1795 resulted from the questionable policy of repealing the maximum laws when the country was in the midst of a costly war. Necessity required the continuation of control until the war was over, once the system had been established. Repudiation of the policy resulted in the temporary withholding of supplies in anticipation of higher prices, and in attempts to purchase all available supplies on the part of the consumers. In the midst of a great war, can it be expected that farmers and consumers suddenly freed from restraint would react otherwise? I am inclined to attribute

[1] *J. Déb. et Déc.*, Vol. LXIX, pp. 355-358.
[2] *Réaction Thermidorienne*, Vol. II, p. 429.
[3] *Les Subsistances dans le District de Versailles*, Vol. II, p. 291.
[4] *C. P. S.*, Vol. XIII, pp. 749-754.
[5] *Le Comité des Subsistances de Toulouse*, p. 118.
[6] However, see *Recueil des principaux Textes concernant, l'Economie Rurale, Commission de Recherche*, 1907, pp. 350-351. (A law against such desertions of farms is given.)

the troubles of 1795 not so much to the maximum policy as to the premature discontinuance of that policy.

The Government, in repealing the maximum legislation in December, repudiated the system of restrictions; but it required the fulfillment of requisitions already made. A system of preemption for the Government at market prices was substituted. Weary of the exactions demanded by the system of control, the public was anxious to be freed from all restrictions; but their fears of famine increased with the approach of the days of freedom. Their fears were well founded. The farmers refused to provision the markets; requisitions were vexatious and were disregarded. The Government resorted to a new system of control, more exacting but less effective than the earlier system.

About the scarcity of subsistence in 1795, there can be little doubt. Lefèbvre writes that the fear of starvation began to cause trouble in Bergues late in 1794.[1] The peasants refused to accept the depreciated paper money. Similar apprehensions were prevalent in Versailles.[2] A great fear was evident in Paris; the police inspectors received more numerous and more sincere complaints in February, March, and April than ever before.[3] The authorities of Chaumont complained of an unusual increase in prices and an unprecedented disappearance of commodities.[4] The Committee of Public Safety granted many subsidies to the Provinces for the purchase of bread.[5] The rations of bread outside of Paris were smaller than ever in 1795.[6] The army partook of the general distress.[7]

The Government renewed its old requisitions and ordered new ones throughout 1795. The absence of a consistent policy made the fulfillment of these requisitions very difficult. Evasion was easy when the cultivator was granted the privilege of withholding six months of supplies.[8] The circulation of grains beyond the

[1] Les Subsistances dans le District de Bergues, Vol. I, pp. lxxxvi–lxxxviii.
[2] Les Subsistances dans la District de Versailles, Vol. II, pp. 350–351, 354–359.
[3] Réaction Thermidorienne, Vol. I, pp. 406–492, 500–517, 560, 652–663.
[4] Les Subsistances en Céréales dans le District de Chaumont, Vol. II, p. 437.
[5] C. P. S., Vol. XIX, p. 510.
[6] C. P. S., Vol. XIX, p. 793; Vol. XXI, pp. 348–350; Vol. XXIII, p. 232.
[7] H. Bourdeau, Les Armées au Rhin au Début du Directoire, pp. 307–308, 310–311.
[8] Les Subsistances dans le District de Bergues, Vol. I, pp. lxxxix–xc.

limits of each municipality was beset with difficulties.[1] Requisition that had become more frequent and more harassing, had also become more difficult to enforce.[2] Even more heroic measures brought little success. The administrators of Versailles, for example, required the farmers to fetch one-fortieth of their crops to the market on every tenth day.[3] On January 22 the Convention ordered the arrest of all cultivators who were in arrears to the Government.[4] In March, the failure of requisitions received much attention.[5] Lecointre informed the Convention that the right of requisition was publicly sold, and that various officials sold requisitioned commodities at double the price of requisition.[6] On March 23 the Committee of Public Safety requisitioned one-fifth of all the grains and vegetables in all the departments subject to demands for the provisioning of Paris and the army.[7] This law was evidently not enforced, for soon after the Government voted another decree which allowed the officials of the granaries of Paris to withhold two months of provisions if they sent the remainder to Paris.[8] The representatives of the Government with the armies of the North and of the Sambre-and-Meuse complained of the illusory character of the requisitions.[9]

The kaleidoscopic changes of measures, the rapid movements from one policy to another, distinctly more rapid than had been the case in 1793–94, attest the weakness of the Government and the failure of the requisitions. The changes occurred so quickly as to warrant a presumption that most of the measures had failed. The Government ordered a new "census" of grains as of May 21. Each locality was to retain enough to sustain itself until the harvesting of the next crop.[10] On July 22 the Convention instituted a Patente law, requiring a license for the privilege

[1] *Les Subsistances dans la District de Bergues*, Vol. I, p. xcv.
[2] *C. P. S.*, Vol. XIX, pp. 407, 480–492, 510–511, 560–561, 577, 685–686, 724.
[3] *Les Subsistances dans le District de Versailles*, Vol. II, pp. 352, 354–359.
[4] *C. P. S.*, Vol. XIX, p. 619.
[5] *Ibid.*, Vol. XX, pp. 730–731, 752.
[6] *Moniteur*, Vol. XXIII, pp. 438–440.
[7] *C. P. S.*, Vol. XXI, pp. 261–262.
[8] *Ibid.*
[9] *Ibid.*, p. 540.
[10] *Recueil, Céréales*, pp. 252–253.

of dealing in grain. This was an attempt to regulate the grain trade.[1] The Commission for provisioning the market in a circular of August addressed to the administrators of the departments, suggested a systematic provisioning of the market as a method of reducing prices.[2] The Committee of Public Safety on August 24 put the army at the disposal of the local authorities to insure the enforcement of requisitions.[3] The Convention also adopted its former policy of frowning upon sales outside of the market.[4]

In the autumn, with excellent crops and a marked reduction of the scale of the war, want disappeared.[5] The dangers of famine were over. The armies continued to suffer, however, from the demoralization caused by the policy of control. Jourdan, a great general of the Revolution, said in February, 1796: "The army has subsisted for a long time only on requisitions, but these requisitions have destroyed all the resources of the country. The supply of meat is inadequate; it has been maintained so far only by taking away supplies in sections where there remained only the beasts necessary to cultivate the land."[6]

4. SIGNIFICANCE FOR THE ASSIGNATS

Writers often assume that the Government introduced price-fixing to enhance the value of the Assignat in terms of commodities.[7] That assumption is untenable. The debates that led up to the maximum contain nothing that supports that contention. The members of the Convention did not realize, before the introduction of the system, that maximum prices might affect the value of the Assignat to a significant degree. The system of maximum prices, however, sustained the value of all the Assignats that circulated; and since the Government's power of spending was limited only by its needs and powers of requisition, the system proved to

---

[1] *Recueil, Céréales*, pp. 256–257.
[2] *Ibid.*, pp. 260–261.
[3] *Ibid.*
[4] *J. Déb. et Déc.*, Vol. XXVI, pp. 23–27.
[5] *Réaction Thermidorienne*, Vol. II, pp. 724, 746.
[6] H. Bourdeau, *Les Armées du Rhin*, pp. 307–308.
[7] See for example Marion's opinion given in an earlier part of this chapter, and Mallet du Pan's opinion given in Chapter II.

be lucrative. Since the Government expended a large proportion of all of its receipts on subsistence and supplies which were put at its disposal at prices only moderately above those of 1790, the Government suffered a relatively small loss from the depreciation of the Assignats. Whereas prices otherwise might have increased 2 or 3 times, or even more in 1793–94, actually the Government paid but 33⅓ per cent additional in most instances. The Treasury expended 82 millions (stable value) in the purchase of two-thirds of the bread and a small proportion of the meat consumed in Paris in 1795. To clothe and feed an army of 1 to 1½ millions — 2 or 3 times the population of Paris — probably required an additional 200 millions.[1] Requisitions presumably enabled the Government to obtain its supplies at *market* prices in 1795, but these prices were notoriously below *competitive* ones. The difficulties encountered by the Government attest the low prices of requisitioned commodities. Did not maximum prices and requisitions enable the Government to carry on undiminished warfare during the period of regulation in spite of marked decreases in the stable value of public revenues?

Marion asserts that the maximum, a procedure to stop or conceal the depreciation, soon proved powerless and injurious. Hawtrey is of the opinion that the strong Government during the Terror profiting from maximum prices, a forced loan, and military success, was responsible for the enhancement in the value of the Assignat. Blanc was unequivocal: the maximum prices infused new life into the Assignat, and, thus strengthened, it became a lucrative resource, which enabled the Government to carry on its wars successfully. In a sense all these writers are inaccurate. An increase or decrease of the value of the Assignat becomes almost meaningless under such conditions. The Assignat was not a uniform monetary unit. For the Government ten livres in 1793 would purchase the provisions which seven and one-half had purchased in 1790; but the system of rationing forced the public to hoard a large proportion of their money, and thus their Assignats lost a much larger part of their value. An Assignat at the disposal

---

[1] The Government at one time admitted that the army was consuming the equivalent of the pre-war consumption of meat. *C. P. S.*, Vol. XVII, pp. 176–180.

of the Government was not of equivalent value to one at the disposal of the public. The value of the Treasury's Assignat was increased at the expense of the public's; the Government had a prior lien on all necessities and services. Without the privilege of a prior lien on commodities and of an artificial reduction of the prices of commodities and wages, the Government would have required many more Assignats to make a particular payment; and the public would have competed more strenuously for the available supplies. The necessity for more Assignats would have resulted in a cumulative increase in the issues, and they would have depreciated in 1793–94 as rapidly as they did in 1795. The average private consumer did not gain from the restricted issues made possible by control, because the Government had a prior lien on supplies. Actually, the system of regulation made it possible for the Government to command sufficient purchasing power without the necessity of resorting to the immoderate issues required in 1795. Blanc and Hawtrey are probably correct in so far as they attribute victory to maximum prices; but they are hardly justified in discussing without some caution the general appreciation of the Assignat during this period. As the Government requisitioned increasing supplies and services, the Assignats privately held represented a smaller proportion of the total stock of commodities. The Assignat belonging to the Government appreciated; the average Assignat at the disposal of the public depreciated.

With requisitions, and maximum prices below market prices, supplies of commodities were increasingly withheld from the market. A scarcity of commodities was apparent even before the maximum period. The additional hoarding of supplies under the maximum system and the losses resulting from the Government's prior lien on supplies were costly for private holders of Assignats. The resulting fall in the value of the aggregate of Assignats is to be set against the increase in value of disbursed Assignats caused by the reduction in prices made possible by control.

My historical survey of the subsistence question points to the following periods as those of scarcity and trouble:

		Value of Assignat (Local Tables) Per Cent
1792	January-March (War in April)	88. in December, 1791
	September-November (Decision of	75. in March, 1792
	December 8 to continue non-regu-	72. in August to
	lation of the grain trade)	75. in December
1793	January-April (Outbreak of war with England;	75. in Dec., 1792 to
	first maximum in May)	58. in April, 1793
	May-August (Detrimental effects of an inefficient	58. in April to
	system of control)	39. in August
1794	July-December (Downfall of Terrorists and weak-	40. in June to
	ening of their economic system)	28. in December
1795	January (Repeal of maximum laws and scarcity)	28. in December, 1794
	-November	to .8 of 1 per cent in November, 1795

When subsistence was scarce, or when the public feared for its food supplies, the Assignat depreciated rapidly. The only exception seems to have been the last few months of 1792; but in that period the subsistence problem was not very troublesome. The disturbances were serious, however, and the discussions attracted much attention. Moreover, the increase in the value of the Assignat of 3 per cent is rather misleading. Compare the increase of 3 per cent with that of 14 per cent according to the Treasury figures for the price of gold and silver, and it will be evident that if the prices of gold and silver were excluded from consideration in the local tables, a depreciation would have been found for this period. It does not necessarily follow that in each case the state of the subsistence market was the initial cause of the changes in the value of the Assignat. Doubts about the possibilities of procuring subsistence in 1792 and 1793, for example, might have been a mere accompaniment of the proximate possibility of war early in 1792 and in 1793.

No single factor can explain the depreciation at any one time. Nevertheless, it is my opinion that the state of the subsistence market was a factor of prime importance in each of the periods mentioned. The depreciation of July to December, 1794 — the limited meaning of changes in the value of the Assignat during this period is stressed — was genuine because the system of control broke down sufficiently so that people could spend Assignats with a tolerable amount of freedom; and the depreciation was caused largely by their haste to buy subsistence. The same remarks pertain to the first four months of control: the control was ineffective, and the public was able to spend freely. Only because this freedom was effectively limited in the next year or so did the disbursed Assignat become so valuable.

The Assignats were worth nothing if they could not buy bread, the substantial and almost the exclusive necessity of life. The inelastic and dwindling supplies of bread concomitant with the inelastic demand evidenced in the increasing offers of Assignats, were fatal. In 1795 the scarcity of subsistence and the surplus of Assignats were especially apparent. I believe that the conditions of famine were one of the most important causes of the depreciation during the final eighteen months of depreciation. Moreover, the necessity of buying subsistence for from one and a half to two million people, was the most important single cause for the increased issues of paper money.

CHAPTER VII

CAUSES OF DEPRECIATION

(*Through the Terror*)

THE termination of the Terror is an appropriate and convenient place to divide the study of the causes of depreciation. Before Robespièrre fell, the Assignat maintained a relative stability compared to what was to follow; depreciation was not as decided nor as uninterrupted as in 1795. The termination of the Terror resulted, also, in a discontinuance or an ineffectiveness of the economic policies of the Terror, which was of vital significance for the Assignat.

1. THE OPINIONS OF PRESENT DAY WRITERS

The French, in general, assume depreciation without a conscious attempt to explain it. We may say that the more important French authors have a fatalistic theory of paper money depreciation. Depreciation was inevitable; an explanation is unnecessary. Levasseur, Stourm, and Gomel offer virtually no explanation.[1] Blanc attributed the high prices to the excessive issues of paper money, and (true Jacobin that he was!) to the actions of the monopolists.[2] But the depreciation of the Assignat was evidently another problem for Blanc; for he attributed the depreciation largely to counterfeiting and to the extensive offering of foreign credits for Assignats.[3] Colson wrote that the depreciation was inevitable because the Assignat had no value of its own; a sale of land was necessary to redeem it.[4] Jaurès avoids an explanation by telling us that the Assignat did not depreciate during the

---

[1] Subercaseaux attributes the depreciation to excessive issues and loss of confidence. *Le Papier-Monnaie*, pp. 155 156.
[2] L. Blanc, *L'Histoire de la Révolution Française*, Vol. II, pp. 587–588.
[3] *Ibid.*, pp. 583–584.
[4] A. Colson, "Tableaux des Billets de Confiance Émis dans les 83 Départements," *Revue Numismatique*, 1852, p. 263.

first four years.[1] Marion, a carping critic of the Assignats, contributes the following general theory of depreciation.

"In pretending to impose on rural populations this 'signe' which they never desired, and because of which they concealed their products, the Revolution burdened itself with a frightful task; and it is well to say that the Assignat did more harm than good. With the Assignat came a latent civil war, sometimes open, also, between the rural inhabitants refusing to accept, and the cities pretending to force them." Evidently Marion believes that the antagonism of the farmer did much to undermine confidence in the Assignat.[2]

Illig, a German, scorns the influence of land sales on the value of the Assignat. Since the new creations far outnumbered the burnings, the sales of land were of secondary importance. He finds it necessary, however, to abandon the quantity theory (at least in this simple form) for an explanation of the increase in value during the Reign of Terror. He attributes that increase to the fearless policies of the Government.[3] Because he emphatically believes that the Assignats moved in complete harmony with the foreign exchanges, he contends that any factor that influenced the exchanges affected the value of the Assignat.[4] In particular, Illig mentions counterfeiting and the purchase of necessities as factors that contributed to the depreciation of the exchanges.[5]

Hawtrey's attack is brilliant always, but vulnerable at times. The early depreciation, in his opinion, was caused largely by the disproportionate issues of large denominations. The precipitate depreciation of the spring of 1792 and of the first eight months of 1793 are described as speculative excesses, and the reactions from these declines, the appreciation of the fall of 1792 and of the last four months of 1793, are, therefore, easily explained. Hawtrey asserts that the economic conditions did not warrant the low values of the spring of 1792 and the summer of 1793. For both periods, also, he is of the opinion that the appreciation was par-

---

[1] J. Jaurès, *Histoire Socialiste*, Vol. II, p. 111.
[2] M. Marion, *Histoire Financière*, Vol. III, p. vii.
[3] H. Illig, *Das Geldwesen Frankreichs*, pp. 73–76.
[4] *Ibid.*, p. 71.
[5] *Ibid.*, pp. 71–72, 78.

tially a depreciation of gold. In the earlier period, he points to the depreciation that accompanied the business expansion in England; and in the later period, he points to the measures taken against the precious metals. Hawtrey finds an explanation for the depreciation after the maximum period in the rapid consumption of hoarded balances and in the frenzied competition of traders in re-stocking.[1] I have commented on Hawtrey's presentation in Chapters III, IV, and VI.

To Falkner, a Russian, belongs, in my opinion, the distinction of having contributed the most subtle, as well as the most ingenious explanation of depreciation. In so far as Falkner presents one explanation, it may be called a juristic-quantity theory of depreciation. He explains the relatively high value of the Assignat until July, 1790 by the fact that the Assignat was primarily a capital investment, rather than a circulating medium. The discontinuance of interest payments resulted in a further fall of 5 per cent from August to December, 1791. Falkner explains the retention of a relatively high value until May, 1791 by the displacement of the metallic money and the assumption of the monetary function by the Assignat.[2]

The fall to a low value of 57 per cent within the next year, however, requires a different explanation. Since the increased circulation of money does not offer an adequate explanation, he shifts his attention to the political and economic conditions of the period. Note, nevertheless, the important modifications: "Only thanks to the comparison with gold and silver and to the cost of gold and silver, are 'Kreditpolitische' variations in the value of paper money without a corresponding change of their supplies possible; for the whole value of the circulating media is a stable amount which equals the value of the supply of goods to be exchanged. But when the metals circulate alongside of the paper money, a relative depreciation of one kind of money is possible."[3] In other words, Falkner implies that an increase in the value of the Assignat without a corresponding decrease in the supply of paper money was

[1] R. G. Hawtrey, *Currency and Credit*, 1st ed., pp. 248–249.
[2] S. U. Falkner, *Das Papiergeld der französischen Revolution 1789-1797*, pp. 34-40.
[3] *Ibid.*, pp. 39-41.

possible only because the metals were deprived of some of their monetary employments. The factor of confidence is evidently of no importance. If gold and silver had not circulated alongside of the Assignats, no political or economic event, in Falkner's opinion, could have brought about a reduction in the value of the paper money without a proportionate increase of the supplies of money.

In explaining the appreciation of the latter part of 1793, Falkner repeats his emphasis of the increased monetary functions of the Assignats, now substituted for gold and silver banned by a strong government. The increase in depreciation that began in the middle of 1794 and extended through the beginning of 1795, should not be attributed to the political and economic conditions, for they had improved. Since the metals had entirely disappeared, an explanation in terms of quantities issued was now acceptable, says Falkner: "The increase of the aggregate supply found its compensation in a corresponding decrease in the value of each piece."[1] In May and June, 1794, the Assignats in circulation were three times as great as the normal monetary circulation, and each Assignat had a value of one-third of the gold livre. The return of the metals in 1795, he continues, caused a more rapid depreciation of the Assignats than a consideration of the quantities issued, alone, would lead one to expect. Moreover, the value of the Assignat, in competition with the metals, depended exclusively now on its capacity to acquire goods, and to express the value of the goods.[2] (One may wonder from what source the Assignat acquired its value previously if not from its capacity to acquire goods, present or future.)

2. An Explanation of Depreciation

A. First period — 1790-91 [3]
At the end of the period:

> Notes emitted, 1860 millions.
> Notes in circulation, 1490 millions.
> Value at end of period (local tables), 86 per cent.
> Value at end of period (Treasury figures), 77 per cent.

---

[1] S. U. Falkner, *op. cit.*, 49.
[2] *Ibid.*, pp. 52–53.
[3] See Chapter I for some additional consideration of this period.

Before the Revolution, the amount of money in circulation has been estimated at approximately 2000 million livres. That a reduction of the circulation by one-fourth was accompanied by an apparent depreciation, requires an explanation.[1] Gold and silver had not completely disappeared; for purposes of hoarding and of making foreign remittances, the metals were in strong demand. The preponderance of large denominations of Assignats made the metals indispensable for some payments. The Government, itself, both often insisted on metallic payments and often disbursed gold and silver.[2] Also, from the beginning an element of the population distrusted the Assignats and hastened to disburse them.[3] The resulting dissipation of balances, the continued competition of gold and silver, the unavailability of the Assignat for small payments, as well as its unfitness for hoarding, resulted in a smaller quantity of money functioning as effectively as a much larger quantity had functioned previously. An American contemporary whose memories of the American Revolutionary Currency were still fresh, admonished the French that the precious metals might disappear before an equivalent issue of paper money appeared because paper money circulated more rapidly.[4]

Did the Assignat depreciate in 1790–91?[5] Certainly, no testimony is available of an increase in the price level.[6] The lack of confidence, and the competition of gold and silver may explain not why the Assignat depreciated, but why the aggregate of Assignats, equivalent to but 75 per cent of the money circulating before the Revolution, did not appreciate. The local values based on the prices of commodities, lands, and gold and silver, reflect a loss of but 14 per cent at the end of this period as compared to a loss

---

[1] Cannan suggests that paper money is conveniently held and hence that the introduction of an inconvertible paper money results in more money (paper plus gold and silver) being carried around. E. Cannan, *Money*, 4th ed., rev., p. 46.

[2] P. V., Vol. LXIX, 761.

[3] See *Opinion sur les Assignats* (Lille), pp. 5–7, for the attitude of the provinces; also P. V., Vol. XXI. (M. La Galissonnière, p. 12.) On September 24, 1790, the vast majority of 33 cities declared themselves opposed to paper money.

[4] P. V., Vol. XXIX, "Au Peuple Français sur les Assignats," p. 16.

[5] I consider this question in Chapter IV, also.

[6] The increased price of meat in Paris early in 1791 was caused by the peculiar conditions of the meat market. Actes de la Commune, 2d series, Vol. I, pp. 412, 484; Vol. II, pp. 129–133.

of 23 per cent for the Treasury values of gold and silver. The year 1791 was one of high land values. (The price of land increased at least as much as the price of gold and silver.) But it is doubtful whether quotations for land received much consideration in the construction of the tables for this early period; hence I am of the opinion that the higher values of the local tables are explicable by the failure of the prices of commodities to rise. The value of the Assignat in gold and silver fell to 77 per cent (as given by the Treasury table); and if the value of Assignats in commodities had remained at 100 per cent, its value should have been 88½ per cent according to the local tables. This result rests on the assumption of equal weights to (1) gold and silver prices and to (2) commodity prices in the construction of the local tables. The local tables actually gave a value of 86 per cent. This apparent depreciation was, therefore, little more than an appreciation of gold and silver.[1] Gold and silver were scarce because they were widely hoarded, because the exchanges had depreciated sufficiently to make the exportation of metals extremely lucrative,[2] and because the Government required gold and silver for certain indispensable payments.[3]

Fear had contributed to a gradual disappearance of the metals, and, therefore, to a correspondingly intense need for some additional money even before the Assignat had appeared.[4] The Government created the Assignat for other purposes, but incidentally it in large part replaced the metals. The Government, primarily because of its destitute state, and only secondarily because of its desire to keep the paper money out of the hands of the poor, manufactured large denominations preponderantly. The metals remained the exclusive medium for small payments.[5] Those who

---

[1] Dupont attributed the premium on gold and silver to their scarcity and utility for wage payments. *Moniteur*, Vol. V, p. 303; Lavoisier attributed the depreciation partially to an appreciation of gold and silver. G. Lavoisier, *L'État des Finances*, pp. 64–65.

[2] Bergasse demonstrated in 1790 that a saving of 8 per cent was made by shipping gold instead of purchasing exchange. *Protestation de M. Bergasse contre les Assignats-Monnaie*, 2d ed., pp. 25–26.

[3] The army expended 4 millions in the purchase of precious metals in 1791. P. V., Vol. LXIX, 761, Tables.

[4] *P. V. Ag. et Com.*, Vol. III, pp. 316, 522.

[5] The municipality of Toulouse regulated (of necessity) the price of bread both in numéraire and in paper. *Le Comité des Subsistances de Toulouse*, p. iv.

maintain, with Jaurès, Levasseur, and Hawtrey, however, that the inconvenient size of the denominations were in the main responsible for the early depreciation are largely in error, because the depreciation was one in terms of the prices of gold and silver and of the exchanges, rather than in the prices of commodities. Also, as I have indicated in Chapter III, the lack of confidence evident in the depreciation of the exchanges can be explained by the sporadic attacks on the land security.

This absence of depreciation in a country which still remembered the disturbances caused by Law, is worthy of comment. During this period the Government attempted to overcome the deficiency of small denominations. A decree of October, 1790 and of May, 1791 authorized the creation of Assignats of fifty and of five livres. The substitution of Assignats of smaller denominations for gold and silver did not bring about price increases. Probably the most satisfactory explanation of the stability of this period is to be found in the general belief that the Assignat with its land security was anything but a replica of Law's dreaded paper. Falkner's assertion that the Assignats did not depreciate at the beginning of this period because they constituted a capital investment, contains a semblance of truth. But the rentes were depreciated approximately one-half at the beginning of this period; attempts to borrow failed miserably. It is possible that the land security, the interest on the early issues, and the possibility of using Assignats later to pay debts, accounted for appreciable purchases of Assignats for investment purposes. The faith in the security and the need of a substitute for the metals were, however, probably the two most important factors contributing to the stability of 1790-91.

The demand for money was probably greater in 1790-91 than in the years preceding the Revolution. The subsistence markets were normal again. Agriculture prospered as a result of the freedom from taxation, the liberty of cultivation, and the recently acquired immunity from many feudal exactions. Jaurès, as against Young, Levasseur, White, and Poinsard, contends that industry at least held its own.[1] The liquidation of the privileged "Jurandes

[1] A. Young, op. cit., Vol. I, pp. 609-610. E. Levasseur, op. cit., Vol. I, p. 59.

and Maîtrises," the free access to any industry, the encouragement offered by the new patent system, the abolition of the feudal rights of transportation, weights, sales and the like, and the abolition of all internal custom duties, all contributed to the development of industry.[1] The depreciation of the exchanges offered a bounty on exports that stimulated manufacturing and offset the loss caused by the reduction of the purchasing power of the upper classes. Internal trade increased as a result of the unified customs system. The discontinuance of the collection of "péages et octrois" was also helpful.[2]

The relative stability of the Assignat during this period is the more remarkable in the light of the many attacks upon it. The numerous attacks of the pamphleteers emphasized in particular the weakness and fictitiousness of the security.[3] Doubts of writers of the prominence of Bergasse, Condorcet and Calonne as to the availability of the lands, made an impression.[4] In spite of these attacks, the general confidence in the security was not appreciably impaired. The rapid sales of land in 1791 are evidence of this.

The political outlook was dark; war with Austria and Prussia threatened throughout 1790 and 1791. To many, the success of the Revolution seemed not at all assured. The signs of internal insecurity and friction were apparent everywhere. The financial

A. D. White, *Fiat Money Inflation in France*, p. 33. L. Poinsard, "Le Crédit Public pendant la Révolution," *La Révolution Française*, Vol. XV, pp. 248–249. J. Jaurès, *op. cit.*, Vol. I, p. 78; Vol. II, pp. 254–255.

[1] *Recueil, Céréales*, pp. 211–217.

[2] *Recueil des Principaux Textes Concernant le Commerce, Commission de Recherche*, 1912, pp. 32–33, 40–43, 78–107.

[3] See Actes de la Commune de Paris, Vol. V, pp. 378, *et seq.*; Vol. VI, pp. 98–100, 138–143. "Addresse de la Ville de Lyons," p. 9. C. A. Calonne, *De l'État de France*, pp. 88–89, 94–96; Condorcet, *Nouvelles Réflexions sur le Projet de Payer la Dette Exigible en Papier Forcé*, pp. 5–6; De Montlosier, *Observations sur les Assignats*, p. 8; "Debates of March, 1790" in P. V., Vol. XIV; *Examen Impartial du Projet d'un Nouvelle Émission d'Assignats par un Négociant de Bordeaux*, p. 14; *La Fameuse Semaine*, pp. 15–18; *Les Provinces à l'Assemblée Nationale*, pp. 9–23; *Mémoire sur la Vente des Biens Ecclésiastiques*, p. 12; *Opinion de l'Évêque de Nancy*, pp. 2–8; *Opinion de M. l'Évêque d'Autun*, P. V., Vol. XXXI, p. 7; *Opinion de la Chambre de Commerce de Lyon*, p. 11; *Projet d'un Décret d'Éprémesnel*, September 20, 1790; *Réplique de M. Bergasse à M. de Montesquiou*, pp. 18, 43, 81–83.

[4] See the Actes de la Commune, Vol. V, pp. 371–374, 494–505, for an insight into the excitement caused by Bergasse's publication. (This includes a masterly attack on the Protestation de M. Bergasse contre les Assignats-monnaie.)

situation was bad; the Government had destroyed the antiquated taxes without as yet providing adequate substitutes.[1] The Assignat, to the extent of two years of ordinary revenues, had been employed for the reduction of the public debt. Complaints of counterfeiting — a substantial danger because of the crude mechanical execution — were frequent.[2] That the Assignat remained at par during this period is a tribute to the "land idea," as well as a reflection of the intense need for a circulating medium; perhaps, also, the sluggish movement of prices and the heavy sales of lands are relevant considerations. The increased demand for money — for the improved conditions of trade and agriculture were of more importance than the questionable decrease in manufacturing, then of minor importance — deserves notice. The public was not only willing to accept the Assignat as a medium of exchange, but to some extent, was willing to hoard it.

B. Second period — January–May, 1792
At end of period:

    Notes emitted, 2200 millions.
    Notes in circulation, 1660 millions.
    Value at end of period (local tables), 72 per cent.
    Value at end of period (Treasury figures), 58 per cent.

In the early months of 1792, there developed a depreciation in terms of commodity prices. Political conditions, no doubt, affected the price level. After January it became apparent that the outbreak of war was imminent. Hence the public disbursed their Assignats quickly and hoarded commodities. The same fear induced the farmers and traders to hoard their supplies. The results, it will be recalled, were food riots everywhere, impeded circulation of products, and higher prices. The fear of starvation made the people anxious to exchange their Assignats for food at a material loss.

People were beginning to lose confidence in the paper money. The Minister of War complained in January of the refusal of the

---

[1] M. Lecouteul attributed the depreciation to the uncertainty of the new tax system. *Moniteur*, Vol. VIII, p. 325.

[2] "Rapport au Nom des Comités des Finances, des Rapports et des Assignats, réunis," P. V., Vol. LXV, pp. 4–6; also Arch. Parl., Vol. XXXIV, p. 580.

meat contractors to accept the Assignats.[1] Clavière commented on the increasing number of houses built, of dwellings furnished lavishly, and of new local enterprises—all symptoms of the distrust of the Assignat, for the people were anxious to invest their Assignats in something stable.[2] The Minister of Interior received complaints from a local official of the refusal of workers to accept them.[3] The Committee of Agriculture and Commerce was informed in April that farmers were selling grain at prices reduced by one-half, upon the condition that payments be made in gold and silver. The Government recognized the depreciation officially in June by conceding increases in pay to its military personnel.[4] Marshal Luckner held the absurd opinion that an increase in pay would be a deterrent to desertions and would halt the depreciation, because the men would be more likely to hoard their Assignats.[5] Narbonne, the Minister of War, promised contractors an indemnity for possible losses caused by the future depreciation of the Assignat.[6] A large coal corporation demanded one-half of the sales price of coal in numéraire, in order to be able to pay one-half of its wage bill in numéraire.[7]

The economic conditions, in most respects, improved during this period. The Government was provisioning the army without much difficulty. M. Lacuée reported that the army had a half year's supply of grains on hand on May 27.[8] Foreign trade increased in spite of the prohibition of many exports.[9] Arthur Young found improved conditions of manufacturing, stimulated, in his opinion, by the lower real wages.[10] The Minister of Interior, however, believed that because the public expended an increased proportion of its income on bread, the activities of manufacturing

---

[1] Arch. Parl., Vol. XXXVII, pp. 625-626.
[2] E. Clavière, De la Conjuration contre les Finances, p. 20.
[3] Correspondance du Ministre de l'Intérieur, p. 283.
[4] Arch. Parl., Vol. XLV, p. 502.
[5] Ibid., Vol. XXXIX, pp. 55-56.
[6] Rapport Présentée sur le Compte Rendu par M. Narbonne, p. 14.
[7] C. Schmidt, Un Projet de Nationalisation des Mines d'Anzin en 1792, Commission de Recherche, 1910, pp. 234-235.
[8] Arch. Parl., Vol. XLIV, pp. 163-164.
[9] Ibid., Vol. LVI, pp. 650-651; also Jaurès, op. cit., Vol. II, pp. 257-258; E. Levasseur, Histoire du Commerce de la France, Vol. II, p. 13.
[10] A. Young, op. cit., Vol. I, pp. 622-623.

plants suffered.[1] A distinguished member of the Legislative Assembly commented on the lack of a circulating medium; the fifteen hundred millions of paper money had a gold value of but seven hundred and fifty million livres.[2] Economic conditions had improved, and, therefore, the demand for money had increased. But the stable value of the money in circulation had fallen.

With the increase in prices the legislators and the pamphleteers took notice of the depreciation for the first time. They were aware of the effects of an increased demand for money on its value. Lebrun proposed to educate the people to invest their Assignats in something other than commodities.[3] M. Philibert recommended an exchange of Assignats for annuities.[4] Cailhasson counselled a sale of "créances nationales".[5] Clavière believed that a sale of paper supported by the lands sold but not yet paid for in full and the creation of a savings bank, would contribute additional employment for the Assignat.[6] To introduce additional channels of circulation for the Assignat, Condorcet pointed out the necessity of exchange bureaus, savings banks, and the sale of a type of second mortgage note secured by payments due for lands sold.[7] Lebrun later proposed a new loan, a lottery secured by the public lands, and sales of the public interest in lands sold but not paid for.[8] Boislandry, however, submitted a bold proposal to demonetise the Assignat. In lieu of an increase in demand, he suggested a reduction of the supplies of money.[9]

The attention devoted to the problem of depreciation by many leaders of French thought reflects the impression made by the depreciation. The constructive criticisms offered, no doubt, attracted attention to the depreciation. Explanations appeared frequently. Cailhasson was of the opinion that the Assignat circulated more rapidly than gold and silver, and that as the Assignat depreciated,

[1] Arch. Parl., Vol. LVI, p. 652.
[2] Ibid., Vol. XLIII, p. 341.
[3] Lebrun, Mémoire Présentée à l'Assemblée Nationale, pp. 4–5.
[4] Arch. Parl., Vol. XXXIX, pp. 136–143.
[5] Ibid., Vol. L, p. 577.
[6] E. Clavière, Conjuration, pp. 67, 72–78.
[7] Arch. Parl., Vol. L, p. 569.
[8] Ibid., pp. 560–566.
[9] L. Boislandry, Considérations sur le Discrédit des Assignats, pp. 16–17.

the velocity of circulation increased even more.[1] Counterfeiting was a recurrent cry.[2] Mosmiron emphasised the excessive issues of paper money — especially of Billets de Confiance — and the decrease in commerce.[3] Boislandry made a brilliant summary of the causes of the depreciation. He stressed in particular the increased circulation as compared to the needs of commerce. Paper circulates twice as quickly as gold and silver, and when depreciation begins, the velocity of circulation increases even more, he said.[4] Members of the Legislative Assembly decried the competition of public securities with the Assignats in the purchase of lands.[5] Some attributed the depreciation to the excessive use of Assignats by the Government for the payment of debt.[6] The failure to collect taxes, an important factor in the depreciation, received some attention.[7]

Laffon-Ladebat offered an explanation for the apparent higher depreciation in terms of gold and silver. The premium on the metals for export purposes should have made them redundant abroad; but moved by fear people everywhere hoard gold and silver, he said. Their price is increased 3 or 4 per cent by the purchase of a million livres. The silver écu is sold at a premium of 70 per cent, and bullion is sold at a premium of 90 per cent.[8] (The continued greater depreciation according to the Treasury figures, compared to the depreciation as measured by the local tables, attest the scarcity of gold and silver.)

The rapid sales of land continued, although the pace of 1791 was not maintained. The withdrawal of Assignats from circulation through land sales had become an important deterrent to depreciation; and the first suggestion of the confiscation of the possessions of the Émigrés injected new confidence into the Assignat. The depreciation, evident in the prices both of commodities and

---

[1] *Moniteur*, Vol. XII, p. 255.
[2] *Papiers de Barthélemy, Ambassadeur de France en Suisse, 1792–1797*, Vol. I, pp. 48, 95, 100, 105.
[3] Arch. Parl., Vol. XL, pp. 497–498.
[4] L. Boislandry, *Considérations*, pp. 7–9.
[5] Arch. Parl., Vol. XLIII, p. 405, Vol. XLV, p. 128.
[6] *Ibid.*, Vol. L, p. 580.
[7] *Ibid.*, p. 577.
[8] *Ibid.*, Vol. XLIII, p. 339.

of gold and silver, was undeniable in the early months of 1792. The political clouds and the accompanying Economic Federalism which manifested itself in the hoarding of supplies by each locality as well as by individuals, were the important causes of the depreciation during this period. The frequent discussion of the depreciation attests the actuality of the problem. Confidence in the Assignat had declined.

C. *Third period — June–December, 1792*

At the end of the period:

Notes emitted, 2750 millions.
Notes in circulation, 2250 millions.
Value at end of period (local tables), 75 per cent.
Value at end of period (Treasury figures), 72 per cent.

This period has generally been considered as one in which the Assignat maintained its value and even attracted increased confidence. The Treasury figures indicate an increased prestige for the Assignat. If we consider the weight given to the price of the metals, however, the local tables reflect a loss of internal purchasing power. Prices of commodities continued to increase. The folly of placing exclusive reliance on the prices of gold and silver is apparent once more. A speculative fall in the price of gold and silver is the explanation of the apparent rise. The important victories of Valmy in September and Jemappes in November reacted on the speculative markets.

Political and economic conditions were fundamentally unsound throughout this period. The increasing power of the extremists, which was evident in the deposition of the king, aggravated the unsettled conditions. The excesses — the September massacres, for example — made the people wary of the future. The indiscreet law of November 19, volunteering French aid to any peoples seeking liberty, made war with England inevitable. Political disturbances reacted on the subsistence market. People hastened to dissipate their balances but found inadequately provisioned markets.

At least three items are to be set on the other side of the ledger. First, the state of the finances was improving: tax yields were more satisfactory, absolutely and relatively; and the Government discontinued the disbursement of Assignats for debt payments. Second, the appropriation of the vast lands of the Émigrés strengthened the security and resulted in an increased confidence in the paper money. Third, the demand for money was increased by the prevalence of speculation.[1] The unprecedented development of speculation led to the imposition of a tax on all transfers of securities.[2]

D. Fourth period — January–August, 1793

At end of period:

Notes emitted, 4950 million livres.
Notes in circulation, 4050 million livres.
Value at the end of the period (local tables), 39 per cent.
Value at the end of the period (Treasury figures), 22 per cent.

The faith in the French Republic fell to a new low point during this period. January brought the execution of the king, and February the bread riots and the opening of hostilities with England. The upheavals in Vendée began in March, only to be followed by Doumouriez's treasonable desertion the next month. May and June contributed the victory of the bloody Commune in the overthrow of the moderate Girondists, and on the other side of the ledger, a victory over the insurrectionists at Nantes. Three decisive military defeats were the lot of the Government in the month of July, which also saw the introduction of the Reign of Terror. And finally in August came the surrender of the largest fleet of France with the capitulation of Toulon, as well as the uprising in Lyons. Much confidence was not likely to be placed in the Revolutionary money under such adverse conditions.

It will be recalled that the subsistence market was in a deplorable condition. Prices were rising, and farmers were concealing their supplies. The law enacted in December emphasizing the necessity of free circulation, had been ineffective. The first maximum in May resulted from the intolerable conditions prevalent everywhere. Certainly the maximum, as a practical system, can

---

[1] Deslandres discusses the increase of speculation, *Du Crédit Public*, pp. 23–26. E. Clavière estimates that Parisians speculated in three hundred millions of securities yearly. *Lettres à Cerutti*, pp. 109–113

[2] See A. Mathiez, *Un Procès de Corruption sous la Terreur. L'Affaire de la Compagnie des Indes*, pp. 16–23.

be disregarded until the end of this period. (It probably accentuated the deficiencies.) The hoarding and the sluggish movement of subsistence from locality to locality were important causes of depreciation. As the farmers and dealers refused to sell, the people became more anxious to buy.

The insecurity during this period led to a reduction of the supplies and sales not only of grains but of all commodities, and hence the field of employment for money was reduced. Laws against the hoarding of commodities were driving many out of business. The impassable state of the roads — an incessant complaint, but more frequent since the beginning of actual warfare — made commerce difficult.[1] With war on every frontier, foreign merchandise could only enter through contraband channels. Foreign commerce suffered a marked decline in 1793.[2] The large supplies of commodities hoarded by the Government deprived private individuals of their use; and both because the Government purchased at low prices, and because it often eliminated the middlemen, these activities made possible economies of cash.[3] Only the increased speculation offset to any degree the curtailment of the demand for money in other channels.[4] Because the market for land became glutted, and because the public lost their enthusiasm in the midst of insecurity, the rate of sales of lands declined and hence the Assignats lost an important source of employment. People looked to the land sales to absorb the surplus of Assignats; and since land sales were declining, the discovery of new methods of consuming balances of Assignats was necessary. The fear of a counter-revolution made the public more anxious to invest their paper money in commodities instead of in land.[5]

Cambon carried through a program to check the private use of the precious metals; but it was not successful until the next period. The Government prohibited payments in gold and silver in fulfillment of private contracts and prohibited the sale of numé-

---

[1] *Rapports des Agents du Ministre de l'Intérieur*, pp. 272–274.
[2] M. J. Peuchet estimated the decline in foreign trade in 1793 at 50 per cent, *Statistique Elémentaire de la France*, p. 482.
[3] *Les Représentants du Peuple en Mission*, Vol. III, p. 485.
[4] A. Mathiez, *Un Procès de Corruption*, p. 32.
[5] Arch. Parl., Vol. LXVI, p. 73.

raire on April 8, 1793.[1] The Committee of Public Safety alleged that this action was absolutely necessary; the monthly requirements in numéraire for the army alone were thirty million livres.[2] In 1795 Cambon's version of the discontinuance of specie payments, however, was that the measures were taken because the Government, with but six hundred thousand livres of metals on hand, was making monthly commitments of fifteen millions in numéraire.[3] The significance of the regulation lies, as Hawtrey affirms, in the artificial depression of the prices of gold and silver and in the consequent appreciation of the Assignat. Or we may say that the Assignat was strengthened by the additional monetary employment thus thrust upon it. Hawtrey assumes from changes in the value of the measure employed that the value of the Assignat has changed. One may point to the change in the demand for the paper money and arrive at the same conclusion. For this period, however, the laws of discrimination against the precious metals were of little practical significance, because without the unstinted support of a powerful government, they were not enforceable.[4] (During the next period, the Reign of Terror, they were enforced.) As gold is driven out of circulation by official interference, Assignats are substituted, and, hence, the demand for them is increased. But during a period of price control when the Government virtually determines how many units of money are to be disbursed and at what rate, the demonetisation of gold and silver may have no net effect on the value of the paper money. The relatively greater depreciation given by the Treasury figures is probably explicable by the extreme depreciation of the exchanges; the Treasury employed the exchanges as a measure of depreciation during the latter part of this period.

This period was productive of many plans for improving the position of the Assignat. Most of the proposals were made on the assumption of an excessive supply and suggested methods of reducing it. The Provisional Executive Council instructed the commissioners in Belgium to put Assignats into circulation in Bel-

[1] Arch. Parl., Vol. LXI, pp. 592–595.
[2] C. P. S., Vol. III, pp. 241–243.
[3] J. Déb. et Déc., Vol. LXVII, p. 220.
[4] Arch. Parl., Vol. LXV, pp. 108–110.

gium.[1] Malthieu emphasized, in January, that security and good order were prerequisites for the rapid sales of land.[2] Many of the plans embodied proposals to accelerate the rate of sales of the lands. The failure to maintain the rapid pace of 1791–92 in the sales of land removed an obstacle to depreciation. In February Clavière proposed to reduce the creation of Assignats by paying the soldiers in overvalued copper coins. He also favored a new loan redeemable in numéraire.[3] Chabot, on the same day, recommended that the Treasury issue "créances" on designated lands and a general loan hypothecated on the public lands.[4] Ramel made a report for the Committee of Finance on April 23. The Committee proposed to hasten the sale of lands and to economise on Assignats by paying all public creditors in a debt paper to be acceptable in payment for lands, if accompanied by an equal offering of Assignats. The Committee expected that by the introduction of these methods, together with the collection of arrears in taxes and the sales of annuities, the circulation would be reduced by more than two milliard livres.[5] The Committee on Assignats and Money (Balland reporter) expressed an independent opinion. Its proposals included a sale of the Government's interest in lands sold but not paid for, a premium for anticipatory payments on land purchases, and the sale of a security to yield 5 per cent interest.[6]

Legislation progressed, also. A forced loan, the subject of a long discussion, was approved in the latter part of June.[7] The Government on July 1 decided to exploit the creditors of the army by paying them in the future in "Reconnaissances de Finance," a non-circulating paper.[8] Cambon modified a decree ordering the demonetisation of all Royal Assignats of fifty livres and above, to include only denominations of one hundred livres and above. This dishonest proposal by which the Government aimed to demonetise all the Assignats of large denominations created before August,

[1] C. P. S., Vol. I, p. 431.
[2] Moniteur, Vol. XV, pp. 103–104.
[3] Arch. Parl., Vol. LIX, p. 209.
[4] Moniteur, Vol. XV, p. 599.
[5] Arch. Parl., Vol. LXIII, pp. 153–155.
[6] Ibid., pp. 171–172.
[7] Moniteur, Vol. XVI, p. 723.
[8] Ibid., Vol. XVII, p. 22.

1792, received official sanction on July 31.[1] Cambon presented a remarkable report on the Grande Livre on August 15. It included many suggestions for the reduction of Assignats. He hoped, by creating the Grande Livre for recording and consolidating the public debt, to reduce the Assignats in circulation, effect a reimbursement of the debt, and accelerate the sale of public lands.[2] All these proposals and laws had a common end, the reduction of the money in circulation. One method of enhancing the value of paper money is to reduce the circulation; a reduction in quantity generally has direct effects on prices; and, also, confidence is increased.

The apparently hopeless political outlook with war on every frontier, with Dumouriez's treachery, with civil war in the West and a latent civil war in Paris, contributed to the phenomenal fall of the Assignat during the first eight months of 1793. The question of redemption (except through the sale of lands) was irrelevant for the Assignat. Adverse political events depressed the value of the Assignat because (1) adversity meant that increased issues would be necessary in the future; (2) the overthrow of the French Republic entailed the loss of the lands of the Church and of the Émigrés, and hence (in the minds of the people) the worthlessness of the Assignat, and, finally, because (3) a weakened political situation had an unfavorable effect on the subsistence markets.

The increased issues were no doubt a factor in the depreciation, but many other factors require emphasis. Depreciation would certainly not have proceeded so far had each inhabitant felt assured of his subsistence. The collection of taxes declined during this period, for the losses from increased depreciation more than offset the nominal increase of the public revenues. A perusal of the charts in Chapter II will convince the reader of the retrogression of taxation during this period: Both the stable values and the proportion of all revenues raised by taxation fell disastrously. The needs of increased warfare further exhausted the Treasury. The demand for money decreased because of the curtailment of commerce and industry and the decrease of land sales. In short, this

---

[1] *Moniteur*, Vol. XVII, pp. 278–280.
[2] *Ibid.*, pp. 408, 790.

was a period of disastrous depreciation caused by the adverse economic, political, and financial conditions. Nor did the partial demonetisation and other questionable practices of the Government contribute to the confidence in the paper money.

E. Fifth period — September, 1793–July, 1794
End of period:

Notes emitted, 8450 million livres.
Notes in circulation, 7200 million livres.
Value (local tables) in March, 46 per cent; in July, 41 per cent.
Value (Treasury figures) in December, 48 per cent; in July, 34 per cent.

The Terror was effective. Maximum prices and rationing were realities in spite of many violations. As has already been said, to refer to an increased value for the Assignat during this period is not strictly accurate. Writers express amazement at the renewed confidence in the Assignat. I doubt whether it increased in value as much as they believe. The local figures reflect a maximum increase (March) of but 7 per cent; the Treasury figures, however, reflect a maximum increase (December) of 26 per cent. The latter increase is explicable largely on the grounds of the depreciation of gold and silver and of the exchanges. The failure of the local figures to give a greater increase in value for the Assignat, is puzzling. The exclusion of consideration of controlled commodities is one explanation; the ineffectiveness (?) of the maximum is another possible explanation. Writers who employ the price of metals or the exchanges as a measure almost universally speak of the increased value of the Assignat during this period. But the Treasury figures merely reflect the fall of the exchanges to some extent a movement of the gold points — and perhaps the demonetisation of gold and silver. The local tables are not particularly helpful here either. Convinced that the maximum was tolerably effective, I believe that the local tables do not give the actual increase in value for the *disbursed* Assignat. The increase of 7 per cent is not an adequate allowance for the decrease in the value of gold and silver. If we ascribe to the prices of gold and silver and of land their probable weight, it appears that, according to the local tables, the prices of commodities increased. This apparent anomaly may be due to an exclusion of the prices of controlled commodities. My conclusion is that the value of the disbursed Assignat was increased by control.

However, the actual price level was of secondary importance. For all practical purposes, a large proportion of the Assignats had no outlet. The Government not only decided how many Assignats should be spent for all the necessary and semi-necessary commodities, but practically decided how much was to be expended on any particular commodity. The propriety of speaking of an increase or decrease in the value of the Assignat under these conditions is questionable.

Political conditions were sound. A strong central government with the Committee of Public Safety at its helm dominated the entire situation. The policy of terrorism was successful in all its ramifications. The military policy, devised and enforced by the genius of Carnot, bore its fruits on every frontier. The vigilant "représentants du peuple en mission" helped to maintain the vigor of the policies of the Central Government in every hamlet of France.

The circulation increased steadily, in spite of the fact that the needs of war were met to a greater extent than in the previous period by taxation and by the spoliations of the Government. The stable value of tax receipts increased noticeably, and even the proportion of all revenues raised by taxation showed an appreciable increase. (See charts in Chapter II.) The receipts from the sales of lands were large absolutely, but not relative to the increased issues. The Terrorist Government confiscated large areas of lands and other forms of wealth, which it added to the security behind the Assignats. But in the midst of the Terror sales fell appreciably.

The discriminatory regulations against the metals bore fruit during this period. But the net effect of these measures was of little practical significance. The value of the Assignat was scarcely affected by the demonetisation of gold and silver. Less Assignats were available for hoarding, because more served as money; but the Government practically determined both the number of Assignats to be expended, and the value of every Assignat disbursed, except, perhaps, those expended for a few luxuries. The only significant reduction in the circulation resulted from the demonetisation of the Royal Assignats; the other measures taken during the previous period had little effect on the circulation. A forced circulation in Belgium and Holland absorbed a relatively unimportant quantity of Assignats.[1] Certainly, the absence of a policy of control would have resulted in an appreciable increase in the prices of necessities; for land sales, the demonetisation of gold and silver (a measure of economy for the Government) and the increased tax receipts did not prevent an increase in the circulation which was caused by increased public expenditures.

Complaints of the violation of the laws relating to gold and silver were infrequent after September.[2] The death penalty was voted for quoting two prices (paper and metallic), for discrediting the Assignats, for refusing to accept the Assignat, and for accepting it at a discount.[3] The Government ordered a complete demonetisation of gold and silver in December.[4] The public was admonished that all metals discovered concealed in the earth, caves, interior of walls, floorings, or pavements would be confiscated.[5] Cambon in 1794 demanded an inventory of each individual's wealth.[6] The laws were apparently enforced. Two public contractors, Levy and Elie, suffered a penalty of six years of detention for demanding payments in numéraire.[7] The Revolutionary Tribunal of Paris was responsible for several convictions: Twelve men were guillotined for hoarding gold and silver; the court pretended to see an intention of remittance to the enemy. (No proof was adduced, however.[8]) The court sentenced a few other dealers to death even though the purchase of gold had been in behalf of the Government.[9]

Because the supply of commodities was reduced, the demand for

---

[1] *C. P. S.*, Vol. XV, p. 536.
[2] Caron finds but one complaint. *Paris pendant la Terreur*, Vol. II, p. 361.
[3] Arch. Parl., Vol. LXXIII, pp. 406–407.
[4] *Moniteur*, Vol. XVIII, pp. 565–567.
[5] *Ibid.*, p. 416.
[6] *J. Déb. et Déc.*, Vol. LV, p. 202.
[7] Arch. Parl., Vol. LXXX, p. 160.
[8] P. H. Wallon, *Histoire du Tribunal Révolutionnaire*, Vol. IV, pp. 331, 343.
[9] *Ibid.*, pp. 461–462; also see Vol. II, pp. 513–514, 527; Vol. III, pp. 454, 464–465, 474; Vol. IV, p. 210; Vol. V, p. 282.

money fell. The maximum resulted in the storing of a large proportion of the available supply of commodities. A decree against the hoarding of commodities that included a death penalty for violations, had a calamitous effect on trade. Since the operation of the Grand Livre made dealings in Government securities impossible except by book transfers, the demand for money was further reduced. The closing of the bourses and the almost entire disappearance of speculation had similar effects. Because of extended war operations within and without, production fell.[1] Some commodities disappeared from the ordinary channels of trade, notably, copper, soap, fats, oil, beer, whiskey, and even meat.[2] The system of maximum prices made the continuance of the exportation of commodities impossible. France could not afford to sell to foreigners at maximum prices.[3] The result was a signal decrease in foreign trade which left the country unable to pay for its imports. The incessant warfare damaged the roads and thus hampered internal commerce. The net effect of the decreased employment for the Assignats was to make more available for hoarding and for the limited supplies of luxuries. Had the possession and evidence of much wealth not been incongruous with personal safety, more of the surplus Assignats would have been invested in public lands.

The relatively few Assignats expended on controlled commodities — relatively few certainly when the money in circulation was three or four times that of 1789, and the supplies at the disposal of the public were considerably less — retained a high value. The Government, in particular, profited from this system. In view of the restricted fields of employments, as contrasted with the vast increase of the supplies of currency, who can truthfully say that the value of the average Assignat increased during this period?

One more incident is of some interest for this period. Barère,

---

[1] In March, 1794, Cambon announced an increase of 700,000 men in arms in the previous year. A total of 1½ millions were under arms. *J. Déb. et Déc.*, Vol. LVIII, p. 22. The Minister of War received an appropriation of 20 millions in March to pay for losses suffered from the invasions. *Ibid.*, Vol. LVII, p. 194.

[2] Montgaillard, *L'État de France en 1794*, pp. 39–43.

[3] The maximum law of September 29, 1793 contained a provision prohibiting the exportation of the 29 controlled commodities during the continuance of war. *Recueil des Principaux Textes concernant le Commerce*, p. 162.

whose influence on the economic policy of the Terror was probably unsurpassed, made the following interesting statement in his memoirs: "History knowing and revealing all will tell us how the last Committee of Public Safety signalled its existence by squandering one hundred millions of metals that the Committee of Finances had amassed by the cares of Cambon and Ramel and had placed in the caves and rooms of the Treasury, to replace the Assignats when their retirement was begun."[1] If Barère is to be trusted, the Terrorist Government was making provisions for a return to a metallic standard. The accumulation of gold and silver under the favorable conditions of demonetisation was not difficult. The repudiation of the policy of isolation made the expenditure of this accumulated treasure necessary.

[1] *Mémoires de B. Barère*, Vol. I, p. 92.

CHAPTER VIII

CAUSES OF DEPRECIATION
(After the Terror)

1. An Explanation of Depreciation

F. *Sixth period* — *August, 1794–December, 1795*

	1794		1795			
	Aug.	Nov.	Feb.	May	Aug.	Nov.
Notes in circulation:						
Milliards of livres	7.6	8.0	8.8	11.4	16.4	19.7
Values: Local tables	39	32	22½	11	3½	.8
Treasury tables	31	24	17	7½	3	.8

THIS is the period of spectacular depreciation. It aroused the legislatures to a rather sustained interest in the financial situation. The fall of the Assignat was virtually uninterrupted from August, 1794 to March, 1796, when the Mandat was substituted. This chapter covers only the period to December, 1795 because the three following months formed a period of transition in which the Assignat was of secondary importance. With the downfall of Robespièrre on July 28, 1794, the enforcement of the economic policies of the Terror weakened. As a practical system, we can disregard the maximum system after July. The repeal did not occur until the latter part of December however. Issues followed one another rapidly; and as depreciation proceeded unabated, more issues were necessary to consummate the pretentious program of the Government. In 1795 the depreciation advanced more rapidly than in proportion to the increase in circulation. The rapid fall in the value of the Assignat made the financial position of the Government a trying one. As the Treasury attempted to recoup itself for losses caused by depreciation by creating more money, depreciation proceeded even more rapidly.

The Assignat had to compete with gold and silver once more early in 1795. The metals trickled in from hoards and from abroad. The premium on the metals exceeded that on the exchanges; hence their importation became profitable. The loss of the exclusive monetary privilege contributed to the depreciation of the Assignat. The decreasing stable value of the paper money made the reintroduction of gold and silver imperative, but their presence made a recovery unlikely.

The revocation of the maximum laws brought disaster in 1795. Farmers, craving freedom and anticipating higher prices, took advantage of the more lenient attitude of the Government and refused to sell on the market. The Government requisitioned large supplies of commodities for the use of the army. The markets were scantily provisioned. As the people hastened to disburse their Assignats for the limited supplies of commodities, the Assignats depreciated; and as they became aware of the plenitude of paper and the scarcity of commodities, the depreciation was accelerated.

One possible cause of depreciation, the "au cours" payments, which will receive some attention in Chapter IX, is merely mentioned here.[1] For the details, the reader is referred to that chapter. The Government had made some irresolute attempts to collect revenues in kind in 1793–94. The reduced value of the Assignat, together with the rigidity of the French tax system, resulted in serious reductions in the stable value of public receipts. By 1795 plans for the collection of public revenues "au cours" were common. The problem had its ramifications in many private transactions also, and "au cours" payments became the specific for many of the injustices caused by the rapid depreciation. Because "au cours" payments required more Assignats, it may be supposed that their introduction would result in an increase in their value. Perhaps; but the discussion of "au cours" payments, especially as regards public transactions, was disconcerting to the public. They involved a partial demonetisation. Even an official recognition of a depreciation that every one was aware of, made the public doubt the Assignats more. Perhaps the success of a plan whereby the Government received its tax and land payments in Assignats "au cours", might have rehabilitated the state

---

[1] When payments are adjusted according to the changing value of the paper money, "au cours" payments are employed.

of the finances and hence have bolstered up the value of the Assignat. But success never came of any of these plans before the Assignat was beyond saving.

Supplies were scarce during this whole period. The Convention requested all its committees and members to aid in the rejuvenation of agriculture, industry, science and commerce.[1] Cambon also diagnosed the situation in September, 1794: A reduction of consumption was necessary. Agriculture and commerce required protection (security) to attain a flourishing state.[2]

Eschassériaux, for the Committee of Public Safety early in October, said in part: "We must create a vast plan of commerce, interior and exterior; we have to render agriculture flourishing and generate in France a rapid and concerted movement which would announce to the universe that even in the midst of the most astonishing revolution, we can undertake the most extended and advantageous relations."[3] The Convention approved of these resolutions, and agreed with the Committee, "that every citizen who imports raw materials deserves well of his country".[4]

Johannot, also, in a remarkable report presented in behalf of four committees, dwelt on the inadequate supplies as a major cause of the low value of the Assignat. He said that production was still inadequate, that transportation was disorganized; and that sea insurance rates were prohibitory. Foreign trade and speculation had suffered annihilation as a result of a misconceived public policy. He concluded with recommendations to allow the free exportation of numéraire and to guarantee imports against public requisitions. Cambon came to a somewhat similar conclusion when he stated that the high prices were due in part to the deficiencies caused by the occupation of one-fifth of the workers with military pursuits. In his opinion, the increase in prices had been well-nigh universal — in Germany, Spain and Piedmont, as well as in France.[5] Although Cambon was willing to concede on another occasion that the depreciation had been caused in some

[1] *Recueil des Principaux Textes concernant l'Industrie*, p. 292.
[2] *J. Déb. et Déc.*, Vol. LXIV, pp. 137–139.
[3] *Ibid.*, p. 397.
[4] *J. Déb. et Déc.*, Vol. LXVII, pp. 62–82.
[5] *Moniteur*, Vol. XXIII, pp. 394–395.

small measure by rumors of demonetisation, he maintained that the major cause was the scarcity of livestock and agricultural products.[1]

The Government persisted in its efforts to re-establish foreign commerce. In December, 1794, it conceded the right of using foreign balances for the purchases of commodities abroad.[2] The suppression of the Secret Committee of Six early in 1795, which body had been created to inspect all correspondence with foreigners, was equivalent to raising the sequestration of the property of foreigners.

The survey of prices for March–April, 1795, undertaken by the Committee of Public Safety, included some speculations on the part of the district agents as to the causes of the high prices. Many of them attributed the increased prices to the decrease in supplies. The high prices in the District of Ormont were caused in part by the scarcity of agricultural implements — the forges were producing war supplies — and, in part, by the demoralization of the transportation facilities.[3] The agents found that the exhaustion of food supplies, the destruction of factories and of manufactured goods, the interference with transportation facilities, and the concealment of subsistence, all contributed to the depreciation of the Assignat in the Department of Loire-Inférieure.[4] The agents in the District of Rouen believed that the depreciation resulted from excessive issues, but that scarce objects suffered a disproportionate increase.[5] The high prices in the Department of Vosges were attributed to the requisitions which forced the farmers to demand high prices in private sales as compensation for the low prices received for the requisitioned supplies. The report also referred to the lack of subsistence, the surplus of Assignats, and the difficulty of procuring raw materials.[6]

Early in 1795 the officials with the Army of the Pyrenees com-

---

[1] *J. Déb. et Déc.*, Vol. LXVIII, pp. 230–233.
[2] *C. P. S.*, Vol. XIX, pp. 614–615.
[3] P. Caron, *Une Enquête sur les Prix après la Suppression du Maximum, Commission de Recherche*, 1910, p. 401.
[4] *Ibid.*, p. 338.
[5] *Ibid.*, p. 387.
[6] *Ibid.*, p. 401.

plained bitterly of its destitute condition. The impassability of the roads and the sea blockade made the material position of the soldiers a trying one.[1]

In April Pelet made a report for the Committee of General Security, in which he, also, emphasized the unusual dearth of commodities. Commerce and manufacturing are languishing; the hoarding of commodities is the rule; an equilibrium between needs and products, and between "signes" and products is indispensable. He also emphasized the disproportionate circulation of paper money. Pelet continued: "A month, a day, an hour passes and prices increase in such a frightful manner that the greediness, the real dearth, the lack of public confidence, and the worry about the present and future are all evident."[2]

The wars and the Revolution had a calamitous effect on production. The cumulative results of this long period of turmoil were now apparent. The sale of live stock was a serious evil, difficult to eradicate.[3] An investigation of the Committee of Public Safety revealed that the number of pieces of woolen cloth manufactured in France had decreased from 2.6 millions in 1793 to 800,000 in 1795; and that the number of workers attached to this industry had fallen from 594,000 to 320,000.[4] A study in 1796 comparing conditions before the Revolution with those in 1796-97, was even more gloomy.[5] The value of the production of cloth in the Department of Corrèze had fallen from 80,000 livres to 10,000 livres.[6] No tapestry establishments were in operation in the Department of Creuse in 1796-97 as compared to 700 before the Revolution.[7]

The officials of the Department of Moselle related a lugubrious tale: The Town of Henry suffering from the effects of the war, the requisitions, and the interruption of communications, lost its cloth

[1] J. N. Fervel, *Campagnes de la Révolution Française dans les Pyrennées Orientales*, Vol. II, pp. 270–271.

[2] *J. Déb. et Déc.*, Vol. LXX, pp. 270–271.

[3] *Les Conséquents du Maximum pour l'Agriculture, Commission de Recherche*, 1908, pp. 219–221.

[4] *Une Enquête du Comité de Salut Public sur la Draperie en L'An III, Commission de Recherche*, 1913, p. 377.

[5] G. Schmidt, *Un Essai de Statistique Industrielle en L'An V, Commission de Recherche*, 1908, pp. 11–205.

[6] *Ibid.*, p. 28.

[7] *Un Essai de Statistique Industrielle*, p. 35.

trade. The lack of free communication, the forced loan, the maximum, and paper money were the explanations offered for the reduction of production in Metz. Absolonne, a citizen of Fontoy, who normally employed 1200 men, had to abandon all his pursuits on account of losses caused by the maximum and paper money.[1]

The impassable state of the roads and the high price of labor and of raw materials were given as the causes of the reduction of the number of workers in the cloth industry in Lille (Department of Nord) from 360 to 60.[2] A commune (Arms) of the Department of Pas-De-Calais reported no reduction in the number of workers. The Canton of Arms included the woolen, hat, tannery, sugar refining, paper and soap industries among its destroyed or partially destroyed industries. Poor transportation was the chief cause of complaint.[3] The City of Mans (Department of Sarth) reported a reduction of trades from 54 to 7 or 8 and of masters from 274 to 40.[4]

The dangerous shortage of supplies was no mere fantasy. De Larevillière-Lépaux tells us late in 1795 that "the canals were not operating, the bridges were destroyed, the roads were impassable, and the relay of 'postes' abandoned".[5] The Committee of General Security in November complained of the exhausted state of the supplies of subsistence, coal and wood.[6] The wretched condition of the roads made the provisioning of Paris impossible in the opinion of the Minister of Interior.[7] The Army of the Rhine endured hunger as late as 1795: the soldiers received a daily pittance of eight ounces of bread. Kleber's troops were without shoes and coats.[8]

Consider what was said in Chapter VI on the scarcity of 1795 — in particular on the supplies in the market — and consider the additional facts presented here; and it will be clear that the scarcity of supplies was of vital significance in 1795. As a result of the continued requisitions, the reactions from the rigid control of the

[1] *Un Essai de Statistique Industrielle*, pp. 42–48.
[2] *Ibid.*, pp. 79–109.
[3] *Ibid.*, pp. 146–167.
[4] *Ibid.*, pp. 196–205.
[5] *Mémoires de Larevillière-Lépaux*, Vol. I, p. 319.
[6] *Recueil des Actes du Directoire Exécutif*, Vol. I, p. 29.
[7] *Ibid.*, pp. 34–35.
[8] H. Bourdeau, *Les Armées du Rhin au Début du Directoire*, pp. 90–100.

maximum period, the cumulative effects of four years of extensive warfare and the wretched conditions of transportation, supplies were far below their normal level. I have been interested here primarily in supplies other than subsistence: the peculiar conditions of the subsistence market, the frenzied competition to buy subsistence at any cost — treated more fully in Chapter VI — are even more vital considerations for the problem of depreciation.

It will be recalled that even during the period of maximum prices, an illegitimate system of trading had developed. A new class of middlemen had undertaken to buy commodities at the maximum and to resell at a profit. In the early months of 1795 speculative transactions of every conceivable nature flourished. Each commodity passed through the hands of an increasing number of middlemen before it reached the final consumer. Did this increased speculation not lead to an increased demand for money and a decline of prices? The increased demand for money, however, was offset often by the increased supplies of commodities offered for the money and, hence, taken off the market. This speculative demand probably did help to bolster up the value of the paper money when commodities not actually in the possession of buyer or seller were purchased. Against this, however, we should consider the tendency toward increased prices caused by the wholesale movement from productive enterprises to the unproductive pursuits of speculation and gambling. I lean strongly to the conclusion, however, that the spectacular development of the speculative middleman gave the Assignat an additional employment of some importance that helped to maintain its value.

There is no doubt about the facts. The officials of the District of Allier-Montmarault complained that meat passed through the hands of ten middlemen before reaching the army.[1] An unusually large number of markets sprang up in the Department of Charente-Inférieur. These markets attracted large numbers from productive enterprises.[2] Boissy d'Angas told the Convention that he agreed with Smith on the beneficial effects of speculation, but the remarkable development of buying and selling things not in

---

[1] P. Caron, *Enquête sur les Prix, Commission de Recherche*, 1910, pp. 16–17.
[2] *Ibid.*, pp. 78–79.

the seller's possession drew people from industry, and that, therefore, he recommended a meticulous regulation of speculation.[1] The police inspectors of Paris also complained of the large increase in the number of middlemen.[2] The legislators, by authorizing the reopening of the Bourse and the free sale of all merchandise, hoped to eradicate any unnecessary speculation.[3]

But speculation continued. Lehardy pointed out that speculation continued to increase, that the middleman's work was becoming increasingly popular, and that buying on a margin was more common than ever.[4] The Committee of Finance attributed the high prices to the increased number of middlemen and the increase of speculation.[5] The Convention devised a "Patente Taxe" for the purpose of reducing speculation and the hoarding of supplies.[6] Vernier was of the opinion that the speculators and engrossers were sending prices up; for the same commodity often passed through twenty hands. "The entire community was establishing itself as business houses and violating the laws of commerce shamelessly."[7] On the recommendation of three of its committees, the Convention decided early in September to prohibit the sale of gold and silver outside of the bourses, to make illegal all sales of commodities not actually in the possession of the seller, to inflict a penalty of two years detention for any violation, and to inscribe "Agioteur" (speculator) for public display on the chest of the convicted person.[8] The sale of metals not actually in the possession of the seller was prohibited once more on October 20.[9] In November Eschassériaux, the spokesman of the Committee of Five, estimated that the same product exchanged hands twenty times in the same day. The Committee was of the opinion that the rapidity of turnover of commodities was the main cause

[1] J. Déb. et Déc., Vol. LXIX, pp. 180–184.
[2] A. Schmidt, Tableaux de la Révolution Française, Vol. II, p. 356.
[3] C. P. S., Vol. XXII, pp. 658–660.
[4] Moniteur, Vol. XXIV, p. 445; J. Déb. et Déc., Vol. LXXI, pp. 330–335.
[5] J. Déb. et Déc., Vol. LXXIII, pp. 138–140.
[6] Recueil, Industrie, pp. 246–249; J. Déb. et Déc., Vol. LXXIV, p. 437.
[7] J. Déb. et Déc., Vol. LXXIV, p. 437.
[8] Ibid., Vol. LXXV, pp. 196–199.
[9] "Notes sur la Législation et l'Administration de la Monnaie," Bulletin d'Histoire Économique, 1911, pp. 387–389.

of the scandalous increase in prices; it asserted that no one worked in the big cities any more.[1] The police denounced the increased speculation in wheat, flour and rice on the Bourse.[2] The editors of the *Gazette Française* were puzzled by the large number anxious to buy land in contrast with the small amount of land on sale, and at the vast number of sales of all kinds as contrasted with the little actually produced and consumed.[3]

Up to this point I have discussed the conditions of the subsistence market, the reduction of supplies, and the discussion and operation of "au cours" payments as the causes of the depreciation of this period. The increased demand for money as a result of the increasing participation of the public in speculation alone tended to sustain the value of the Assignat. The failure of the Government to sell its lands profitably during this period, as well as the reduction of the land security, were additional causes of depreciation. I dealt with this subject more fully in Chapter III. A few additional points are of interest here.

The restitution of the possessions of those condemned during the Terror became an issue in the fall of 1794, and this probably contributed to the depreciation of the Assignats. The Convention in November, 1794 raised the sequestration of the possessions of the condemned.[4] In March, 1795, Boissy d'Angas proposed a decree authorizing the restitution of the lands already appropriated by the Government. Against the argument that the restitution would reduce the security against the Assignats and hence result in high prices, he argued that a restitution was indispensable for the maintenance of any confidence in the paper money, for no one has confidence in a money issued by a dishonest government. Schmidt estimated that the restitution, which the Convention approved in April, deprived the Assignats of one-third of their security.[5]

A law enacted in May, 1795 authorized the sale of lands for Assignats at seventy-five times their annual revenue in 1790. This

[1] *Moniteur*, Vol. XXVI, p. 498.
[2] C. Schmidt, *Tableaux*, Vol. II, p. 444.
[3] *Réaction Thermidorienne*, Vol. II, p. 444.
[4] *J. Déb. et Déc.*, Vol. LXV, pp. 612–614.
[5] A. Schmidt, *Paris pendant la Révolution*, Vol. II, pp. 394–399.

ill-advised attempt to dissipate the resources certainly detracted from the confidence in the Assignat. D'Ivnerois, a discriminating critic of France's financial policies, maintained that the restitution of the lands of the condemned, and the failure to perpetuate the policy of lawless appropriations enforced during the Terror, were fatal to the Assignat.[1]

The political situation was excellent in some respects and weak in others. Military success was France's lot on every frontier throughout this period. A glorious peace with Prussia and Holland was obtained in the spring of 1795. But the friction between the Conventionalists and Constitutionalists, a relic of the Terror, weakened the Government internally; and the weakened financial condition jeopardized the continuance of any government. As depreciation increased, it became increasingly difficult to print a sufficient quantity of notes to meet expenditures.

The attempts of the Government to extricate itself from its financial difficulties, form an interesting chapter in the history of this final period.[2] The lack of a consistent policy, the failure to agree on any policy, and the fact that hopes raised with each proposal were only to be shattered soon after, were all effective in contributing to a more rapid depreciation of the Assignat.

Cambon harped upon the necessity of rigid economy in November, 1794.[3] A proposal, emanating from Fayou, to sell small lots at twenty times the "prix d'estimation", met with little favor.[4] Tallien and Pelet agreed that the excessive issues were responsible for the rapid depreciation, and the former predicted that victory would be accompanied by decreased expenditures and hence by a reduction of the money in circulation.[5]

---

[1] F. D'Ivnerois, *A Cursory View of the Assignats*, pp. 3–4. This episode is also discussed in Chapter III.

[2] Nowak, in discussing recent monetary reforms in Poland, describes the two schools of thought clashing for control. The organic school demands economy and increased taxes, and opposes monetary reform before the budget is balanced. The technical school proposes stern measures: the valorisation of taxes, centralisation of devisen, and the parallel emission of two monetary units. G. Nowak, "La Réforme Monétaire en Pologne," *Revue d'Économie Politique*, 1924, pp. 809–810.

[3] *Moniteur*, Vol. XXII, p. 427; the *Journal des Débats et Décrets* gives another version. Vol. LXV, pp. 638–640.

[4] *J. Déb. et Déc.*, Vol. LXIII, p. 519.

[5] *Ibid.*, Vol. LXV, pp. 637–638.

On January 2, 1795, Lequine suggested various methods of reducing the circulation by increasing the receipts from the sales of lands. A premium on anticipatory payments, a repeal of the 2 per cent registration tax on the sales of land, and an extension of the time of the acceptance of payments of "Inscriptions on the Grande Livre" were suggested.[1] Cambon, by special legislation, attempted to assure the people of the official repugnance for any plan of demonetisation. The Committee of Finances, through its reporter, Cambon, proposed a lottery secured by the unsold lands, and a system of bounties on all anticipatory payments on lands already sold.[2] But Cambon and his Committee had lost their magic. His proposals were met by many counter-proposals, and only after much delay did the Convention accept part of the program of its Committee.[3] A lottery of public lands, a sale of paper secured by lands sold but not paid for, economies in public expenditures, a more rapid sale of lands, and a more rapid collection of payments due on lands were suggested in a semi-official plan.[4] The land security held a very prominent position in almost all proposals for increasing the value of the Assignat.

Johannot, in behalf of the Committees of Public Safety, Legislation and Finance, read an influential report on April 15, 1795. The proposals included an issue of Cédules d'hypothèque (a mortgage note on public lands), on the security of which new Assignats were to be issued; the freedom of stipulation between individuals of metallic or paper payments; and, finally, the return to a régime of absolute freedom. The Committee hoped that its plan, if successful, would result in an increase in the value of the Assignat, and that the Government would thus atone in part for "having deprived the holders of the Assignats of part of the purchasing power of the money in their possession, as new ones were issued".[5]

A law of April 25 allowed free dealings in gold and silver.[6] The

---

[1] *Moniteur*, Vol. XXIII, pp. 126–127.

[2] *Ibid.*, pp. 393–395.

[3] *J. Déb. et Déc.*, Vol. LXIX, pp. 98–99, 118–119, 127–128.

[4] *Observations Présentés par le Conseil de Commerce Au Com. P. S.*, pp. 1–8.

[5] *J. Déb. et Déc.*, Vol. LXXI, pp. 25–27, 39–40; *Moniteur*, Vol. XXIV, pp. 228–229.

[6] *Ibid.*, pp. 309–310.

increased competition of the precious metals, thus encouraged, was unwelcome to the supporters of the Assignats. The stable value of the aggregate of paper money began to fall early in 1795. The competition of a few hundred million livres of gold and silver was of fundamental importance, since the stable value of the paper money was but one hundred and fifty million livres in November, 1795; even in May it had been only one milliard livres.[1] (Two thousand million livres of precious metals were in circulation in 1789.)

When the stable value of the paper money in circulation falls to 200 million livres, the reappearance of, say, 200 million livres of gold and silver is of greater relative significance than when the paper money in circulation retains a much higher aggregate value. A falling stable value — so far as it is not offset by an increased rate of circulation — in itself tends to react favorably on the value of paper money, for a genuine scarcity of circulating media is experienced. By the reappearance of gold and silver it is deprived of some of this potential value, but it is to be remembered that the gold and silver will not circulate as rapidly as the paper money.

In May a strong agitation for a tax in kind, promoted by Bourdon and Dubois-Crancé, held the attention of the Convention. The latter emphasized the need of a substitute for additional Assignats and requisitions.[2] Johannot opposed this proposal for a "return to the hated Dîme," proposing instead to reduce expenses and to issue Cédules d'hypothèque.[3] Dubois-Crancé said that the purchase of subsistence was costing the Treasury 1200 million livres annually, while the Contribution Foncière was yielding but one-thirtieth in purchasing power of what was anticipated in 1790. The price of a quintal of wheat was 10 livres in 1790 and 300 livres in May, 1795. Bourdon proposed that the tax be reassessed in order to obtain the equivalent in wheat of the amount

[1] The concept, stable value, has received some consideration in Chapter II. Briefly, it connotes the value of the aggregate of paper money in circulation obtained by multiplying the number of units by the value of each unit in relation to its value before depreciation had begun. Thus, if the circulation were 8000 millions in 1794, and the value were 25 per cent, the stable value would be 2000 millions.

[2] *Moniteur*, Vol. XXIV, pp. 449–451.

[3] *Ibid.*, pp. 396–397.

expected in 1790.[1] Jean Bon Saint-André, borrowing from these proposals for a tax based on the price of wheat, suggested a general scale of depreciation for all public and private payments. When a scale of depreciation was agreed to in June the plans of Johannot and of Dubois-Crancé were put aside temporarily.

Proposals to demonetise were made more frequently in May. Haussman suggested that all Assignats of 5 livres and above should hereafter be acceptable at only three-quarters of their value.[2] Bourdon, among his other proposals, advised that all holders of Assignats should be forced to exchange them at the rate of five-eighths in bonds and three-eighths in Assignats. Gaston openly supported a complete demonetisation and the substitution of numéraire.[3] The Government took a hazardous step on May 11 in demonetising the "Assignats à Royal Face" of denominations from 10 to 100 livres.[4] The supporters of this measure hoped that a reduction of the circulation by 1025 millions would result. Vernier, for the Committees of Finance and Public Safety, told the Convention that a complete demonetisation would be an extreme measure. He continued, however, by describing the various methods of demonetisation: a demonetisation of certain denominations; a reduction of a percentage of the nominal value of the paper money; a complete demonetisation accompanied by a return to the metallic system; the American scheme of taking advantage of the depreciation, and reimbursing the creditors of the Government — in Vernier's opinion the French had not reached that stage of dishonesty; and, finally, a demonetisation by progression.[5]

A serious outbreak occurred in Paris on 1 Prairial (May 23), and the Convention temporarily diverted its attention from financial matters. The lapse was harmful because the Government put through the disastrous law of 10 Prairial, which provided for the sale of land at a ridiculously low price.

[1] *Moniteur*, Vol. XXIV, pp. 397–399, 440.
[2] *Ibid.*, p. 396.
[3] *Ibid.*, p. 444.
[4] *Recueil, Monnaie*, pp. 358–359. It will be remembered that the notes of 100 livres and above had already been demonetised.
[5] *Moniteur*, Vol. XXIV, pp. 680–682.

A writer in June made a novel suggestion in proposing a divorcement of the monetary quality of the Assignat from the "security" quality. De Valence believed that the holders of the Assignats were entitled only to the security and hence proposed to give them but one year in which to buy lands.[1]

The search for a palliative continued through 1795 with little evidence of success. Many diversified plans were suggested, but few ever attained the stage of enactment. A lottery of public possessions received the approval of the Government on May 27.[2] The Convention assented to a tontine and a 3 per cent loan of a milliard on July 13.[3] The often discussed "taxe en nature" became effective in a modified form in the new Contribution Foncière voted on July 21. The passage of the new Foncière was an acknowledgment of the failure of the earlier attempt to collect the public revenues "au cours".[4]

By July the Assignat was depreciating so rapidly that the Government prohibited debtors from paying their debts before the date of maturity of their obligations.[5] Although many, slow to perceive that depreciation was to continue, had hastened to take advantage of the depreciation by anticipating payments, a more astute element postponed payments of foreign and local bills in the hope of further depreciation. The Government thereupon ordered that bills be deposited and paid within three days of the date of maturity.[6]

Pancoucke, a writer of high reputation, proposed early in September (1) to demonetise 10 milliards of the Assignats by a redemption in gold bonds at their market value (30 to 1); (2) to substitute 333 millions of Cédules d'hypothèque (secured by the land) for the demonetised Assignats; (3) to retire the large Assignats — largely in the hands of the rich; and, finally, (4) to open a land bank, which was to advance 300 million livres to the Government.[7]

[1] De Valence, *Essai sur les Finances*, XII–XIV, XLV–XLVI.
[2] *J. Déb. et Déc.*, Vol. LXXII, p. 543.
[3] *Ibid.*, Vol. LXXIII, pp. 354–357.
[4] *Ibid.*, Vol. LXXIV, pp. 440–441.
[5] *Moniteur*, Vol. XXV, pp. 236–238.
[6] *Recueil des Principaux Textes Concernant le Commerce*, pp. 249–250.
[7] C. J. Pancoucke, *Nouveau Mémoire sur les Assignats*.

The Convention, occupied in the summer and early fall with the new constitution, devoted comparatively little time to the pressing needs of finance. There is no evidence of a single significant success for the many plans put into operation in 1795. The administrative machinery of the Government was weak. The Convention relied on Assignats more than ever, with some aid from continued requisitions. Legislation against the evil speculators, responsible for this depreciation in the opinion of many, was enacted repeatedly during the second half of 1795. The Convention attempted to dispose of the houses in Paris owned by the Government, requiring payment within a few weeks.[1] On October 25 the Convention approved an extraordinary war tax of twenty livres for each livre of assessment for the Foncière.[2] The Legislature approved several other extraordinary measures on November 15: some taxes to be collected in numéraire; a pronouncement once more in favor of the collection of public receipts "au cours"; a 3 per cent loan to be paid, principal and interest in numéraire; a milliard of Cédules d'hypothèque for extraordinary expenses; and a sale of forests and "mobilier" in metals or "au cours."[3] The Government soon recognized the folly of issuing a loan, payable in gold and silver, but receivable in Assignats of a market value of 1 per cent of their nominal value.[4] The final decree on the Cédules, voted on November 25, authorized the conversion of Assignats into Cédules at the market value of the Assignats and the expropriation of the Government from any parcel of land at any offer to pay the "prix d'estimation" in Cédules.[5]

When the value of the Assignat was reduced to less than 1 per cent of its nominal value, proposals to demonetise were made almost daily. Lafon-Ladébat suggested that all notes lose their monetary values in four months, for the announcement of such a program would cause people to hurry to pay off their debts, and hence the value of the Assignat would increase.[6] He did not di-

---

[1] *J. Déb. et Déc.*, Vol. LXXV, pp. 180–184.
[2] *Ibid.*, Vol. LXXVI, pp. 541–542.
[3] *Ibid.*, Vol. LXXVII, pp. 234–241.
[4] *Ibid.*, pp. 2, 19, 100.
[5] *Moniteur*, Vol. XXVI, pp. 542–543, 546, 558.
[6] *J. Déb. et Déc.*, Vol. LXXVII, pp. 206–208.

vulge whether the demonetisation was to be in effect only temporarily. De Valence proposed virtually a complete demonetisation in suggesting a compulsory exchange for a government bond which was to yield 1½ per cent.[1]

A measure, enacted on November 20, to suspend the sale of lands, "to assure the holders of the Assignats that they will invariably have the portion of security which is legitimately due them", helped to impart the final blow.[2] I have considered elsewhere the forced loan of six hundred millions that was voted at this juncture. It was not a striking success. Who can doubt, after considering the nature of these many attempts to resuscitate the Assignats, that they only accelerated their depreciation?

The political situation — especially on the frontiers — did not warrant this unprecedented loss of confidence in the Assignat. The increase of speculation was not a negligible factor in helping it to retain its value longer. The state of the subsistence market, the disorganization of the productive processes, the deplorable financial conditions resulting from the lax administration and the inability to concur on a definite program, the reduction of and loss of confidence in the security, the proposals to demonetise, and, finally, the renewed competition of gold and silver, all detracted from the confidence in the Assignat and contributed to the headlong depreciation. Depreciation proceeded much more rapidly than would be expected from a mere consideration of the issues: the depreciation by the end of this period was at least twelve times as great as might be expected from a survey of quantities in circulation. The lack of confidence in the paper money, as evidenced by the desire to be rid of it, reflected the composite effect of all of these forces, and is of much greater significance than mere quantities.

SUMMARY

No comprehensive and systematic treatment of the depreciation of the Assignat has yet been made. Many writers on the subject take depreciation for granted. Why stop to explain the depre

---

[1] C. M. de Valence, *Observations Addressés au Directoire Exécutif*, p. xvii.

[2] *J. Déb. et Déc.*, Vol. LXXVIII, pp. 19–20.

ciation of a paper money issued to excess? An uninterrupted fall, in the opinion of some, was inevitable. Hawtrey's emphasis on speculation is helpful, although he does not consider speculation in all its ramifications. The most serious deficiency in Hawtrey's treatment — to be expected in a brief essay — is his failure to consider the many forces that affected depreciation. Falkner makes a brilliant contribution in pointing out the necessity of considering the availability or unavailability of the metals for satisfying the demand for money.

One explanation of the depreciation was and is fully appreciated. The economists, the writers on public finance, and the monetary theorists have all expressed (or implied) an adherence to the quantity theory. Their allegiance to that theory often explains a neglect to inquire further into the process of depreciation. As has been indicated, however, the writers and thinkers of the Revolution found much that was not explicable in terms of quantity. Lavoisier, for example, considered the moral effects of additional issues; Johannot commented on the depreciation, incomprehensible on a consideration of quantities alone, when Doumouriez betrayed his country. A brilliant essayist, Boislandry, formulated a comprehensive list of the causes of depreciation that a writer of today, better versed in monetary theory, might well be proud of. The man in the street did not miss an opportunity to scoff at the quantity theory; he pointed out, for example, that in May, 1796, the price of the louis was 9000 livres, whereas when the money in circulation had been three times as great, the price was but 2000–4000 livres.[1] A police reporter made note not only of the fact that prices fell with the capture of Amsterdam early in 1795, but that the populace expected that a fall in prices would follow a great victory.[2]

Wagner[3] and Mitchell[4] have made familiar the thesis that changes in the value of money are caused in large part by changing political fortunes. But Ferraris, whose treatise on paper money

[1] A. Schmidt, *Tableaux*, Vol. III, p. 205.
[2] *Réaction Thermidorienne*, Vol. I, p. 453.
[3] A. Wagner, *Die russische Papierwährung*, pp. 141–143. Also, *Sozialökonomik*, Part II, Vol. II, pp. 698–700.
[4] W. Mitchell, *A History of the Greenbacks*, especially Part II, Chapter III.

still remains one of the great works in the field, was critical of Wagner's position.[1] Mises observes that military success was accompanied by final depreciation during both the French and American revolutions.[2]

Wagner and Mitchell employed exchange and gold quotations as measures of depreciation. These markets are speculative and reflect the changing military and political situation well; in fact, one is easily misled by appreciable movements that are not easily explained by changes in fundamental conditions. But perhaps the most important explanation of the differences between Wagner and Mitchell, on the one hand, and Ferraris and Mises on the other, is that the former dealt with periods in which the depreciation was moderate, or at least not extreme. They did not have in mind periods in which the financial strain was so great that the creation of artificial purchasing power became the dominating factor in the situation. I agree with Wagner and Mitchell that a favorable political event would have an advantageous effect; but Wagner, and especially Mitchell were inclined to overemphasise the effects of the changing political situation.

What has been neglected in the explanations of the depreciation of the Assignat? There has been unquestionably a failure to consider adequately the problem of the supply of commodities, or, more comprehensively, of the demand for money. War, internal insecurity, and misguided public policies, all contributed to the reduction of supplies. But the effects of these forces varied so that the demand for money was not constant during this period. A careful consideration of the demand for money is indispensable for an estimate of the residue of damage caused directly by the Assignat.

Closely related, and yet a problem that requires special analysis, is the problem of subsistence. The Economic Federalism,[3] the disorganized conditions of transportation, the effects of the public control and of the warfare, all require analysis. The singular syn-

---

[1] C. F. Ferraris, *Moneta e Corso Forzoso*, pp. 25–29.

[2] L. Mises, *Die geldtheoretische und geldrechtliche Seite des Stabilisierungsproblems*, pp. 18–19.

[3] A phrase descriptive of the attempts of localities to prevent free economic relations with outside communities.

chronization of the periods of rapid depreciation and of lack of subsistence, forces the writer to the conclusion that the unhappy state of the subsistence market was a factor of fundamental importance for the value of the Assignat. An Assignat that could not buy bread was indeed worthless and the holder was willing to offer an increasing number of paper livres until he could procure the necessary subsistence. That the French expended perhaps two-thirds of their incomes on bread, is significant.[1]

The purchase of subsistence required a large proportion of the resources of the Treasury. A writer estimated the monthly cost of the distribution of bread at 546 million livres in 1794–95.[2] The cost of feeding Paris in 1795 equalled one-tenth of the total expenditures of the Government.[3] Dubois Crancé, a well informed contemporary, estimated that two-thirds of the daily expenditures of the Government in the spring of 1795 were consumed in the purchase of subsistence, and by that time the circulation had been enriched by 6 milliards (more than one-half of the total) as a result of governmental expenditures for subsistence.[4]

Thirdly, consider the effect of the land security, which received some attention in Chapter III. The study of the Assignats demands more than an acquaintance with present-day monetary theory: it requires an insight into the conditions during the Revolution. A study of the daily life of the Revolution confirms the impression that the fundamental source of the confidence in the Assignat lay in the land security that strongly supported it. The man in the street believed that the waste of these resources was equivalent to a demonetisation of the Assignat. Does any one suppose that the crafty legislators of the Revolution persistently advertised the abundance of the land security for the mere joy of the computation? We may not go all the way with D'Ivnerois who said that "The confiscations in 1793–94 kept the Assignat at its high value during the Terror", but we cannot doubt either the purpose of the confiscations of the possessions of the Émigrés and of the condemned, or the aid rendered the Assignat by these addi-

---

[1] See Arch. Parl., Vol. LIV, p. 691; Vol. LXXII, pp. 397–398.
[2] A. Schmidt, *Paris pendant la Révolution*, p. 16.
[3] *J. Déb. et Déc.*, Vol. LXXX, pp. 364–365.
[4] J. Jung, *L'Armée et la Révolution*, especially Vol. II, chapter VI.

tions to the security. A minute study of all the specifics, suggested or carried through from 1794 to 1796, reveals that very few of them were not proposals to increase the receipts from the sale of lands. Can we give full confidence to the many writers on the Assignats who either neglect or dogmatically dismiss the very important influence of the land security on the value of the Assignats? So much for the more important sins of omission.

I have not intended to make this chapter on depreciation either a refutation of the quantity theory, or an encomium of it. I hold only that a discussion merely on the basis of quantities leads us nowhere. Subsistence, supplies, security, taxation, and the other factors at work, all finally affect the value of money through changes in the quantity of paper money thrown on the market or through any of the other variables in the equation of exchange. Quantities issued are of little significance without a consideration of the varying haste with which they are disbursed. The most effective way of paying homage to the quantity theory is to disregard it in its superficial form; but in apparently disregarding it, to study the forces at work — forces that finally become effective through changes in the supplies of and demand for money.

Criticisms of the quantity theory have been numerous in recent years. One of the by-products of this criticism has been a change in emphasis from quantities to balances. Aftalion points out that large variations in prices in the war and post-war period were accompanied by small variations in the supplies of money issued.[1] Gide observes that the countries of the greatest inflation were not those of the highest prices.[2] Bonnet observes that inflation remained inoperative because the public was unable to dispose of its large balances.[3] Hahn points out that individuals who received additional cash were more likely to save than spend.[4] They are all seeking for an explanation of the failure of the rigid quantity theory. Herrmann expresses the difficulty well: depreciation does not necessarily follow inflation, for inflation may be latent.[5]

[1] A. Aftalion, "Les Expériences monétaires récentes et la Théorie Quantitative," Revue d'Économie Politique, 1925, p. 666.
[2] C. Gide, "Notes on financial and monetary Situation," p. 4. Memorandum presented to the Brussels Conference, 1920.
[3] G. E. Bonnet, La Politique anglaise d'Assainissement monétaire, pp. 40–41.
[4] A. Hahn, Geld und Kredit, p. 132.
[5] K. A. Herrmann, Die Zukunft des Goldes, p. 78.

CHAPTER IX

SOME EFFECTS OF DEPRECIATION

1. DEBTOR-CREDITOR RELATIONS[1]

Two distinct problems are involved. People who had made advances when the currency was at a relatively high value were entitled to protection from payments in a cheap or worthless money; and debtors who had borrowed in a depreciated or almost worthless money had to be saved from the unfair demands for metallic reimbursements when the country returned to a metallic standard.[2] For the most part this section concerns itself with the latter problem, but the first problem is touched upon incidentally.

A brief chronological résumé of the history of paper money during the French Revolution may be helpful here. The Assignats were first put into circulation early in 1790. They maintained a reasonably high value until the end of the maximum period (December, 1794). The value of the paper money fell from 30 per cent in January, 1795 to 20 per cent in April, 1795, and to 1 per cent in November, 1795. The authorities were forced in December, 1795, in order to buy the necessities of war, to issue a new species of paper, the Rescriptions. The Rescriptions, or rather the Promesses de Rescriptions, were rigidly limited in quantity, and were redeemable in gold. The Mandat, or Promesse de Mandat, appeared in March, 1796, and depreciation attended its very inception. The Government recognized this depreciation as early as July, 1796.

---

[1] This section was written in 1925. Hargreaves' excellent study has since appeared. (E. L. Hargreaves, *Restoring Currency Standards*. London, 1926.) The two studies largely supplement each other. Hargreaves is primarily interested in the legislation affecting the relations of debtors and creditors. He bases his study on the statutes as given by Duvergier, and, to some extent, on the interpretation of the courts. I am concerned with the history of the legislation, its repercussions on the value of the Assignat, and with the economic effects of the scarcity of currency. (See especially pages 54 to 68 of Hargreaves' study.)

[2] A. Wagner, *Sozialökonomik*, Part II, Vol. II, p. 720.

The local tables of depreciation were prepared in order to reduce the confusion and inequalities that spread into private transactions. From the beginning of 1792 the Assignat was not accepted in private transactions at its full value. The Government contrived many severe penalties to enforce the acceptance of Assignats on equal terms with gold. Nevertheless, the Government was forced, as early as December, 1791, not only to buy at increased prices, but even to allow indemnities both for the future internal depreciation in the case of domestic contracts, and for the future depreciation of the exchanges in the case of foreign purchases.[1]

It is apparent that in some instances, in contracts voluntarily made with the Government, some account was taken of present and future depreciation. Were the contracts amended when their spirit was seriously modified by depreciation? Caron has reprinted an interesting and relevant document in the 1913 volume of the publications of the Commission des Recherches. It is a letter and an accompanying memoir that were submitted to the Committee of Public Safety in August, 1795.[2] The house of Desjardins et Faure et Desjardins fils had contracted, in February, 1793, to furnish the house of Pierre Courajod et Cie with three bills of exchange on Madrid. Before the latter could realize on these bills, the war with Spain had begun. Spain sequestered all alien property, including alien credits. Courajod et Cie sued for recovery in 1793. The troubles in Lyons — the city where the transaction had occurred — delayed a decision until Messidor 3 (June, 1795). The tribune decided that Courajod et Cie were to be reimbursed not only for the nominal amount of Assignats delivered to Desjardins, but were to receive an amount equal to the real value of the Assignat in February, 1793. The memoir also revealed that the court overruled an earlier verdict on a similar question and verdicts rendered on the same point both in Marseilles and Paris. The question of the effects of depreciation on contracts was evidently a prominent one in the local courts, and

---

[1] *Rapport Présentée sur le Compte Rendu par Narbonne*, p. 14.
[2] P. Caron, "Le Commerce Lyonnais et la Dépréciation des Assignats," *Bulletin d'Histoire Économique de la Révolution*, 1913, pp. 190–209.

at least one local tribunal dared to modify the terms of a contract where the *spirit of the contract* had been altered.[1]

The whole economic system was collapsing in 1795 as a result of the disorganization and inequities caused by the precipitate depreciation. The revenues received by the Government in depreciated Assignats were lavishly disbursed, much to the dissatisfaction of the public creditors, the rentiers and pensioners in particular. The landed proprietors, facing bankruptcy, protested in vain against the payment of rents in depreciated Assignats. When the Assignats began to depreciate rapidly, debtors hastened to settle long standing debts. Larevillière-Lépaux, describing conditions late in 1795, remarked that as a result of the rapid depreciation, "All public credit was dead and all confidence shattered; cash sales alone were made in private transactions, or with interest charges that rendered every transaction impossible or ruinous".[2]

The rapid depreciation of the Assignat concerned the Government largely because of the shrinkage in its revenues. A Government that had imprisoned men for the unpatriotic offense of not accepting the Revolutionary money at par, hesitated to recognize the depreciation officially. Necessity, however, demanded action. Johannot, in April, 1795, in behalf of the Committees of Public Safety, of Commerce, of Legislation, and of Assignats dwelt on the necessity of encouraging honesty in transactions between individuals and between individuals and the Government.[3] The Assignats were depreciating so rapidly that the raising of revenue by the use of the printing press was proving unsatisfactory; and receipts from land sales and taxes were contributing little substantial revenue.

Suggestions were made that the Government might benefit from a recognition of the depreciation of the Assignat. Two serious objections had to be answered. Would not an official recognition of depreciation put an additional burden on the already overworked Assignat? Many recognized that the stable value of the aggregate currency had decreased rapidly, and that any

[1] Hargreaves says that prior to 1795 the courts refused to recognise depreciation. *Op. cit.*, pp. 66–67.
[2] L. Lépaux, *Mémoires*, Vol. I, especially Chapter XVII.
[3] *J. Déb. et Déc.*, Vol. XXI, p. 25.

legislation that might result in an increased demand for it would be inadvisable.[1] The twenty milliards of Assignats in November, 1795 had a stable value of less than one hundred millions. That is to say, the depreciation proceeded much more rapidly than could be explained by the proportionate increases in circulation. The metallic currency before the Revolution totalled two milliards. The increased velocity of circulation in 1795 and the partial return of the metals could scarcely offset a loss of over 95 per cent in the stable value of the currency. The danger was a genuine one. The Government was forced to concede a postponement of "au cours" payments early in 1796 because of the lack of circulating media.[2] (With "au cours" payments, the Assignat would not be accepted at its nominal value, but rather at its depreciated value; and, therefore, more Assignats would be necessary to make a given payment.) Similar action had to be taken in February, 1797.[3] A second objection was offered by others. Might not an official recognition of depreciation be a final blow to the rapidly depreciating paper money? At least two pamphleteers had such premonitions.[4]

A more careful definition of the concept, scarcity of currency, is perhaps necessary. A scarcity is genuine only in the sense that the public is unwilling to accept a rapidly depreciating paper money, even to make necessary payments in the future. The public learns to economise on balances held and thus minimises the losses from depreciation. Hence, in large part, a reduction of the stable value of the currency is offset by an increase in the rate of consumption of balances. The scarcity results from the fact that people begin to lose confidence at a more rapid rate than balances can be economised. Assuming that the confidence of the public is further shaken by the announcement of "au cours" payments, they become even less willing to accept and hold paper money; and whether the currency becomes less or more overworked will depend upon whether the further growth of confi-

---

[1] *Moniteur*, Vol. XXVI, pp. 630–632; Vol. XXVIII, p. 68.
[2] *Ibid.*, Vol. XXVII, pp. 433–434.
[3] *Ibid.*, Vol. XXVIII, p. 558.
[4] P. Capon, *Observations sur le Mode de Paiement de Quatrième Quart des Biens Nationaux*, pp. 3–5; Derant, *Un Dernier Mot en Faveur des Mandats*.

dence will have a greater or less effect than the increased demand resulting from the introduction of "au cours" payments.

In 1794 the Government had demanded payments in kind for all rents on its domains. This decree proved ineffective. A bill requiring all payments to the Government to be made according to a scale of depreciation was approved in June, 1795. Houses and factories subject to the Contribution Foncière were excepted from the rigorous payments demanded by this law. A circulation of 2000 million livres was deemed the normal circulation. Each taxpayer or public debtor was to pay 25 per cent additional for each 500 million livres additional to the 2000 million in circulation at the time the tax was due or the contract made.[1] The Government modified the June law and ordered the taxpayers, in July, 1795, to pay the Contribution Foncière, one-half "au cours" and one-half in kind.[2] The frequent proposals for the collection of public contributions "au cours" affirm the failure of the earlier measures.[3]

The solution of the problem was delayed somewhat by the Mandat experience. The depreciation of the latter, however, began early. The farmers of public lands on June 27, 1796 were ordered to pay one-quarter of the amount of their lease for the year (1795–1796) in kind. The remaining three-quarters were to be remitted in paper money according to the price of wheat, the assumption being that each livre would purchase 10 pounds of wheat, as in 1790. Thus, if 120 livres were payable in that manner (lease of 160 livres), and if the price of wheat were 50 centimes (one-half livre) a pound, then the farmer was to pay 600 livres in cash $(10 \times \frac{1}{2} \times 120 = 600)$.[4] In the next few months the Government passed legislation demanding payment for land sold since March, 1796 and for taxes in numéraire or in paper "au cours."[5]

---

[1] *Moniteur*, Vol. XXV, pp. 13–16.

[2] *J. Déb. et Déc.*, Vol. LXXVII, pp. 377–380.

[3] *Ibid.*, p. 237; also see Chapter VIII. Behnsen and Genzner rightly maintain that attempts to collect public revenue "au cours" are fraught with difficulties; for the public, suffering a serious reduction in its standard of living, aims above all to economise on tax payments. H. Behnsen und U. Genzner, *Die Folgen der Mark-Entwertung*, pp. 77–78.

[4] *Recueil des Principaux Textes concernant l'Économie Rurale, Commission de Recherche et de Publication des Documents*, 1907, pp. 388–389.

[5] *Recueil, Monnaie*, pp. 434, 436, 437, 440.

The Government legislated to prevent the decline in the real value of its receipts before it offered any relief to its functionaries and creditors. Cambon pleaded for them in the latter part of 1794.[1] He argued that the farmer had been favored by a new maximum, but that no relief had been offered to the public creditors. The Treasury, in July, 1795, declared invalid some contracts made by the representatives "en mission" with the army of the Sambre-et-Meuse, because they stipulated that supplies should be paid for at prices based on the future exchanges on Amsterdam.[2] But such action at this time was exceptional; the Treasury had to be more generous as a rule toward public contractors, if the armies were to be provisioned and clad. Vernier informed the Convention in April, 1795 that payments for public contracts had been stipulated in numéraire or "au cours" for some time.[3] At a relatively early period of the depreciation of the Mandat, the Directory entrusted the Minister of War with the power of revising contracts when depreciation made such revision expedient.[4]

Public employees had to be conscripted. Often the public authorities had no alternative but to supplement the wages in depreciated paper with a few ounces of bread. Early in 1796 the employees surrendered these meagre rights to payments in kind on the unfulfilled promise of payments in a stable currency.[5] Gerod commented on the ineffectiveness of the measures voted to relieve the public employees down to May, 1797.[6] This legislation, never put in practice, included the law of June, 1795, doubling salaries; the law of August, 1795, authorizing the payments of salaries one-half in grain; and, finally, the law of October, 1796, granting to public employees one-half of their salaries in numéraire.

The abominable treatment of the rentier constituted one of the tragedies of the Revolution. An offer of help was proffered to the

---

[1] *J. Déb. et Déc.*, Vol. LXV, p. 715.

[2] *C. P. S.*, Vol. XXV, pp. 321–322.

[3] *J. Déb. et Déc.*, Vol. LXXI, pp. 79–83.

[4] *Recueil des Actes du Directoire Exécutif*, Vol. II, p. 539.

[5] F. D'Ivernois, *Histoire de l'Administration des Finances pendant l'Année 1796*, 2d ed., pp. 55–56.

[6] *J. Déb. et Déc.*, Vol. XCV, pp. 209–210.

rentier in June, 1795, but was not to become effective until March, 1796. The *Moniteur* of November 25, 1795 announced a bounty of ten times the amount due for the year IV (1795–96) to all rentiers and pensioners. (The Assignat had fallen to 1 per cent of its 1790 value by November, 1795.[1]) The *Moniteur* evidently reported this law erroneously. This relief was granted only to rentiers with rentes yielding one hundred livres or less annually. The percentage of bounty decreased with the increase in the amount of income realised from rentes.[2]

Gerod announced to the Anciens in January, 1797 that the rentiers had been promised relief by the legislators, but that they had been deprived of this help because of the financial difficulties of the Government. Although a law of October, 1796 had provided that the rentiers were to receive one-sixth of all the ordinary receipts, they had received but one million francs in three months.[3] The Government then gave the rentiers the privilege of converting their credits in numéraire for the year IV (1795–96) into partial payments for land.[4]

Many of the journals and contemporary pamphlets bewailed the sufferings of the rentiers. In particular, a lawyer named Ollivier supported their contentions. He demanded privileges for rentiers in their relations with their creditors, similar to those taken by the Treasury in its relations with rentiers. Since the Treasury had retained the privilege of paying in a worthless paper, Ollivier contended that the rentiers should not be deprived of similar privileges toward their creditors. The Government had paid the rentiers in a worthless paper; but when metallic payments became the rule, it defaulted.[5]

The question of farm leases requires separate consideration because it was impossible to readjust farm leases according to the laws of adjustment (to be explained) for other private transactions. Farm leases were generally made for periods of nine years.

[1] *Moniteur*, Vol. XXVI, p. 558.
[2] *J. Déb. et Déc.*, Vol. LXXXI, pp. 179–180. This was an innocuous law since the Assignat was worth about 1 per cent of its nominal value at the time and was soon to become worthless.
[3] *J. Déb. et Déc.*, Vol. XCI, pp. 148–150.
[4] *Ibid.*, Vol. XCII, pp. 390–393.
[5] Ollivier, *Rentiers de l'État et Observations sur le Rapport de Paradès.*

Life tenures were rare. Depreciation had made farming profitable. The Government found it necessary, in demanding payment for the Contribution Foncière in kind from the proprietors, to order the farmers to pay their rents in a similar manner. Later legislation revealed that this law had proved ineffective.[1] A law authorizing the payment of rents on public lands in kind was also ineffective.[2]

A decree of June 17, 1795 authorizing a readjustment of farmers' rents, was equally ineffective.[3] It was decided (August 26, 1797) that leases made before January 1, 1792 and after July 25, 1796 — considered periods of relatively stable monetary conditions — were not to be readjusted. Leases made between the date of the maximum and before July 25, 1796 were to be reduced by a table of depreciation to the 1790 rental values.[4] A return to metallic payments would have caused hardships otherwise. (Evidently no provision was made for the period between January, 1792 and May, 1793.)

Because the problem was not settled by the law of August 26, 1797, a more serious attempt was made in July, 1798: A reduction according to the local values of the Assignat (local tables) might be made in the case of nine-year leases, if the proprietor were agreeable; or payments might be made in gold or silver if the farmer were willing. If both were unwilling to abide by these provisions in the case of nine-year leases — that is, if the proprietor were unwilling to adjust the lease according to the local table, or the farmer were unwilling to adjust by paying full metallic values for the amount of the lease — then an expert was to decide. An expert was to decide the issue in any case for longer leases.[5]

A very important moral and economic problem was raised by the accelerated rate of depreciation of the Assignat. Debtors took advantage of the low value of the paper money to pay off long time debts. A dramatist of the day has left us a play written around this theme. M. Deslandres, formerly a flourishing mer-

---

[1] *J. Déb. et Déc.*, Vol. LXXII, pp. 300, 377–380.
[2] Arch. Parl., Vol. LXXVIII, pp. 61–65.
[3] *Moniteur*, Vol. XXV, pp. 13–16.
[4] *Recueil, Économie Rurale*, pp. 396–398.
[5] *Ibid.*, pp. 398–400.

chant, has been virtually ruined by the maximum and the stagnation of trade resulting from a fluctuating standard. When the Louis was quoted at 5000 livres — a depreciation of over 99½ per cent — he sees an opportunity to retrieve his fortune by repaying a business debt of 6000 livres. The play concerns itself largely with the calumnies suffered by M. Deslandres.[1]

Debtors hastened to pay their debts in worthless paper. They anticipated large payments when they feared an appreciation of the paper or a return to a metallic standard. The evil developed so extensively that during the period of extreme depreciation of both the Assignat and the Mandat, debtors were barred by law from paying their capital debts.[2] Although this ban was lifted theoretically with the promulgation of the tables of depreciation, the last suspensions of payment were not lifted until December 1, 1797.[3]

The appearance of the Mandat in March, 1796 made it possible to allow the resumption of capital reimbursements suspended in July and December, 1795. The Mandat, it was hoped, would maintain a stable value. A table of reduction was deemed necessary for the liquidation of contracts made during the period of paper money (Assignat) depreciation. This table was voted in Germinal IV (April, 1796). It was based on the price of gold and silver with some adjustments for the prices of commodities.[4] Kaufman thought that the table was partial to the interests of the creditor class. He asserted that when the course of the Assignat was 4 per cent in the departments and 3 per cent in Bâle, these tables of depreciation gave a value of 20 per cent.[5] All private contracts entered into after January 1, 1792 were divided into sixteen classes according to the date of contract.[6] The amount to be reimbursed decreased with the increased depreciation at the time of the agreement. Obligations entered into before January 1,

---

[1] *Appel à l'Honneur* (Anonymous).
[2] *Recueil, Monnaie*, p. 365.
[3] In December, 1796 obligations anterior to 1791 were ordered to be paid, one-third immediately and two-thirds in two years. In February, 1797 this act was modified, *ibid.*, p. 451.
[4] *Moniteur*, Vol. XXVIII, p. 67.
[5] *Ibid.*, p. 153.
[6] *Ibid.*, p. 75.

1792, and those since stipulated in numéraire, were to be settled in Mandats without any reduction. The stringent laws from 1793 to 1795 against contracts stipulating payments in numéraire were thus disregarded. A number of the later laws contained a similar provision legalising illegal contracts.[1]

The rapid depreciation of the Mandat necessitated another suspension of capital reimbursements on 29 Messidor 4 (July, 1796). The lack of coöperation, both within each chamber and between chambers — as well as the intense hostility between debtors and creditors — delayed the legislative passage of the new depreciation tables until 5 Messidor 5 (June 22, 1797). From April to July, 1796, the problem was to protect the creditor from reimbursements in a depreciating paper. (Hence the act of 29 Messidor 4 was passed.) The partial return to a metallic standard in the fall and winter of 1796 presented another problem: now the debtor had to be spared the burden of metallic payments.

The Council of 500 voted in November, 1796 to relieve the debtors from the oppressive weight of metallic reimbursements.[2] In pursuit of its program of relief for the debtors it agreed, on December 2, 1796, to follow the Treasury quotations as its main guide, with the Bâle quotations as a supplementary guide, and to make some allowance for the difference "that has always existed between the value of the Assignat in gold, and its value in commodities".[3] Late in March it was decided that transactions antedating the period of depreciation and those made after July, 1796 were to be liquidated in numéraire.[4] On the 16th of Germinal (April 5) all assignments to creditors since the recent suspension of payments (July, 1796) were declared invalid.[5] Ten days later an official commission proposed the construction of a table of depreciation for every department.[6] The Council of 500 finally adopted a resolution on the 30th of Germinal (April 19) calling for the construction of local tables of depreciation.[7] This resolution,

---

[1] *Lois et Résolutions Complètes sur les Transactions*, p. 2.
[2] *Moniteur*, Vol. XXVIII, p. 497.
[3] *Ibid.*, p. 504. The final bill said nothing of the Bâle exchanges.
[4] *J. Déb. et Déc.*, Vol. LXIV, pp. 163–166.
[5] *Ibid.*, p. 651.
[6] *Ibid.*, p. 666.
[7] *Ibid.*, pp. 671–672.

which subjected private transactions made during the paper money régime to adjustment on the basis of the department tables, became law on 5 Messidor 5 (June 23, 1797).[1]

The right of the State to interfere in private contracts was not conceded without much opposition. Laffon-Ladebat, in a discourse rendered on 28 Nivôse 5 (January 13, 1797) to the Conseil d'Anciens, summed up the case for both the creditors and the debtors.[2] The debtors suffer a loss of value in all their investments, public and private, because of depreciation; and they ought to be relieved from the bondage to their creditors that results from the necessity of repaying in gold and silver for loans contracted in a depreciated paper. The creditors pretend that the State cannot interfere with private contracts; that individual obligations are independent of the Government; that inviolability of property is the essential basis of public association; and, hence, that the debtor must pay the full value of his debt in coin.

A pamphleteer asserted during this controversy that the State could not interfere with contracts that were not fraudulent; and he maintained that the low rates of interest were evidence of the faith of the creditors in non-interference by the Government.[3] This writer evidently held that the creditors charged a low rate because they gambled on the possibility of repayment in metallic money. Low rates were obtained, in fact, only for loans made in paper with the possibility of repayment in metals. They were not low when paper loans were at stake; and, as will be seen in the latter part of this chapter, there is evidence of high rates for metallic loans once the country returned to a metallic standard.

Lataché attacked the proposed law as being unconstitutional on the very day on which it was passed (5 Messidor 5). It was retroactive; it interfered with the rights of private property; and it provided for an unconstitutional usurpation of the judiciary by the legislative power.[4] Mollévaut, a defender of the debtor's interest, rendered the decisive discourse. The most cogent argument he employed involved an appeal to the self-interest of the creditors.

[1] *J. Déb. et Déc.*, Vol. XCIV, p. 462.
[2] *Observations d'un Rentier Viager*, pp. 1–5.
[3] *Réponse à l'Opinion de Duguet sur les Transactions*, pp. 4–5.
[4] *J. Déb. et Déc.*, Vol. XCVII, p. 99.

The creditors could not expect full payments in metals to be made now (1797) for contracts that were agreed to when 40 or 50 milliards of paper money were in circulation. The resumption of payments could be made practicable only by a reduction of the debts by a table of depreciation.[1]

All contracts were not subject to the terms of these tables. Government transactions remained largely independent of them. Farm leases had to be adjusted in a more scientific way in many instances. Transactions agreed to before January 1, 1791, and after 29 Messidor 4 (July 16, 1796) were designated metallic transactions and had to be liquidated with numéraire. Payments for lands alienated during the paper money régime were to be adjusted by experts.[2]

Revalorisation laws are increasingly invoked in order to reduce the injustices caused by the depreciation of paper money and by the reintroduction of a metallic currency.[3] Frederick the Great was responsible for a simple revalorisation law after the Seven Years War.[4] Germany, Poland and Hungary have recently enacted comprehensive laws of that type.[5] The recent Hungarian attempt to deal with this problem is particularly interesting. In introducing its law, the Hungarian Government proceeded on the assumption that a crown was a crown. Adjustments were to be made only in exceptional cases; special consideration was to be given to claims arising from delays in payment; and the courts were to inquire whether, by taking ordinary precautions, contracting parties might have provided for depreciation.[6]

[1] J. Déb. et Déc., Vol. XCVII, p. 101.
[2] Recueil, Monnaie, pp. 476-478.
[3] For a discussion of attempts to obtain a stable measure of value in Central Europe in the last 10 years, see M. S. Braun, "Die Doppelnote", Schriften des Vereins für Sozialpolitik, Vol. CLXV, No. II; also J. Hirsch, Die deutsche Valutafrage, pp. 17-18; and R. Stucken, "Die Werthestündigen Anleihen in Finanzwirtschaftlicher Betrachtung", Schriften des Vereins für Sozialpolitik, Vol. XCVI, No. III. F. A. Leitner (Finanz und Preispolitik, p. 8) discusses various Methods of making contracts that include allowances for depreciation.
[4] L. V. Birck, Scourge of Europe, p. 108.
[5] British Overseas Report on Hungary, 1925, pp. 17-18; R. Lewinsohn, Histoire de l'Inflation, pp. 35-36, 231-232, 327-328. G. Kurntowski, "La Réforme monétaire en Poland," Revue d'Économie Politique, 1924, pp. 525-528.
[6] Economic Bulletin of the Central Corporation of Banking Companies, Vol. II, No. 4 (1926), pp. 35-36.

The Code Napoléon requires that payment be made in an equivalent number of francs, without regard to the changing metallic content of the money. Knapp's position is similar. "The State, therefore, treats the older debts as if the unit of value, a pound of copper, were only a name by the use of which the relative amount of debt was indicated, and which does not mean that in reality a copper was to be delivered."[1] In the course of the debates in Austria in the early part of the 19th century, Gartner maintained that reimbursements should be made "au cours" because the State has no right to hamper the proper fulfillment of private contracts; gold, alone, is genuine money. But the Exchequer contended that money is a medium of exchange, that the State may manufacture it out of valueless material, and that private citizens should not be given preferential treatment.[2] Not until November, 1923, did the Supreme Court of the German Reich abandon the thesis that a mark is a mark.[3] But legislatures have frequently repudiated the Nominalist position, and have attempted to obtain a modicum of justice for debtors and creditors by revising contracts.

No doubt monetary policy has been determined in part by the attitude of the authorities toward the revision of contracts. Did not the tenacity with which devaluation was fought in recent years in both France and Italy arise from the widespread acceptance of the thesis that a franc is a franc or a lire is a lire? Revision of contracts was unlikely; hence deflation was the only possible program until the obstacles of a deflationary policy became apparent to everybody. Wagner proposed deflation for Russia because, in his opinion, an equitable revision of contracts was impossible.[4]

2. TRANSITION TO A METALLIC STANDARD

A country that sees its paper money depreciate continually, and finally depreciate so rapidly that the stable value falls to a very small proportion of the value of the money circulating before

[1] G. F. Knapp, *State Theory of Money*, p. 14.
[2] See V. Hoffman's excellent study of Austria's experiences in the early part of the 19th century. "Die Devalvierung des österreichischen Papiergeldes im Jahre 1811," *Schriften des Vereins für Sozialpolitik*, Vol. CLXV, pp. 108–112.
[3] H. Schacht, *Stabilisation of the Mark*, p. 212.
[4] A. Wagner, *Die russische Papierwährung*, pp. 112–116.

its introduction, sooner or later concerns itself with the possibilities of a return to a metallic standard. The difficulties encountered in the return to a metallic standard make a fascinating chapter in the history of paper money.[1] The required adjustments do not occur automatically as some would have us believe. Falkner writes, "so the speed and completeness with which the flow of metals was brought about, and with which the precious metals were brought back, prove that the money had been hoarded by the French, and that the exportation, which the contemporaries had feared so, had required only a small proportion of the metals."[2]

Thibeaudeau, a contemporary, said that the fear of a scarcity of numéraire was not realized when the paper money petered out; the metals came out of hiding within the next fifteen months and there was no great catastrophe.[3] These statements give too rosy a picture.

Gold and silver were used concurrently with paper money to an unknown degree up to the Reign of Terror. The Terror was successful in eliminating the competition of gold and silver in internal transactions. No sooner did the economic policies of the Reign of Terror lose their vitality, however, than the precious metals began to circulate once more. Later, the law of 6 Floréal 3 (April 22, 1795), which authorized the reopening of the Bourse and guaranteed the freedom of transactions in gold and silver, stimulated their return.[4] Dealers, to an increasing extent, demanded numéraire for their merchandise. The Government required increasing amounts of gold and silver; the Directory demanded a credit of twenty-one million livres in numéraire for the use of four departments in November, 1795; and in the following month it even estimated its annual expenditures at fifteen hundred millions in

[1] Genz once remarked that the dangerous epoch only begins with attempts to bring back normal conditions. A. Wagner, *Die russische Papierwährung*, pp. 4–5.
[2] S. U. Falkner, *op. cit.*, p. 53. B. M. Anderson also exaggerates the ease with which the transition was effected. *Chase Economic Bulletin*, January 12, 1922, p. 44.
[3] *Mémoires*, Vol. II, pp. 29–30. Mises quotes approvingly Thiers' remarks on how easily the gold came out of hoards and from abroad. Mises, *op. cit.*, pp. 10–11.
[4] The English reported important losses of specie from June, 1795 to February, 1797. In particular attention was drawn to the unprecedented losses of February 21–27, 1797. "Third Report of Committee of Secrecy on Outstanding Demands of the Bank of England, 1797," in *Reports of the Committee of the House of Commons*, Vol. II, p. 12.

numéraire. (Of course this does not mean that the Government expected to receive all of its revenue in gold and silver.)

The decrease in the stable value of the paper money which became evident in the early months of 1795, together with the demand which developed for the metals because they were often the exclusive means of purchase, contributed to a marked appreciation of the precious metals.[1] The stable value of the total paper money in circulation fell to a small proportion of the money in circulation before the Revolution. The more rapid consumption of balances, the substitution of numéraire, and the decreased demand for money were not enough to offset the fall in the stable value of the currency; the country suffered from inadequate surplus of cash because it was losing confidence rapidly. It will be recalled from Chapter IV that after the maximum the premium on gold and silver exceeded the premium on the foreign exchanges. This was equivalent to a bounty on the importation of gold and silver. Nevertheless, it is doubtful whether importations of gold and silver, for the next few years at any rate, were of material importance. France, economically disorganized, possessed an insufficient amount of purchasing power to pay for appreciable importations of the precious metals. The demand for French exchange was limited. The fact that the scarcity remained apparent for several years — as will be seen — indicates that the supplies forthcoming from private hoards were inadequate.

A chart follows which compares the Assignats in circulation with their stable value. The latter variable represents the amounts in circulation reduced by the average values (monthly) of the local tables. Note the excess (over the pre-Revolutionary circulation) of the stable value of the currency in the first half of 1794. This apparent failure of the Assignat to depreciate in proportion to the increased issues was due to the maximum system, which resulted in a compulsory hoarding of Assignats and a high value for those disbursed. (In the early years of the recent war, the rate of depreciation did not keep up with the expansion of issues.)

---

[1] Bonn, in discussing similar conditions in post-war Germany, says that, considering the large hoards of cash and the price levels, the money in circulation was not excessive. M. J. Bonn, *Stabilisation of the Mark*, p. 40.

Note also that in 1795 depreciation proceeded more rapidly than in proportion to the increased issues.[1] The stable value of the currency had fallen to perhaps one-twentieth of the pre-Revolutionary circulation by the end of 1795 and the early months of 1796.[2] The marked decrease in the aggregate of monetary paper

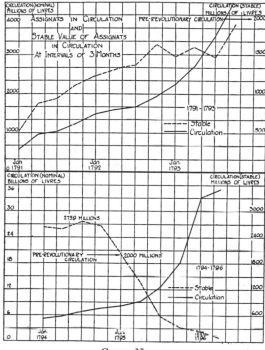

CHART NO. 22

resources (stable) was a severe handicap to the French people. The more rapid circulation of the paper money and the reappearance of some gold and silver remedied the situation to some extent. Contemporaries commented on the lack of money. The introduction of "au cours" payments, in increasing the demand for

[1] Russia had a similar experience recently, as did all countries with advanced depreciation. S. Katzellenbaum, *Russian Currency and Banking 1914-1924*, pp. 94-97.

[2] Compare the reduction in Germany recently. The gold value of the currency fell from 90 marks per capita in 1914 to 1 mark in November, 1923. J. Hirsch, *Die deutsche Währungsfrage*, pp. 17-18.

money in the last months of 1795 and in 1796, made the deficiency apparent.

The decrease in the stable value of a currency during a period of extreme depreciation, however, is not likely to be as great as is generally supposed because the paper money may maintain almost full value for certain public and private payments (debts and taxes, for example). The index numbers or other measures used in the reduction of the nominal values of the currency fail to take into account the value of the paper money for these payments. Keynes points out that the standard of living is reduced by the process of inflation, and, hence, less money is required.[1]

Is there a deficiency or scarcity of money? Karl Marx's contention that the supply of money is adjusted to the demand by automatic changes in the velocity of circulation, is not without truth.[2] But as Aftalion has recently observed, there are mechanical limitations to a very rapid increase in the velocity of circulation, and, hence, he prefers to explain the rapid changes in price levels independently of changes in either money or velocity of circulation.[3] The deficiency of money is genuine only in the sense (as Keynes observes) that people make the mistake of economising monetary balances too much;[4] or that the public is not content to accept money which is rapidly depreciating, and thus is unable to make necessary payments (a variant of Keynes' point); or, finally, there may be genuine deficiencies of a temporary nature because changes in rate of consumption of monetary balances are not adjusted rapidly enough to changes in the price level. But an increase in the value of the money or in the rate of disbursement of balances should follow.

As already noted, Rewbell's proposal in June, 1795 for a scale of depreciation for payments to the Government was based on the idea that prices increased in proportion to new issues. Every debtor or taxpayer was to pay one-quarter additional for each five hundred millions in circulation beyond the pre-Revolutionary circulation of two thousand millions at the time the contracts for

[1] J. M. Keynes, *op. cit.*, p. 44.
[2] K. Wicksell, *Vorlesungen*, Vol. II, p. 170.
[3] F. Aftalion, *Monnaie, Prix et Change*, pp. 198–199.
[4] J. M. Keynes, *op. cit.*, pp. 46–47.

land purchases were entered into or the taxes became due.[1] But more discriminating observers were aware that depreciation was proceeding more rapidly than in proportion to increases in the circulation. Prunélé expressed the opinion that prices had increased more than in proportion to the new issues because of the ease of counterfeiting, the loss of confidence in the security, the immoderate emissions, and, finally, the excessive consumption of commodities.[2] Savary informed the Convention in July that the depreciation had advanced more than in proportion to the increase in the circulation.[3] A report of October 16, emanating from four committees of the Convention, referred to the inadequate supplies of Assignats in the light of an unprecedented demand for money caused by the high level of prices.[4] The supporters of a new maximum recognized that prices had increased much beyond 10 times, although the circulation had increased but tenfold, and, therefore, recommended, as a compromise, a maximum of 10 times the prices of 1790.[5] Lebrun demonstrated on December 3, 1795 that 30 milliards of Assignats were equivalent to but 300 or 400 millions of silver.[6] On the same day Lafon-Ladébat told the Anciens that 6.4 milliards in February were equivalent to 1600 millions in real value, that the 7.6 milliards circulating in March were equivalent to 1200 millions in real values, the 13 milliards in June were equivalent to 260 millions, and that 20 milliards currently in circulation had a value of but 150 millions.[7]

Proposals to return to a metallic standard began to attract attention in the spring of 1795. Thus Gaston in May openly proposed a return to a metallic standard.[8] By November an official committee recommended measures for augmenting the supplies of precious metals.[9] In the hope of increasing the confidence in the Assignat, the Council of 500 determined in November on an early

[1] *Moniteur*, Vol. XXV, pp. 13–16.
[2] A. M. E. Prunélé, *Fortunes*, pp. 17–18.
[3] *Moniteur*, Vol. XXV, p. 236.
[4] *Ibid.*, Vol. XXVI, p. 219.
[5] *J. Déb. et Déc.*, Vol. LXXVI, pp. 506–507.
[6] *Ibid.*, Vol. LXXVII, pp. 178–179.
[7] *Moniteur*, Vol. XXVI, pp. 620–624.
[8] *Ibid.*, Vol. XXIV, p. 444.
[9] *J. Déb. et Déc.*, Vol. LXXVII, p. 234.

destruction of the Assignat plates.[1] In Dupont's opinion no more than 300 millions of numéraire were circulating in France in December, 1795.[2] The Committee of Five made some suggestions as to how to encourage the metallic circulation.[3] Evidently little numéraire circulated in Paris, for Lebrun, Commissioner of Finance, estimated that most of the 200 or 300 millions of numéraire in France circulated in the provinces.[4]

The rapid depreciation of the paper money had reduced the Government to an unenviable position, because the most important source of revenue (paper money) was yielding little. The Government resolved on heroic measures. In December the Directory submitted a proposal for a forced loan. The failure of this remedial measure is discussed in Chapter II.[5] Then it postponed payments on past obligations.[6] Forty millions of Assignats were the only assets available on January 13, 1796; the Government thereupon created a new species of paper money, the Rescription, which was to be employed for the payment of all outstanding obligations in stable currency of 150 livres or more.[7] On January 20 the Treasury issued a proclamation on the Rescriptions now ready for circulation: They were to be issued in denominations of from 1000 to 50 livres, to be receivable at all public offices, and were "to partially relieve the lack of numéraire".[8] The Minister of Finance was ordered on February 20 to calculate and arrange in order of urgency all the arrears up to February 18, but was to withhold payment for the present.[9] The first 30 millions of Rescriptions were used sparingly indeed.

But the Treasury remained empty. Camus suggested the discontinuance of the sales of land. Dubois-Crancé, emphasizing the lack of metals, proposed a tax in kind that was to yield 1500

1 *J. Déb. et Déc.*, Vol. LXXVIII, pp. 79–80.
2 *Moniteur*, Vol. XXVI, pp. 681–682.
3 See also C. M. A. De Valence, *Observations Addressées au Directoire Exécutif*, p. xvii; *Moniteur*, Vol. XXVI, p. 501.
4 *Ibid.*, p. 614.
5 See *Actes du Directoire Exécutif*, Vol. I, pp. 296–298.
6 *Recueil, Monnaie*, p. 405.
7 *Ibid.*, p. 402.
8 *J. Déb. et Déc.*, Vol. LXXX, pp. 121–122.
9 *Ibid.*, Vol. LXXXI, pp. 135–156.

millions of gold livres indispensable for the next campaign.[1] Many demanded that the Assignats be retired and exchanged for new Assignats stamped and reduced in quantities. The stamped Assignats, alone, were to retain the monetary function. The sponsors of this plan generally also emphasized the need of a "special" security for them.[2] The Committee of Finance of the Council of 500, however, adhered to a few hackneyed proposals: an elimination of speculation, renewed sales of land with provisions for rapid payment, vigorous measures for the collection of the Forced Loan and of back taxes, and "au cours" payments for many debts to the Government.[3] The Committee and its foremost critic, Dubois-Crancé, agreed as to the scarcity of numéraire. But Crancé criticized it for not recognizing the impracticability of "au cours" payments when the country was handicapped by a scarcity of money.[4]

Although the program of the Committee had already been accepted in part by the Legislature, the Directory, dissatisfied with the rate of progress, proposed on March 9 an issue of 600 millions of Mandats.[5] The plan of the Directory was not unlike the earlier proposals to stamp a limited number of the Assignats which were to be secured by designated lands. For the Assignats were to be exchanged for Mandats which were to be supported by a special security.[6] Seven days later the Legislature conceded to the Directory the privilege of issuing 2400 millions of Mandats. It was to employ 600 millions for the exchange of Assignats, 600 millions for current expenditures, and 1200 millions for future exigencies.[7] The Legislature bestowed the legal tender quality on the Rescriptions and Mandats and converted the Rescriptions into Promesses de Mandats.[8]

The Mandat never received the popular approval once enjoyed

---

[1] *J. Déb. et Déc.*, Vol. LXXXI, pp. 21–24.
[2] *Ibid.*, pp. 34–35, 53, 60–62, 72–76.
[3] *Moniteur*, Vol. XXVII, pp. 634–637.
[4] *Ibid.*, p. 640.
[5] *J. Déb. et Déc.*, Vol. LXXI, pp. 238–239.
[6] P. A. J. Taschereau on March 5 suggested the redemption of the Assignat by a new paper at 50 to 1. *Il en est Tems encore*, pp. 20–21.
[7] *Moniteur*, Vol. XXVIII, pp. 5–6.
[8] *Ibid.*, Vol. XXVIII, pp. 166–167, *Actes du Directoire Exécutif*, Vol. II, p. 51.

by the Assignat; the public refused to accept it from the very beginning.[1] As Schmidt well observes, by the exchange of the Assignat for Mandats at 30 to 1 when the Assignat was worth less than one-half of 1 per cent of its nominal value, the Government was placing a low value upon them.[2] Freedom of transactions in metals and "au cours" payments in private dealings were officially approved on July 23, a few months after the introduction of the Mandat.[3] On July 25, in the midst of this rapid depreciation, the Government ordered all buyers of land during the Mandat period to pay the fourth (and final) installment "au cours". Capon doubted whether the Mandat would survive the sixteen months allowed to complete the "au cours" payments; and he asserted that the gain to the Government would be negligible because the Mandats thus received would depreciate appreciably before their disbursement.[4] Early in August the Government attempted once more to collect its taxes "au cours."[5]

The stable value of the Assignat was probably no more than 100 million livres when the Mandat was introduced. The issue of Mandats, or, more properly, of Promesses de Mandats, did not begin until April and was not completed until September. The highest monetary value (stable) of the aggregate of Mandats was attained in the middle of September when, as a result of a speculative boom, the value of the Mandat increased from 2½ to 5 per cent, and the stable value of the Mandats increased to 120 million livres. On May 18 the Directory, in a message to the Council of 500, dwelt on the meagre returns to be expected from the Mandats, now depreciating rapidly. Excluding 65 millions, the current value at 340 to 1 of 23 milliards of Assignats in circulation, the Directory anticipated a yield of but 160 millions in stable values from the disbursement of the remaining 1600 millions of Mandats. The Directory assumed in these computations that the Mandats would retain an average value of 10 per cent in the course of their disburse-

---

[1] See *Réaction Thermidorienne*, Vol. III, pp. 128, 157, 198, 222, 227.
[2] A. Schmidt, *Paris pendant la Révolution*, Vol. III, p. 158.
[3] *Recueil, Monnaie*, p. 434.
[4] P. Capon, *Observation sur le Mode de Paiement de Quatrième Quart des Biens Nationaux*, p. 69.
[5] *Recueil, Monnaie*, p. 436.

ment. Eight hundred millions were required for the redemption of the Assignats at 30 to 1.[1] The Assignat, in the opinion of the Directory, was valued at but one-three hundred and fortieth of its face value; the Treasury was, therefore, in receiving the Assignat at 30 to 1, putting a valuation of about 9 per cent on the Mandat, and the 800 millions thus employed would yield but (say) 70 million livres. The authorities did not begin to redeem the Assignats until June.[2]

In June, 1796 the monetary supplies of the country included (1) 100 millions or less of Assignats (stable value), (2) 60 millions of depreciated Rescriptions, and (3) 500 millions of Mandats at an average value of 10 per cent, or 50 millions in stable values. The total of 156 millions — assuming that the Rescriptions depreciated at the rate of the Mandat — constituted the circulating media of the country, with the exception of the scanty supplies of gold and silver that had reappeared.[3] In October, 1795 the Government predicted that the Paris mint in December would have a capacity of 300,000 coins daily.[4] That these new 1 franc pieces circulated at a discount of 2 or 3 per cent as compared to the livre although they contained 1 per cent more of bullion, reflects the lack of faith in the Government.[5] The progress of the manufacture of these coins was very slow, as is evident from the many official complaints of delays in 1795–96.[6] The slowness of the reappearance of the precious metals is apparent if we consider that but 32 millions were coined in 2 years.[7]

The scarcity of money was evident in many ways. Falkner is mistaken in his opinion that by the Mandat period the metals

---

[1] Actes du Directoire Exécutif, Vol. II, p. 408. Wolff predicted in 1920 that the depreciation of the mark would not be so extreme as that of the Assignat, because gold and silver were available when the Assignats disappeared. J. Wolff, Valuta und Finanznot in Deutschland, pp. 69–70.

[2] The depreciation of the German mark was more extreme than that of the Assignat. On October 22, 1923, one gold mark was equivalent to 1 billion paper marks. League of Nations Memorandum on Currency, 1913–23, p. 37.

[3] F. D'Ivncrois (Histoire de l'Administration des Finances pendant l'Année 1796, 2d ed., pp. 92–93) estimated the total at 50 millions.

[4] J. Déb. et Déc., Vol. LXXVI, p. 100.

[5] Ibid., Vol. LXXXI, pp. 166–172.

[6] Actes du Directoire Exécutif, Vol. I, p. 429; Vol. II, p. 87; Vol. III, p. 220.

[7] Moniteur, Vol. XXVIII, p. 710.

had returned and filled all the channels of circulation. Nor can I agree with Marion who says that the Government had only to dissociate the Mandat from gold, *i.e.*, demonetise the Mandat and accept it only at its real value, to bring the metals back.[1]

The Government, in particular, suffered from the lack of numéraire: Saint-Cyr reported that the Army of the Rhin-et-Moselle, hampered by the dearth of metallic money, discontinued its spy work in the Campaign of 1796.[2] Because the farmers refused to accept paper money, the Army of the Rhine had to rely on requisitions once more. The meagre allowance of 600,000 livres of gold and silver in the spring of 1796 sufficed for the most pressing needs only.[3] Napoleon's successful campaigns in Italy in 1796 alone saved the Government from the detrimental effects of an absolute dearth of numéraire. The French representative in Italy wrote in May that they had received 35 millions in gold and silver from Italian sources.[4] But Napoleon, a year later, estimated the total at but 23 millions.[5] Napoleon was concerned with the problem of converting this money into funds in Paris; and he hired Balbi, a banker of Genoa, to solve that problem.[6] However, even Napoleon had been disturbed by the lack of metallic money. Of the 48,000 francs in gold with which he opened the campaign of 1796, only 25 per cent had been contributed by the Treasury.[7] Napoleon complained in May, 1796 that he had been unable to pay his soldiers, and that the Government had failed to keep its promise to remit 30,000 livres for the upkeep of the artillery. That 6 months of active campaigning had cost but 11 millions in cash, had been made possible, in Napoleon's opinion, by the energetic system of requisitions enforced. In 1797 Napoleon was forced to adopt questionable methods to obtain indispensable supplies of cash: Thus, by cajolery and coercion, he succeeded in

---

[1] M. Marion, *Histoire Financière*, Vol. II, pp. 379–380.
[2] G. Saint-Cyr, *Mémoires sur les Campagnes*, Vol. IV. Unable to check page.
[3] H. Bourdeau, *Les Armées du Rhin au Début du Directoire*, pp. 248–249.
[4] F. Bouvier, *Napoléon en Italie*, p. 607.
[5] *Correspondance de Napoléon Ier (1796–98)*, Vol. III, pp. 71, 96.
[6] F. Bouvier, *op. cit.*, p. 95.
[7] M. De Nervo, *Les Finances Françaises sous l'Ancienne Monarchie*, Vol. II, p. 281.

having a note for 22,500 livres accepted by an Italian banking house.[1]

The Directory issued a proclamation on February 3, 1796, authorizing postponement of payments for lands due in Assignats "au cours" or in numéraire, "because of the dearth of gold and silver and the lack of proportion existing between the real value of the Assignats and the needs of the circulation."[2] The Minister of Interior informed the Directory in March that the provisioning of Paris was in danger because of the failure to assemble 2.6 millions in numéraire.[3] In order to encourage the presentation of the precious metals for coinage the Government waived its "droit de fabrication".[4] The police reports often commented on the lack of numéraire.[5] Confronted with a complete loss of the precious metals, the Treasury closed its doors temporarily on August 26.[6] The imperative need of numéraire was one of the factors that helped to lure the Government into the disreputable contract with Dijon and Company.[7] The decree that authorized the demonetisation of the Mandats also conceded a discretionary authority to the public officials "to moderate taxes and surtaxes not acquitted".[8] The Government recognized only too well the difficulty of procuring numéraire.

The scarcity of numéraire was apparent in other ways also. Ollivier compared the interest rate in 1797 with that of 1788:[9]

	Per Cent	
	1788	1797
Bank paper discounted at (per month)....	½	1½
Commercial paper (per month)..........	¼	4 to 10
Mons de Piété (per year)...............	10	does not lend

He attributed these high rates to the scarcity of numéraire; and although we may recognize a confusion of capital and money, the

---

[1] *Correspondance de Napoléon Ier (1796-98)*, Vols. I and II. The first 2 volumes are replete with Napoleon's financial difficulties.

[2] *Moniteur*, Vol. XXVII, pp. 433-434.

[3] *Actes du Directoire Exécutif*, Vol. II, pp. 16-17.

[4] *Moniteur*, Vol. XXVIII, pp. 240-241.

[5] *Réaction Thermidorienne*, Vol. III, pp. 338, 388.

[6] *Ibid.*, p. 405.

[7] *Actes du Directoire Exécutif*, Vol. IV, pp. 443-444.

[8] *Moniteur*, Vol. XXVIII, p. 245.

[9] Ollivier, *Rentiers de l'État*, p. 4.

high rates probably were due in part to the shortage of precious metals.[1] The loans had to be made in metals, which were scarce. The creditor also took an additional risk in that the debtor might find trouble in procuring the metals for reimbursement. Metallic prices in 1795–97 remained consistently below the level of the pre-Revolutionary days. Foreigners often wondered at the cry of famine in the light of the low metallic prices in France. A dinner could be bought at one-third or one-half of the prices of 1788.[2] Taschereau had a premonition that the demonetisation of paper would be followed by a drop in the price level.[3] Pancoucke observed in September, 1795 that prices were considerably lower than in 1789.[4] A few months later, Lebrun, Commissioner of Finance, found in the low prices indubitable evidence of the scarcity of gold and silver.[5]

The more marked appreciation of gold and silver (as compared to the exchanges) and the relatively low metallic prices in France (as compared to the price level abroad) made possible large importations of gold and silver; but they were imported slowly. The Minister of Police complained to the Commissioners of the Directory of the continued hoarding of numéraire.[6] Mollien, a trusted financial advisor to Napoleon, referred to the general opinions of bankers and business men that much of the financial distress up to 1806 was caused by the scarcity of gold and silver.[7]

A contemporary described succinctly the diversified papers circulating from the period when the Assignat disappeared to that when a metallic standard functioned normally again: (1) "*Rescriptions*"; (2) "*Bons*," which were given to the heirs of the condemned and never possessed the legal tender quality; (3) copper coined in large amounts, but demonetised later; (4) "*Ordon-*

---

[1] Probably the most important cause of the high rates was the scarcity of circulating capital. Compare similar conditions in Germany and Austria in the recent post-stabilisation periods.

[2] See the police reports as reprinted by Aulard and Schmidt for numerous references to falling prices in the latter part of 1795, and in 1796.

[3] Taschereau, *Il En Est Tems Encore*, pp. 8–9.

[4] C. J. Pancoucke, *Nouveau Mémoire sur les Assignats*, pp. 4–6.

[5] *Moniteur*, Vol. XXVI, p. 614.

[6] *Recueil, Monnaie*, p. 491.

[7] N. Mollien, *Mémoires d'un Ministre du Trésor Public*, Vol. II, p. 15.

nances," which were delivered to contractors after September, 1796; (5) a paper, redeemable in specie, which was given to contractors in the last few months of the Assignat period.[1]

The Government described an even more heterogeneous collection of circulating media when it announced the renewal of land sales in November, 1796. Recognizing the dearth of numéraire, it demanded but one-half of the sales price in numéraire; the other half was acceptable in any of several forms of circulating media: "*Ordonnances des Ministres*" (for supplies), "*Bordereaux* (accounts) *de liquidation de la dette publique ou de la dette des émigrés,*" "*Bons de requisition ou de loterie,*" "*Ordonnances ou Bons de restitution ou d'indemnité des pertes occasionnés par la guerre,*" "*Inscriptions sur la Grande Livre*"— all of these were to be acceptable substitutes for numéraire up to one-half of the sales price.[2] The Government agreed in February, 1797 to accept the papers designated above up to nineteen-twentieths in payments due on the forced loan.[3]

Mollien described the conditions in 1799 as follows: "The false money (the Assignat) was replaced by the emission of 'pretended values' which could not fulfill the monetary function, because they fluctuated in value: *Cédules d'hypothèque* endorsed by the purchasers of lands, most of them insolvent; drafts on the Treasury without a definite maturity, the recovery of which was as uncertain as the maturity; liens on the *Rentes Foncières,* of which the state pretended to be proprietor, and of which it did not know the debtors; *Titres de compensation* by means of which the rentiers, deprived of payments due from the Government, could similarly free themselves or their friends from the payment of taxes."[4] In 1800 a sinking fund was created to retire the diverse certificates of indebtedness carrying neither a guarantee nor a date of maturity that the Treasury had emitted previously without measure.[5]

---

[1] F. D'Ivnerois, *op. cit.*, p. 93.

[2] *Documents Relatifs à la Vente des Biens Nationaux dans le District de Sens*, pp. cxiv–cxviii; *Documents Relatifs à la Vente des Biens Nationaux, Département d'Ille-et-Vilain*, pp. xxxvii–xxxviii.

[3] *J. Déb. et Déc.*, Vol. XCII, p. 348.

[4] Mollien, *op. cit.*, Vol. I, p. 213.

[5] *Ibid.*

The chaotic condition of the public finances persisted for several years. Barbé-Marbois presented a noteworthy paper in behalf of the Directory on December 20, 1796, which summarized the facts as to the receipts and expenses for the year IV (September, 1795 to September, 1796). The Treasury expended 3.5 billions in Assignats, 152 millions in Mandats, and but 5 millions in numéraire for subsistence. In addition to the customary paper money receipts, Marbois enumerated paper "au cours," receipts from the sales of silver, tangible wealth (furnishings and the like), jewels (15 millions), seizures (20 millions), foreign contributions (the estimate of 240 millions seems grossly exaggerated), sales of commodities and merchandise (60 millions), and requisitions.[1] These figures were supposedly for metallic receipts. The Treasury presented the semblance of a budget for the year V (1796-97). Three months before the end of that year, it announced receipts of 422 millions, almost wholly made up of taxes, and expenditures of 842 millions. The difficulty of procuring appreciable revenues was aggravated by the scarcity of the precious metals.[2]

Perhaps the most spectacular incident in the history of the paper money was the unprincipled manner in which the Government conspired to destroy it. The Government had, it will be remembered, peremptorily revised its contracts with the purchasers of lands in July 1796, and had demanded the last quarter due on the lands "au cours". Handicapped by the lack of numéraire, the authorities hoped that the Mandats remaining in circulation would soon be exhausted by tax and land payments "au cours". The speculators thought otherwise. The remarkable rise in the Mandat from 2 to 7 per cent that occurred in September, and that Falkner attributes to the stationary circulation, was brought about by the activities of the speculators.[3] This rise was a cause of justified consternation on the part of the Government because it feared that the result would be that the Mandats would remain in circulation for a long period of time. Debtors would be enabled to meet their obligations with a relatively small number

[1] Mollein, *op. cit.*, Vol. I, p. 217.
[2] *J. Déb. et Déc.*, Vol. XCVI, pp. 478-483.
[3] The various memoirs on the Dijon affair referred to below, give the detailed history of the period; also Aulard's Police reports are valuable.

of Mandats, and the resumption of metallic payments anxiously awaited by the Treasury, would be indefinitely postponed.[1]

At this juncture (October, 1796) Dijon and Co. entered into a contract with the Treasury which stipulated (1) that Dijon and Co. were to advance to the Government 2.5 millions in écus (silver) without interest; (2) that the Treasury was to provide Dijon and Co. with 100 millions in Mandats, which that organization was to throw on the market to reduce the value of the Mandat steadily, but imperceptibly; and finally (3) that Dijon and Co. were to collect these Mandats from public depositories, and were to pay the Government 1 per cent of the face value of the Mandats thus received. The plan worked well, and the Mandat gradually began to depreciate.[2]

These shameful negotiations of the Government for the destruction of its paper money — not to mention the right delegated to Dijon and Co. to reissue annulled Mandats — soon became public. The press bestowed a plentiful shower of invectives on the Government. The Government in turn attempted to save itself by censuring Dijon and Co. for alleged violations of contracts and subterfuge.[3]

It was so ignorant of its position that Dijon and Co. were able to appropriate 600 millions of Mandats in the possession of the Treasury in 40 departments, despite the fact that the Government did not believe that it possessed even 25 per cent of that amount. (A revision of the contract had conceded to Dijon and Co. the privilege of collecting all the Mandats in 40 departments.[4]) The former confederates of the Treasury were later able to prove that the Treasury had put no limitations on the amount of Mandats to be obtained from these 40 departments.[5] In issuing an order for the virtual demonetisation of the Mandats in February, 1797, the Government repudiated its contract, demanded payment for the first 100 millions of Mandats at 2½ per cent of their face value, and also claimed additional damages.[6] We need only

[1] Dijon et Cie., *Mémoire sur le Traité*, pp. 1-4.
[2] *Ibid.*, pp. 6-13.
[3] *J. Déb. et Déc.*, Vol. XCV, pp. 439-442; *Moniteur*, Vol. XXVIII, p. 709.
[4] H. N. M. Duveyrier, *Résumé du Cause pour la Compagnie Dijon*, pp. 33-39.
[5] Dijon et Cie., *Refléxions des Citoyens*, pp. 47-55.
[6] *Ibid.*

observe that the Government lost its suit to recover for these alleged peculations.

The Assignat depreciated rapidly, and gold and silver failed to appear quickly. The country, therefore, suffered from a serious deficiency of monetary supplies. Industry was hampered by falling prices and inadequate monetary supplies.[1] But the Government in particular suffered. The lack of circulating media aggravated the difficulties of obtaining revenues. In meeting its expenditures, the Treasury introduced a confusing variety of paper payments, and even resorted to acts of bankruptcy. A loss of effectiveness in military operations, as well as in the internal policies of the Government, resulted. The deficiencies of revenue were not wholly due to the scarcity of money; no doubt the continued weak administration in the collection of taxes was not a negligible factor.[2]

[1] C. Schmidt, *Essaie de Statistique Industrielle en l'An V, Commission de Recherche*, 1908. See especially, pp. 146–147 for comments on the low prices of 1796–97. But the entire document reflects the effects of the Revolution and of falling prices and inadequate monetary supplies.

[2] See G. Subercaseaux, *op. cit.*, pp. 312–314, for a discussion of the favoring conditions necessary for a return to normal monetary conditions.

CHAPTER X

FOREIGN EXCHANGES

1. EXPLANATIONS OF THE DEPRECIATION OF THE EXCHANGES

THE depreciation of the foreign exchanges was due partly to the emissions of Assignats. As the paper money depreciated at home, the exchanges, which represented the foreigner's estimation of the value of the Assignat — expressed in relation to the value of the gold or silver in the foreigner's monetary standard — fell. The internal and the external value of the livre, however, did not always move closely together, nor did the fluctuations in the external value necessarily follow those in the internal value. The exchanges were influenced by independent factors, which had little or no repercussion on the internal value of the paper money.[1] Nogaro says that the external value of the Assignat was approximately equivalent to the internal value because the gold market remained active in France during the paper money regime; for the price of foreign exchange was but the price of obtaining gold.[2] But there was a gold market during only part of the Revolution, and the prices of gold and silver, subject to independent forces, diverged widely from the prices of the exchanges and in varying directions. Consider, for example, the demonetisation of gold and the rigorous penalties for exportation during the Terror. More-

[1] Thus Ricardo conceded that a bounty to foreigners would depress the external value of the currency below the internal. *Letters to Malthus* (VII).

A. Halm says that internal prices are affected by the demand for exchange for purposes other than the purchase of commodities (*Geld und Kredit*, pp. 13–14.) But the adjustment of the internal price level may require a long period of time; and before it is consummated other disturbances may arise.

Von Mises takes an extreme position. As the exchanges depreciate, dispensable imports are given up or fall in price and dispensable goods are exported. An unfavorable balance of payments does not explain the divergence between the internal and external value of a depreciated currency. The exportation and importation of commodities are profitable only because of price differences. L. Mises, *op. cit.*, pp. 13–14.

[2] B. Nogaro, *La Monnaie*, pp. 190–191.

over, Nogaro's contention is based on the assumption that the prices of gold and silver were a reliable index of the internal value of the paper money.

As the exchanges depreciated, contemporaries attempted to account for the depreciation. A few attributed it to changes in the internal value of the paper money.[1] The Government has issued too much money, and its value has fallen in terms of commodities and silver, said Mosneron; and since the foreign exchanges merely enable us to exchange our money for the money of the foreigner, our exchanges are depreciated correspondingly.[2] Boislandry concluded that excessive issues of paper money had caused the initial depreciation of the exchanges.[3] Because the new issues had resulted in depreciated exchanges, Solignac proposed to change the mint ratio so as to encourage the importation of silver.[4] A speaker before the Society of 1789 predicted that the exchanges would depreciate as more Assignats were issued.[5]

Speculation was responsible for the depreciation, in the opinion of a notable minority of the contemporaries.[6] Clavière was the most pronounced adherent to this position. Without much effort, he said, our enemies can flood the market with French exchange.[7] He dismissed the notion that the depreciation might have been caused by a change in the balance of accounts; for the large favorable balance of the pre-Revolutionary days could not have disappeared as a result of the extraordinary export of "rentes" and of capital, and of the unusual importations of wheat; hence the depreciation was caused by the speculative activities of the bankers. In a letter to the Legislature, written in December, 1791, he explained that the speculators found in academic books

---

[1] C. Gomel (*Histoire Financière de la Législative et de la Convention*, Vol. II, p. 213), and M. Lefèbvre (*Application du Maximum Général dans le District de Bergues, Commission de Recherche*, 1913, p. 421) express similar views today.

[2] Arch. Parl., Vol. XL, pp. 497–498.

[3] F. L. Boislandry, *Observations sur les Dangers du Papier-Monnaie*, p. 3.

[4] M. F. Solignac, *Observations de M. Mirabeau Relativement à l'Essai sur la Proportion*, p. 11.

[5] *Assignats. Discours Prononcé le 3 Septembre 1790 à la Société de 1789*, pp. 9–11.

[6] Blanc and Jaurès have put much emphasis on this particular explanation. L. Blanc, *Histoire de la Révolution*, Vol. II, p. 629; J. Jaurès, *Histoire Socialiste de la Révolution*, Vol. III, p. 315.

[7] E. Clavière, *De la Conjuration contre les Finances*, pp. 10–16.

reasons for expecting the depreciation of the exchanges, and depreciation naturally followed the often repeated predictions of depreciation. In his opinion hundreds of bills not based on commercial transactions were the subject of speculative activities. Clavière also made the point that although the low exchanges encouraged exports, the increase of exports was limited by the powers of consumption of the French: the French exported only to pay for imports.[1]

Cambon, also, supported the contention that the speculators were responsible for the depreciation of the exchanges. He contributed to the popularization of a myth that Pitt had disbursed five millions sterling for the manipulation of the French exchanges.[2] Fabre reasoned in a similar manner.[3] In the course of the denunciation of the East India Company in 1793, Fabre asserted that one of its objects was to reduce the value of the livre abroad.[4]

To explain the depreciation by changes in the balance of accounts was to offer the most obvious and, perhaps, the most specious interpretation; it was the most usual one, certainly.[5] As early as 1789 Talleyrand explained the depreciation of the exchanges by the exportation of capital.[6] The Count of Custine referred to the last war and commented on the many bills drawn by the army on the Treasury.[7] The payment of interest on the Rentes Viagères (largely held by foreigners) and the sale of French securities by foreigners, attracted the attention of D'Allarde.[8] Bergasse pointed to the lack of faith of foreigners that led to the withdrawal of profits made in France.[9] The increased indebted-

---

[1] Arch. Parl., Vol. XXXV, pp. 495-496.

[2] *Ibid.*, Vol. LXI, pp. 443-444; *Moniteur*, Vol. XVII, p. 101.

[3] *Moniteur*, Vol. XVII, pp. 355-357; also A. Mathiez, *La Révolution et les Étrangers*, p. 148.

[4] A. Mathiez, *Procès de Corruption sous la Terreur. L'Affaire de la Compagnie des Indes*, p. 96.

[5] See H. Illig (*Das Geldwesen Frankreichs*, pp. 71, 77-78) for a recent explanation along these lines.

[6] *Choix de Rapports*, Vol. I, p. 427.

[7] Custine, *Réflexions sur la Proposition du Premier Ministre des Finances*, pp. 14-16.

[8] M. D'Allarde, *Motion sur un Nouveau Régime de Finances*, p. 29.

[9] M. Bergasse, *Lettre à ses Commetans*, p. 44.

ness caused by the excessive and costly purchases of metals abroad by the Government occurred to a few as the salient point.[1] Lavoisier attributed the depreciation of the exchanges to the withdrawal of the income earned in France by the absentees and to the repayment of loans to foreigners.[2] In order to improve the position of the livre abroad, Montesquiou and Condorcet both favored a foreign loan.[3] Deslandres, in 1792, opposed a tax on the profits of companies because he feared that such taxes would lead to a heavy withdrawal of capital and, hence, to a depreciation of the exchanges.[4] In his opinion the depreciation was caused by the recent investments of French bankers abroad in behalf of the Émigrés, and in their own behalf.[5]

Condorcet contributed an able analysis: "But in a foreign country the value of our metals compared to the Assignats can be greater than it is in France. It suffices that the difficulty of exporting bullion or of procuring money to be melted, keeps these three values, naturally equal, from attaining their levels. This difference can and ought to be reflected in the price of the exchanges, of which the depreciation ought not to be attributed alone to the disadvantage of the balance of commerce, nor to other causes which act in the same manner, as, for example, the exportation of the income of the Émigrés, the reimbursements to foreigners, or sales of our investments, or investments abroad, or purchases of bills of exchange."[6]

2. CAPITAL MOVEMENTS

Foreigners had little faith in the ultimate success of the Revolution; and moved by the insecurity, they withdrew large investments in France.[7] French investments were thrown on the markets, and Frenchmen invested abroad. Moreover the harsh treat-

---

[1] Montesquiou (P. V., Vol. LV, Motion of May 17, 1791), and "First Report of Committee of Money" (P. V., Vol. XXXVIII).
[2] M. Lavoisier, De l'État des Finances, pp. 65–66.
[3] M. Montesquiou, Lettre à M. Clavière, pp. 9–10.
[4] G. Deslandres, Du Crédit Public, pp. xxii–xxiv.
[5] Ibid., pp. 84–85.
[6] M. J. Condorcet, De la Disette du Numéraire, Oeuvres, Vol. II, pp. 535–536.
[7] An examination of J. P. Brissot's Point de Banqueroute reveals that foreigners began to lose confidence in France as early as 1787.

ment meted out to the Émigrés also encouraged the exportation of French capital. The vanguard of Émigrés took much cash with them, and they also converted their French possessions into foreign funds. The discriminatory legislation that became particularly obnoxious in the latter half of 1791, drove them out of the country in large numbers.[1] Discussions of sequestrations and, finally, the decision of February, 1792 to sequester the possessions of the Émigrés, forced them to employ every possible method of converting their wealth and income into foreign funds.[2] The rapid depreciation of the exchanges in the latter half of 1791 — a more rapid depreciation of the external than of the internal value of the paper money — is explained largely by the heavy exportations of capital.

How did the Émigrés get their funds out of the country? Many of them collected as much gold as possible, which they carried out of the country. Convictions of Émigrés and their accomplices for smuggling numéraire out of the country were frequent.[3] Many of the two hundred thousand or more Émigrés maintained relations through foreign banking houses (in London in particular) with banks in Paris, which remitted funds to them through their foreign correspondents.[4] As Mathiez has pointed out, most of the French banking houses were of foreign origin. During the Terror repeated exposures were made of illegal methods of transmitting funds abroad. The Government decreed a death penalty for all who attempted to invest their capital abroad.[5] Frequently, however, the French who migrated retained their investments in French industries.[6]

The French Government attempted to discourage the exportations of capital in every conceivable manner. As late as April,

[1] See *Recueil des Lois et Arrêts concernant les Émigrés.*
[2] The Government passed a decree in March, 1793 to the effect that all who were convicted of giving the Émigrés pecuniary aid were to be treated as their accomplices. (*Lois des Émigrés*, pp. 112 113.)
[3] *Histoire du Tribunal Révolutionnaire*, Vol. I, p. 267; Vol. IV, pp. 331, 343; also C. P. S., Vol. XVI, p. 301.
[4] *Correspondance Originale des Émigrés*, Vol. I, pp. 9–10; H. Forneron, *Histoire Générale des Émigrés*, Vol. I, p. 244.
[5] H. Forneron, *op. cit.*, p. 133.
[6] See C. Schmidt, *Un Projet de Nationalisation des Mines d'Anzin, Commission de Recherche*, 1910.

1794, for example, a decree was voted "that no wife or daughter of an emigrant shall be able to marry a foreigner, or leave the territory of France, or sell her possessions".[1] The Government was aware of the influence of capital movements on the exchanges. Attempts were made to borrow abroad in order to improve the position of the Assignat abroad.[2] The Treasury demanded an early repayment of the American loans for a similar reason. From 1790 to January, 1791 the American Government repaid 24.5 of the 31.1 million livres of debt outstanding. Amelot has given us a full report of these payments (effected through banking houses in Amsterdam and Antwerp), and I believe that report, reprinted in the Parliamentary Archives, is the only record of the details of the repayment.[3] It is noteworthy that in December, 1791, when the French exchanges in America were depreciated but 13 per cent, they were depreciated approximately 35 per cent in Bâle, Hamburg and London.[4] Perhaps that is an indication of the influence of the confidence of the American people in the Revolution, as well as of the favorable change in the balance of accounts, resulting from the repayment of these debts.

3. FOREIGN TRADE

The prohibition of the exportation of grains announced in September 7, 1788, was continued during the Revolution.[5] In the course of the Revolution the embargo was extended to many other products; in the early months of 1792 to barley, hay, corn, vegetables, wool, skins, hemp, and cotton; and in May, 1793, iron, copper and lead were added.[6] In the maximum period practically all the exports that had not hitherto been prohibited were added to the non-exportable list.[7] The Government instituted a thor-

---

[1] *J. Déb. et Déc.*, Vol. LVIII, p. 61.

[2] See *Cambridge Modern History*, Vol. II, pp. 296–297.

[3] Arch. Parl., Vol. XLIII, p. 707; E. Pariset, *Journal de Gouverneur Morris*, pp. 178–179.

[4] F. J. Turner, *Correspondence of French Ministers 1791–97*, Vol. II, p. 88.

[5] Arch. Parl., Vol. I, p. 358.

[6] *P. V. Ag. et Com.*, Vol. II, p. 665; *Rapports des Agents du Ministre de l'Intérieur*, p. 86; *Recueil, Commerce*, pp. 116, 149–150.

[7] *Recueil, Commerce*, pp. 155–156, 162; Arch. Parl., Vol. LXX, pp. 427–428.

ough system of control of exports: Americans, for example, who brought precious cargos of food products had to obtain a special dispensation in order to take out a cargo of luxuries.[1] Local governments often took the initiative in prohibiting the exportation of the few commodities that might still be exported legally.[2] But the hopes of the Committee of Public Safety to abolish export trade were frustrated; exports were indispensable as a means of paying for the necessary imports. After March, 1794 the Government allowed the export of all superfluous products. Johannot, in an important report submitted in January, 1795, emphasized the necessity of renewing normal trade relations with foreign countries.[3]

A reform of the tariff system was also attempted; in March, 1791, a thoroughly revised tariff with reasonably low rates was made effective. But as the Assignat depreciated, the tariff lost its effectiveness. In March, 1793 the Government prohibited the importation of velvets, cotton and woolen goods and hats from all countries, as well as all manufactured products from hostile countries.[4] On the other hand, in May, 1793, it removed the tariff on certain necessities: butter, lard, salted beef, arms, munitions and copper.[5] An effective maximum rendered the continued importation on private account of controlled commodities impossible, both because foreigners could not afford to sell at maximum prices and because products imported were subject to requisitions at maximum prices. The only alternative — as will be evident from a later section—was for the Government to import on its own behalf, directly or indirectly. In October, 1794 the Government renounced its right to requisition importations of raw materials,[6] and in November a similar ruling was made for all imports.[7] The duties on several necessities were reduced to one-tenth of the 1791 rate.[8] (The duties had been of little practical importance since 1793 be-

---

[1] *C. P. S.*, Vol. IX, pp. 600–601; see section VI of this chapter.
[2] *Ibid.*, p. 326.
[3] *Recueil, Commerce*, p. 227.
[4] *Ibid.*, pp. 45–48.
[5] *P. V. Ag. et Com.*, Vol. IV, pp. 83–85.
[6] *Recueil, Industrie*, p. 294.
[7] *Recueil, Commerce*, p. 225.
[8] *Ibid.*, p. 236.

cause of the depreciation.) Also, proprietors of funds abroad were allowed to use them to pay for essential imports.[1]

Necker estimated that the pre-Revolutionary imports were 230 millions, and the exports 300 millions, a favorable balance of 70 millions.[2] (Arnould put the favorable balance at 56 millions.[3]) In payment for this excess of 70 millions, Necker estimated that France received 45 millions in bullion, and that but 18 millions of the exports were necessary to pay for insurance, subsidies, shipping, reimbursements of capital, and the like.

Depreciation stimulated exports; for the external value of the currency fell more than the internal value. Exports and imports in 1792 increased to 240 and 210 per cent (respectively) of the pre-Revolutionary figures. The increase in foreign trade was more rapid than the increase in the price level.[4] Exports would no doubt have increased in a more spectacular manner but for the many prohibitions and the economic disorganization. The increase in imports was due to the increased demand for foreign subsistence and raw materials.

The year 1793, with war on every frontier, with the normal economic processes dangerously impaired, and with the system of maximum prices making the continuance of exports of controlled commodities at maximum prices suicidal for the country and the continuance of imports unprofitable to individuals, brought a veritable collapse of foreign trade. According to Peuchet's figures (based on a semi-official report), imports fell in 1793 to 100 per cent, and exports to 110 per cent of the pre-Revolutionary figures.[5] Of course, in quantities there was a material decline after 1788. During the second half of 1793 there was undoubtedly a more marked drop in exports, for the maximum system was more detrimental to the export than to the import trade. Peuchet's figures for tonnage movements in foreign trade are even more significant:

---

[1] *Recueil, Commerce*, pp. 230–231.

[2] J. Necker, *Treatise on the Administration of the Finances of France*, Vol. III, pp. 123, 133–135.

[3] M. Arnould, *De la Balance du Commerce*, Vol. I, p. 63. He estimated the exports for payments for invisible items as but 278 millions for the 73 years before the Revolution. *Ibid.*, Vol. II, pp. 167–168.

[4] *Moniteur*, Vol. XIX, pp. 163–164.

[5] M. J. Peuchet, *Statistique Elémentaire de la France*, p. 483.

the tonnage for 1789, 1792, and 1793 was 2.01, 1.44 and 0.40 million tons respectively.[1]

The scarcity of many necessities, wheat in particular, made the continuance of imports necessary for the success of the Revolution. Throughout the Revolution the Government supplemented private purchases abroad with official purchases. Every conceivable method of payment was used, since exports were virtually discontinued during the maximum period; the payment for imports was a troublesome problem. Purchases of food abroad continued to affect the exchanges adversely. An additional demand for a few millions of foreign bills each month for the payment of necessary supplies was not a negligible factor on the exchange market.[2] (An increase of a relatively small proportion of the total debit items for the year was likely to cause a material depression of the exchanges, because additional French exchange was not required.)

4. Control of the Gold and Silver Market

A debtor purchases a bill of exchange as a substitute for the actual shipment of gold to a foreign country; the transference of a draft of £100 sterling is equivalent to the shipment of £100 sterling of gold. At a relatively early period of the Revolution the Government prohibited the exportation of gold and silver bullion and of metallic money.[3] Because this prohibition made the shipment of gold and silver abroad more difficult (and hence more expensive), a further depreciation of the exchanges was the result. The internal value of gold and silver was depressed, but the value of foreign bills was increased. A depression of the internal value of gold and silver resulted (1) because more gold and silver were made available (as a result of the ban on exportations) for domestic purposes, and (2) because the legislation aiming at the suppression of the internal circulation of gold and silver, made the available sup-

---

[1] Quoted by E. Levasseur (*Histoire du Commerce de la France,* Vol. II, p. 18).

[2] Dubois-Crancé, who was closely conversant with conditions, estimated that obligations in excess of a milliard had been incurred in the purchase of subsistence abroad. T. Jung, *Dubois-Crancé,* Vol. II, p. 217; Pancoucke estimated the unsettled obligations in August, 1795 at 30 millions in numéraire (*Nouveau Mémoire,* pp. 41–44).

[3] *Recueil, Monnaie,* p. 115.

plies rather excessive. In one respect the prohibitory legislation was favorable; more gold and silver were put at the disposal of the Government for foreign remittances — the ban was effective for individuals only — and, therefore, the pressure on the exchanges was reduced. The remittance abroad by shipments of gold and silver constituted a method of pegging the exchanges.

The large purchases of metals abroad in the early years of the Revolution, both for the purpose of obtaining a circulating medium and for the purpose of hoarding a means of payment acceptable abroad, certainly contributed to the depreciation of the Assignats, internally and externally. They required costly outlays of Assignats, and hence led to internal, and, as a result, to external depreciation. Moreover, the pressure on the foreign exchange markets increased, and thus these purchases operating through changes in the balance of accounts, contributed to the decline of the exchanges.[1] The Caisse d'Escompte in a period of four months purchased 40 million livres of numéraire abroad.[2] The Government coined 90 million livres of gold and silver from January, 1791 to September, 1792.[3] With war impending early in 1792, the Treasury purchased large supplies of specie in Holland at an appreciable premium. In 1793 and 1794, when gold and silver were demonetised and when it became a misdemeanor to retain possession of them, the Government repaid an appreciable proportion of its foreign indebtedness by the exportation of the precious metals previously purchased at home and abroad. Not only precious metals, but also jewels, diamonds, and other possessions of the Émigrés were similarly employed.[4] In the spring of 1795 the private exportation of gold and silver was permitted once more.[5] The gold policy of the Government proved lucrative in the later

[1] Sir F. Baring (*Observations on the Establishment of the Bank of England*, pp. 29–30) comments on the importation of gold and silver by the French Government at this time.

[2] P. V., Vol. XX, "Report of May 29, 1790 on the Caisse." M. Marion (*Histoire Financière*, Vol. II, p. 375) says that from July, 1791 to April, 1793, 414 millions were disbursed by the Government for the purchase of 198 millions of metals abroad; M. J. Peuchet (*op. cit.*, p. 473) estimates that 120 millions were consumed in the purchase of metals in the years II and III (September, 1793–September, 1795).

[3] Arch. Parl., Vol. LIX, p. 200.

[4] J. Déb. et Déc., Vol. LVII, pp. 197–199.

[5] P. V. Ag. et Com., Vol. IV, pp. 736–737.

years, for gold purchased at relatively favorable terms in the early years of the Revolution was exported profitably later; profiting from the demonetisation, the Government was able to obtain gold and silver in France at a cheap price.

5. EXCHANGE CONTROL

The preceding section was concerned with one aspect of exchange control; namely, the control of gold movements. In this section I consider the attempts to control and manipulate foreign exchange markets in a more direct manner. Faced with the necessity of obtaining some means of payment for the indispensable imports, the Government seized the papers of all Parisian bankers in September, 1793. Within a few days, however, the Government repudiated this severe policy.[1] The results had evidently been disastrous. Then followed a sequestration of all foreign property in France.[2]

Cambon in December, 1793 dwelt upon the need of gold and silver for payments abroad.[3] However, the Treasury did not rely exclusively on its holdings of gold and silver. The banks throughout the Terror were forced to put at the disposal of the Government all foreign credits available. One coterie of bankers agreed to provide the Treasury with foreign credits of 60 million livres.[4] Gower, the former British Ambassador, evidently relying upon his spy system, said that the Government was able to pay for indispensable supplies by requisitioning 4½ millions of livres daily in gold and foreign bills.[5] Attempts to requisition supplies (wines in particular) were also made for the purpose of paying for imports. The Committee of Public Safety discussed in February, 1794 the terms of payment for all foreign credits appropriated by the Treasury.[6]

The Committee of Public Safety, concerned over the deprecia-

---

[1] *C. P. S.*, Vol. VI, pp. 352–353; P. Caron, *Paris pendant la Terreur*, Vol. I, p. 104.
[2] *Moniteur*, Vol. XVIII, pp. 13–14.
[3] *Ibid.*, p. 566.
[4] See A. Mathiez, "Encore le Banquier Perrégaux," *Annales Révolutionnaires*, Vol. XII, pp. 239–240; O. Browning, *op. cit.*, p. 358; *J.Déb. et Déc.*, Vol. LV, p. 202.
[5] O. Browning, *op. cit.*, pp. 358, 360.
[6] *C. P. S.*, Vol. XI, p. 247.

tion and fluctuation of the exchanges, decided that, since fluctuations were subversive of the morals of the people, the Treasury should set the daily course of the exchanges.[1] This measure, taken early in 1794, was an attempt to manipulate the exchanges and to cheat the owners of foreign bills. At the end of February the Government ordered the preparation of a list of all credits available in France on hostile countries, and also the utilization of diamonds, "mobilier," and the like in payment for the imported commodities.[2] To encourage the importation of necessities, the Government in July gave importers permission to pay for commodities imported from warring countries at one-third above the pre-Revolutionary par of exchange.[3] (Evidently control had been pushed vigorously.) I cannot say whether Cambon's announcement in October, 1794 of a payment of thirty millions on government indebtedness (largely to Swiss speculators) was an untruth, or whether the measure was taken to instill some confidence among foreigners in the Assignat.[4] An attempt to lift the sequestration of foreign possessions was unsuccessful in November, 1794 in spite of the support of Johannot, Cambon, and three of the most powerful committees of the Convention.[5] But early in January, 1795, the sequestration was lifted, and the Secret Committee of Six, installed to examine the correspondence with foreigners, was suppressed in February, 1795.[6]

The rapid depreciation of the exchanges in 1795 embarrassed the Government, and it reintroduced rigid control. The authorities frowned upon a growing practice of selling foreign bills that were certain to be protested, with the intention of earning the difference between the value of the Assignat on the day of the sale of the bill and on the day of repayment.[7] To discourage speculation in bills, the Government made the presentation of bills obligatory within three days of the date of maturity.[8] In October, 1795

[1] C. P. S., Vol. XI, pp. 5–6.
[2] J. Déb. et Déc., Vol. LVII, pp. 187–188, 197–199.
[3] Ibid., Vol. LXI, pp. 292–293.
[4] Ibid., Vol. LXII, pp. 7–12.
[5] Ibid., Vol. LXV, pp. 700–701.
[6] C. P. S., Vol. XX, pp. 237–238.
[7] Moniteur, Vol. XXVI, pp. 245–246.
[8] Receuil, Commerce, pp. 256–257.

the authorities ordered the Committees of Public Safety and Finances to appoint a committee which was to calculate and publish the course of exchange.[1] The Government, to prevent speculation in bills of exchange, introduced several regulatory measures.[2] In the same month (October) the authorities prohibited dealings in futures on the exchange market.[3] Sieveking of Hamburg, in a communication to the *Moniteur*, remarked that dealers in Hamburg were prepared to sell bills on Paris of a maturity of a few months at 25 per cent below the current rate for demand bills.[4]

6. Control of Trade

This section reveals in detail the minute control of foreign trade — and, perhaps, nationalization — undertaken by the Government, or more definitely, the Committee of Public Safety. A sample of these regulations is enlightening. Faced with the necessity of continuing to import certain necessities and of obtaining a means of payment for these imports, the Government assumed complete control of the export and import trade. Unless otherwise designated, the rulings are taken from the documents pertaining to the Committee of Public Safety (C. P. S.) compiled by Aulard.

August 29, 1793. The C. P. S. allows the Department of Côte d'Or 300,000 livres in numéraire for the purchase of horses in Switzerland at a maximum of 500 livres. The Committee bemoans the fact that foreigners accept only numéraire (VI, 192).

October 6, 1793. The War Department demands wheat and rice for 600,000 men for a period of 4 months; one-half is to be procured in Dantzig, Hamburg, and other places in the North; and the other half is to be procured in Sicily, Genoa, and other cities of Italy. The Minister of Interior has ordered 5,000,000 quintals of wheat from Italy; the Citizen Delamorre is commissioned to purchase wheat in Copenhagen up to a value of 100,000,000 livres in Assignats; the Citizen Abbema is to purchase wheat up to a

---

[1] *J. Déb. et Déc.*, Vol. LXXVI, p. 294.
[2] *Recueil, Commerce*, pp. 257–263.
[3] *J. Déb. et Déc.*, Vol. LXXVI, pp. 423–430.
[4] *Moniteur*, Vol. XXVII, p. 234.

value of 12,000,000 livres in Assignats from Northern ports; and an agent is dispatched to America to hasten the shipment of grain and flour contracted for in June. The Minister of Interior is in communication with a Prussian business man associated with a house in Paris, who is to import wheat from Poland. As soon as the ports of the Mediterranean are open, 40,000 quintals in Genoa will be available. Public contractors have agreed to provide the Government with 220,000 quintals of grain from the Archipelago and the Levant. The Committee awaits 10,000 barrels of flour, 50,000 quintals of wheat, and 25,000 quintals of rye from Desjardins, its agent in America. It generously agrees to accept 4 times the quantity contracted for (VII, 249–251).

October 8, 1793. Although the Army of Italy has had a credit established with the House of Tue at Genoa for the purchase of grains, wool, lead, and shirts, it seeks additional foreign exchange credits (VII, 317–318).

October 25, 1793. The C. P. S. reports the exhaustion of the supplies of live stock, but plans to import additional supplies from Switzerland and the interior of Germany. The Committee announces that the violation of the maximum is justified in the purchase of foreign supplies. The Compagnie Croze receives an advance of 500,000 livres for foreign purchases (VIII, 96).

November 15, 1793. The Committee agrees to pay for American products (potash, tobacco, oil, sugar, indigo, and the like) already shipped to Havre in gold and silver up to 6 million livres; it decides on the payment in metals to avert further depreciation of the exchanges (VIII, 429–430).

November 16, 1793. Fearing a famine in the South, the Government dispatches a few agents to the United States (VIII, 470–472).

November 17, 1793. Five millions in metals or foreign exchanges are put at the disposal of the War Department for the purchase of horses in Switzerland (VIII, 520).

November 18, 1793. The C. P. S. reaffirms that the Government does not require foreign imports; the country can obtain sufficient supplies from the soil (VIII, 540–541).

November 25, 1793. The Treasury is granted permission to pay bills drawn by agents of the Republic in Leghorn, Lisbon, Genoa, etc. (VIII, 689).

November 30, 1793. No merchandise can go out of the country without the explicit order of the Conseil Exécutif Provisoire, and the approval of the Committee of Public Safety (IX, p. 61).

December 13, 1793. The American ship *Lawrence* is seized; the Conseil Exécutif Provisoire orders the confiscation of the necessities in its cargo, which are to be paid for at their prices at the port of destination (IX, 370–371).

December 14, 1793. The C. P. S. orders the purchase of 40,000 guns at 30 livres each, to be paid for in gold, silver, foreign credits, or commodities (IX, 390–391).

December 16, 1793. The offer of a citizen of Switzerland to furnish the Government with 500,000 quintals of grains for the provisioning of the army is approved (IX, 435–436).

December 17, 1793. The Committee orders the Treasury to remit 800,000 *marcs d'argent de banque* at their present quotation to Chapeau-Rouge, a business man of Hamburg, in payment for the iron, hemp, masts, and wheat ordered by the Minister of Marines (IX, 460).

Preparations are made for the departure of Fauchet. He has 5 millions in gold in his possession for the purpose of purchasing grains (IX, 476).

The Committee orders the Minister of Foreign Affairs to buy as much powder as possible in Switzerland by the use of commercial or diplomatic methods (IX, 514).

December 23, 1793. The Conseil Exécutif Provisoire allows "pommade, poudre d'odeur, eau de senteur et rouge" to be exported to Basle (IX, 621).

February 4, 1794. The second 500,000 livres (metallic) are put at the disposal of Pourtalès for the payment of grains and guns to be purchased in Switzerland (X, 676).

February 5, 1794. The C. P. S. orders the Treasury to pay 300,-000 livres in Swiss Exchange and 100,000 livres in bills on Hamburg, to be charged to the account of the Minister of Foreign Affairs with the Treasury (X, 707–708).

February 8, 1794. The Committee orders the former Company

of Africa to renew relations with the Levant, Barbary States, and Turkey in order to buy grains and other necessities for the Committee of Subsistence (X, 771–773).

February 14, 1794. The Committee of Subsistence and Provisioning is delegated to purchase 2200 pairs of shoes and some copper from Switzerland, payment to be made in numéraire (XI, 143–144).

February 24, 1794. The Committee allows J. Levan to export 100,000 livres of luxuries on the condition that he import 100,000 livres of necessities. Luffert is permitted to export 1 million in gold to Switzerland (XI, 360).

Permission is granted to neutral ships that bring in necessities to take out luxuries (XI, 367).

February 28, 1794. For the assistance of purchasers from Switzerland, Germany, and Italy, the C. P. S. orders the establishment at "Saint-Louis" of an agency for the exploitation of all methods of payment (XI, 449–450).

The Committee puts 90,000 livres in numéraire at the disposal of the Committee of Subsistence and Provisioning to be used for the payment for cheese to be imported by Benjamin Fer (XI, 470–471).

March 5, 1794. Oil and soap are hereafter to be put on the free list even if they come from hostile countries (XI, 442).

March 6, 1794. The Committee approves a contract between business men and the Department of Gard; the syndicate of business men is to purchase 500,000 livres worth of grain in Genoa (XI, 572).

March 10, 1794. An American captain is permitted to leave Bordeaux with whiskey and wine on the promise to return within 7 months with wheat, flour, coffee, sugar, and the like (XI, 631).

March 11, 1794. The Convention approves the exportation of superfluous products and luxuries in the future (*Recueil, Commerce, p. 181*).

March 13, 1794. The C. P. S. decrees, in order to encourage agriculture and manufacturing and to effect payment for necessities imported, the encouragement of the exportation of superabundant commodities:

1. Bordeaux is to provide the Treasury with 20 millions in foreign exchange credits within a period of 9 months. The city is to export sugar valued at 4 millions, 4 millions in whiskey, 8 millions in coffee, 2 millions in manufactured commodities, and 2 millions in miscellaneous products.

2. Marseilles is to provide 15 millions by exporting 6 millions in copper, 3 millions in sugar, 2 millions in whiskey, 3 millions in wine, and 1 million in luxuries.

3. Nantes is to provide 10 millions for the Treasury by exporting 5 million livres in coffee, 3 millions in sugar, and 2 millions in wine.

4. Various miscellaneous products not necessary for the war may be exported, but the exporter must furnish the Treasury with two-thirds of the value of the exports in bills of exchange or necessities within 8 months of the date of exportation (XI, 670–672).

The Committee accepts the offer of a coterie of business men of Bordeaux to import 100,000 bushels of wheat at a cost of approximately 2 million livres, payment to be made in 3000 tons of merchandise, one-third in whiskey, one-half in fine wines, and one-sixth in luxuries (XI, 672–673).

March 20, 1794. The Government orders the remittance of 13 millions of numéraire to Switzerland for the purchase of provisions (XII, 67).

March 23, 1794. The Committee designates the commodities (luxuries) that may be exported freely, and the commodities (semi-luxuries) that may be exported on approval (XII, 170–171).

March 25, 1794. The representative with the Army of Italy announces the disbursement of 4 millions in numéraire for the provisioning of the Army of Italy (XII, 170–171).

April 15, 1794. The Committee orders the transference of 11 millions in gold and silver to 4 designated cities for the purchase of meat abroad (XII, 600).

April 16, 1794. The Committee of Subsistence and Provisioning is to select 2 firms in each of the principal cities abroad, which are to supervise and direct the activities of the French agents in their localities. The same Committee is to deposit 5 millions with a bank in Hamburg and a similar amount with a bank in Genoa, and is to economize its disbursements of metals (XII, 615–616).

April 19, 1794. Five millions in numéraire at the disposal of the Agent of the Committee of Subsistence and Provisioning in Marseilles are to be used for the provisioning of the South (XII, 683).

April 25, 1794. The Committee dispatches 2 agents to Constantinople and to the cities of the North to dispose of diamonds valued at several millions (XIII, 50–51).

May 1, 1794. The C. P. S. advises the Committee of Subsistence and Provisioning to keep merchants informed of the needs of foreigners, to effect other methods of coöperation, and to avoid needless competition (XIII, 181).

(After this day, frequent permits are given for the exportation of luxuries. I have attempted to make note of but few of these decrees.)

May 3, 1794. The Directory of the District of Marseilles is ordered to remit to the government agent in Africa 580,000 piastres of bills of exchange on Tunis, Leghorn, and Constantinople (XIII, 240).

May 19, 1794. The Committee entrusts Goyneau with a mission to the United States for the purpose of forming commercial liaisons; and also to exchange wines valued at 50,000 livres and 150,000 livres of credits (on the United States) for grains of an equal value (XIII, 715–716).

May 30, 1794. The free exportation of numéraire is to be conceded to any merchant who imports necessities as an agent of the Government when the contract for the importations stipulates payment in numéraire (XIV, 19–21).

June 14, 1794. Lubbert and Dumas of Hamburg are permitted to purchase 112 casks of wine in France with the proviso that they pay in bills of exchange (XIV, 317).

July 15, 1794. The authorities entrust the Committees of Provisioning and Commerce and Public Revenues with the responsibility for the exportation of merchandise of a value (metallic) of 30 million livres which is stored in public warehouses (XV, 21–22).

July 19, 1794. The Committee orders the transference of 4 millions of numéraire to Bourdon at Bâle for the purchase of horses (XV, 279–280).

The C. P. S. dispatches J. Combe to Boston to coöperate with J. Swan and Schwitzer (XV, 334).

July 24, 1794. The Committee exempts all but the 16 largest ports from the task of making a daily report of exports and imports (XV, 404).

July 26, 1794. The Government orders the Treasury to remit 1 million livres in numéraire (one-tenth in merchandise) to the Barbary States and the Levant for the purchase of grains (XV, 445).

August 20, 1794. The Treasury is authorized to remit (1) 300,000 to 800,000 *marcs banco* to Abbema et Fils; (2) 60,853 livres to S. Williams and Company of the United States; (3) 850,000 livres (metallic) to its agent in Brest, and 2.6 millions to its agent in Bordeaux, both to the credit of Swan and Schwitzer (XVI, 234).

August 30, 1794. The Treasury is to remit a bill for 888,000 livres to Abbema at Bâle (XVI, 417).

September 1, 1794. The Committee of Commerce and Provisioning is to purchase silver plate up to a maximum value of 2 million livres which is to be exported in payment for necessities (XVI, 452–453).

September 9, 1794. The Treasury is asked to pay Erhard, Borel et Frères 243,000 livres (value metallic) in Switzerland for copper and nails imported (XVI, 600).

September 11, 1794. The Treasury is to pay Pierpont of New York 132,055 livres with a bill on Hamburg for a cargo imported, the commercial agent of Nantes 100,000 livres (metallic value) for flour from America, and Higginson of the United States 332,211 livres for merchandise imported (XVI, 634–635).

September 14, 1794. Goddard and Co. are permitted to export merchandise of a value of 1 million livres from France; it is to be sold abroad in behalf of the Republic (XVI, 698).

September 15, 1794. The Committee approves a contract with Leveillard and Co. of Philadelphia for the purchase of wheat, flour, meats, salted fish, oil, potash, etc.; payments are to be made with bills on Hamburg (XVI, 723).

October 18, 1794. The Committee orders the Treasury to ship diamonds to the value of 2.2 millions to Durazzo of Genoa (XVII, 504).

November 10, 1794. Dealers are encouraged to export wines on the proviso that they import grains, rice, and vegetables (XVIII, 61–63).

November 17, 1794. The National Treasury is ordered to hold 15 millions in numéraire in readiness, which are to be employed without delay in the acquisition of grains in Genoa and the Barbary States (XVIII, 197).

November 24, 1794. The District of Grenoble receives 3 millions for the purchase of subsistence abroad (XVIII, 320).

December 6, 1794. Carnot informs the representative with the Army of the Alps and the Army of Italy that 18 million livres have been sent to these armies: 16 millions in numéraire and 2 millions in diamonds (XVIII, 556).

December 26, 1794. The Commune of Bayonne receives 6 millions in Assignats for the purchase of grains abroad. (Many similar bounties were given in this period.)

January 3, 1795. Requisitions of wines, whiskey, and other superfluous products for exportation are to be continued (XIX, 238).

January 7, 1795. The Treasury is to remit 10 million livres in Assignats to Lubbert and Dumas for the purchase of grains ordered by the Committee of Commerce (XIX, 326).

January 10, 1795. The Treasury is to remit 1,083,314 livres to Murray of the United States of America in payment for hemp and iron valued at 227,496 livres metallic (XIX, 394).

January 12, 1795. Bills of exchange received by Bordeaux, Nantes, and other cities are hereafter not to be subject to requisition.

The Committee of Provisioning is authorized to pay Clark of Boston for part of his cargo with bills on Hamburg, and the remainder in whiskey and wines (XIX, 431).

January 29, 1795. All agencies of commerce in foreign ports are suppressed (XIX, 743–744).

March 15, 1795. Three million livres to the credit of the Department of Gard are to be transferred to Andre, banker of Paris, in order that he be enabled to pay a bill drawn on him by agents commissioned by the Department of Gard to purchase subsistence in Genoa (XXI, 128).

May 5, 1795. Garnier and Co. of Paris make an agreement with the Commission of Provisioning to import in their behalf a million quintals of wheat at 25 livres a quintal, 400,000 quintals of hay at 18 livres a quintal, and 600,000 quintals of grass at 18 livres a quintal; they are to be paid in numéraire or in Assignats according to the course of exchange of Paris on Bâle (XXII, 688–690).

7. COMPREHENSIVE ANALYSIS

The foreign exchanges depreciated early; in particular, this holds for the London exchanges. It is worth noting (chart follows) that it is not a matter of indifference which exchange market is considered for the year 1790–91. Falkner's attempt to prove that external depreciation did not precede internal depreciation is subject to criticism on several grounds: (1) The selection of March 1790 as a base is arbitrary; (2) a generalization from the exchange values on Amsterdam is not safe — a comparison with the London exchanges would give a different result; (3) but most important, if Falkner should compare the foreign exchanges with the internal price level instead of with the price of gold and silver in 1790–91, he would find a marked lag in internal depreciation. The second chart, which brings together the comparatively strong exchange quotations of Bâle and the Treasury values, does not support Falkner's contention. Exchange quotations are difficult to procure for the Reign of Terror; fortunately, Bailleul published the exchange quotations on Bâle for that period.

The first of the charts on the exchanges extends only to the Reign of Terror; the second carries the study on to the end of the Assignat period. The continuance of the war with England resulted in a discontinuance of the London quotations. In the third chart I have substituted the Treasury figures of gold and silver. On this chart the variables are represented in multiples of their par values; i.e., a value of twenty for Bâle means that the exchanges on Bâle were at twenty times their par value, a premium

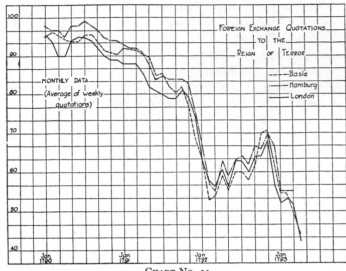

CHART NO. 23

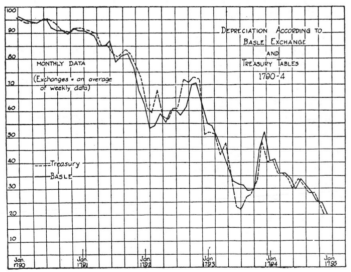

CHART NO. 24

of 1900 per cent. The difference between the premium on the metals and on the exchanges becomes apparent early in 1795, and, with few exceptions, the divergence becomes greater.[1] Gold and silver became more valuable in Paris than the right to procure gold and silver abroad, because the attempt of France to return

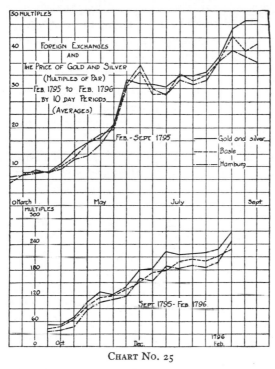

CHART NO. 25

to a metallic standard resulted in an abnormal demand for the metals; and, of course, the facilities for procuring the metals were not normal.

A perusal of the preceding charts will make it evident that until May, 1793, the exchanges depreciated more rapidly than in proportion to the increase in metallic prices. Moreover, before any increase in the prices of commodities had occurred, the exchanges

[1] The foreign exchangequotations are taken in the main from the weekly quotations in the *Moniteur;* some supplementary quotations come from Bailleul (in particular during the Terror).

had depreciated appreciably. To obtain an idea of the greater external depreciation of the Assignat (as compared with the internal depreciation), it is only necessary to refer to the chart in Chapter V (page 121) in which I compare the value of the Assignat according to the Treasury tables (prices of gold and silver), and according to the local tables (prices of gold and silver and of commodities). The depreciation from 1790 to May, 1793, as evident from the local tables, was not nearly as great as the depreciation according to the Treasury tables.

During the early period of the history of the Assignat, the discriminatory legislation against the precious metals had not yet become effective; hence the prices of gold and silver should give a rough index of the prices of foreign currencies. However, even in these early years the exchanges depreciated more rapidly than the Assignats depreciated in terms of gold and silver. The relatively high values of the local tables are explained by the failure of commodity prices to rise as rapidly as the prices of gold and silver. Why did the exchanges depreciate so rapidly, comparatively speaking? A lack of confidence among foreigners in the ultimate success of the Revolution is to be considered. But in my opinion, the fundamental factors that contributed to this more extreme depreciation of the exchanges in 1790–93 were, first and most important, the exportation of capital; second, the large purchases of wheat abroad; and third, the impediments put on the exportation of gold. Any increase in the price of foreign exchanges caused by the third factor may in part be interpreted as a movement of the gold points. If gold were available for export in large quantities, the scarcity of *devisen* and, hence, the depreciation of the exchanges would have been in part averted.

The movement of the exchanges during the period of maximum prices (May, 1793 to December, 1794) requires a more extended analysis. The prices of gold and silver were depressed during this period as the result of a vigorous public policy, and the values of the Assignat indicated by gold quotations remained considerably above the values given by the Treasury tables. I attributed (Chapter IV) the comparatively low values of the Treasury tables to the fact that they represented exchange quotations during this period, and the exchanges had fallen rapidly. A comparison of the Bâle quotations and the Treasury values does not fully confirm this conclusion, as the Bâle exchanges remained above the Treasury values. However, the excess of the prices of gold and silver over the Treasury values was twice as great as the excess of the Bâle quotations over the Treasury quotations, and the exchanges on Bâle were without doubt less unfavorable to France than any other exchanges during this period. Illig has collected the exchange quotations in Hamburg on Paris; and they correspond closely to the Treasury values.[1] Since the Treasury announced that its quotations during this period were based on the price of paper which it had to buy, it seems probable that they represented an average of the cost of purchasing foreign bills. It is also probable that the powerful Government was able to purchase foreign exchange at advantageous terms.

Whereas the Assignat appreciated in terms of gold and silver, and whereas commodity prices were reduced to a level little above that of 1790, the livre depreciated to 22 per cent of parity during this period, and the maximum was but 43 per cent. The exchange market was almost completely divorced from the gold market. What explains this disastrous external depreciation?

The miscreant who was convicted of attempting to take gold and silver out of the country during the Terror might well pay with his life. The risks involved made the exportation of gold and silver a costly process. In other words, the depreciation of the exchanges was in part a movement of the gold points. The failure of the exchanges on Bâle to fall more rapidly was probably in part due to the greater ease of smuggling gold into Bâle. The more effective such interference with gold exports becomes, the greater becomes the divergence between the price of gold and the price of foreign exchange.

Other factors, however, probably had even more weight. A greater relative loss of confidence among foreigners resulted from the doubtful future that France faced with wars raging both at home and abroad. Also, the attempts to manipulate the foreign

[1] S. V. Falkner, *Das Papiergeld der Französischen Revolution*, p. 38. (Falkner used Illig's figures.)

exchanges and to sequester foreign credits were harmful. Since the export trade was practically annihilated, France had to find some other means of payment for her imports. Many ingenious methods were devised to procure the necessary exchange, such as the appropriation of all foreign credits, borrowing from foreign banking houses and commercial firms, and the rationing of available supplies of foreign credits. Nevertheless, the change in the balance of accounts caused by the decline of the export trade did result in a decided pressure on the exchange markets. Great as the depreciation (external) was during this period, it doubtless would have been greater had it not been for the heroic measures enforced by the Committee of Public Safety.[1] The exchanges were pegged by the shipments of gold, silver, precious stones and superfluities, and by borrowing abroad. The Government took complete control of the exchange market.

In 1795, for the first time, the premium on the exchanges was less than the premium on gold and silver. (I doubt, however, whether the premium on the exchanges was less than the increase in internal prices for any extended period.) As the country attempted to return to a metallic régime, the value of the precious metals increased. With the stable value of the paper money falling rapidly the need for a circulating medium became so great that foreigners soon found that they could more profitably pay French debts by the shipment of gold — where gold could be safely taken out of the country — than by the purchase of French exchange. During this period the Assignat was more valuable in terms of commodities than in terms of gold and silver. (See chart comparing the local tables and the Treasury quotations in Chapter V.) The premium on the exchanges was less than the premium on gold and silver; but it is doubtful whether the exchange quotations were as much above the Treasury (gold and silver) figures as the local tables were. The decline in the internal value of the Assignat

---

[1] In the opinion of Mises, the prohibition of imports results in an increase in the purchasing power available for other commodities, and hence prices rise and exports decline. Hence these attempts to bring prices and exchanges down are unlikely to be successful. But Mises argues on the assumption that the exchanges do not depreciate as prices rise, and that the distribution of commodities at home is not controlled. L. Mises, *op. cit.*, pp. 20–26.

was not as great as its decline abroad; but the difference was reduced. The reduction in the difference may be attributed to the speculative reactions from the maximum in the commodity markets and the general scarcity of supplies. As I have indicated in Chapter VI, however, the increase in the internal price level was apparently higher in the early months of 1795 than the increase in the price of gold and silver.

In this chapter I am concerned with the factors that influenced the exchanges independently, and hence with an explanation of the deviations of the external depreciation from the internal depreciation. The part that internal depreciation played in inducing external depreciation, receives little space here. Rather, changes in the balance of accounts and in the gold points have been emphasised. That changes in the external depreciation often reacted on the internal depreciation, is apparent from what goes before. The costly purchase abroad of commodities by the Government absorbed large quantities of Assignats. The demand for foreign exchange was, therefore, inelastic; and as the exchanges depreciated, more Assignats were required. A loss of confidence abroad was also likely to affect confidence at home.

CHAPTER XI

SUMMARY

THE Assignats were primarily a financial resource: the nominal amounts issued, reduced to the values of 1790 by a table of depreciation, were equivalent to seven years of ordinary revenues of the pre-Revolutionary era. The Assignats were freely disbursed for the payment of the Government's obligations in the early years of the Revolution; and they contributed most of the public revenue during its later years. Taxation contributed a small but not negligible proportion of the total revenues, and, it is to be emphasized, this proportion varied, increasing notably in 1792. Both the value of the later issues of paper money, and the importance of tax receipts suffered because of the depreciation. Only the system of price control saved the country.

The maintenance of the land security unimpaired was an indispensable condition for the retention of confidence in the paper money. Regardless of the validity of the contention that the Assignat and a parcel of land of equivalent value were identities, the general assent to that contention did help to instill confidence in the paper money. The people believed in the land security; it transformed the Assignat in their eyes into circulating land. Redemption was a reality. Land sales absorbed large quantities of Assignats, especially in the first three years of their history. A more provident policy on the part of the Government — a policy of security, of protection to purchasers of lands instead of a policy of terrorism for all with visible means of wealth, and of non-interference with agricultural prices — would doubtless have resulted in larger and more profitable sales of lands. But, of course, the system of price control is justified on other grounds.

The undiscriminating use that has been made of the various measures of depreciation, is lamentable. We ought not only to be aware of the attributes of the measures we employ, but also to be wary of unconscious shifting from one measure to another. The movement of the prices of commodities provides us with the most acceptable of all measures, in spite of weighty theoretical objections. The prices of the foreign exchanges and of gold and silver were affected by independent forces, with the result that they deviated appreciably from the corresponding values for the prices of commodities. Insufficient attention has been given to the problem of the selection of the most appropriate measure of depreciation. The depreciation of the Assignat in 1790–1791 that writers discuss, probably did not occur. A premium on the price of gold and of the foreign exchanges emerged, but the general price level remained undisturbed.

The differences in the value of the paper money between the eighty or more departments of France constitute a curious aspect of the history of the Assignat.[1] The variations (according to the local tables of depreciation) attained large proportions: the Assignats in circulation were depreciated from 20 to 80 per cent in different places at the same time. Part of these differences was genuine: thus one section of the country suffered from the lack of supplies, especially of subsistence; in another section, the Assignat had to compete with metallic money; one section of the country had more confidence in the paper money than another. The wide discretion allowed to local officials in the construction of the tables, no doubt, accounted for some part of the vast differences: the apparent discrepancies were in part fictitious. The extremely high values of the Assignats circulating in Vendée, the center of the anti-Revolutionary agitation — in almost every month of the paper money period, an Assignat circulated there that apparently maintained a value above its value in any other department — a noticeable scattering (geographically) of extreme values (both high and low), the large proportion of the discrepancies accounted for by the two extreme deciles — all of these facts substantiate the contention that part of the difference was fictitious. A more gradual tapering off to extreme values might be expected if the

---

[1] A. Wagner observed similar discrepancies in Russia in the sixties of the last century; and Subercaseaux observes them in South American experiences. See G. Subercaseaux, *op. cit.*, pp. 204–205.

variations were wholly genuine. But real differences of large proportions were present; the wide scattering (geographically) of a few sporadic variables, which may be attributed to idiosyncrasies of construction, is not inconsistent with the presence of genuine differences evident from an examination of the geographical concentration of similar values.

The radical members of the Convention, refuting the doctrines of the Economists and borrowing largely from the doctrines of Rousseau, carried through a system of price control and rationing in May, 1793 that endured until December, 1794. The result of the system was that the purchasing power of the Assignats at the disposal of the Government was greatly increased. But with diminished supplies on the markets as a result of the Revolution and wars, as well as of this artificial reduction of the price levels, the buying propensities of the public had to be curbed. The public was prevented from disbursing all of its Assignats; hence it is an error to assume that the value of the Assignat increased during this period merely because maximum prices were depressed. Since a large proportion of all of the Assignats at the disposal of the public were hoarded, it is probably nearer to the truth to say that the value of the *average* Assignat fell. No writer on the Assignats has observed that the increase in the value of the Assignats during this period was in the main a fictitious one. No writer (with the possible exception of Marion and Hawtrey) has even considered the system of maximum prices in relation to the changes in the value of the Assignats; writers have merely observed and commented on the increased value of the Assignat, which was evident in the Treasury figures. Hawtrey advances further than other writers in pointing out that the price of gold was artificially depressed during this period, and, therefore, that the gain of the Assignat was not as great as appeared on the surface. But he is in error to concentrate his attention on the price of gold; and he unknowingly quotes the price of the exchanges and not of gold. Marion attempts to demonstrate that the Maximum was ineffective and hence could not affect the value of the Assignat.

The system of maximum prices encountered innumerable obstacles of an administrative nature; but at least for one year of its existence — notably during the Terror — the maximum was tolerably effective in spite of many violations. The system prevented the farmers from profiting from the curtailed supplies at the expense of the Government and the residents of the cities. The benefits derived by the Government and the urban elements by the increased purchasing power of the Assignats expended, were, without doubt, in part offset by the reduced supplies sent to the markets by the farmers. At any rate, the system enabled the Government to issue additional supplies of paper money without paying the penalty of higher prices, and thus enabled the Government to support fourteen armies, as well as Paris.

Depreciation cannot be understood without a consideration of the many forces at work. The condition of the subsistence market was of fundamental significance. Periods of scarcity were accompanied by depreciation. With the fear of starvation ever present, any deficiency in the normal supplies might cause a wholesale dumping of Assignats. Periods of inadequate subsistence synchronized closely with periods of depreciation.

The Revolution was a period of curtailed production, and, therefore, of reduced supplies. Not only did the Revolution witness increased issues of paper money, but it was accompanied also by a reduced demand for money. The latter factor in itself would have caused a very large fall in the value of the livre. Especially during the latter part of the Revolution, when the cumulative effects of the Revolution, of the extensive warfare, and of maximum prices began to be felt, are the reduced supplies to be considered. An explanation of depreciation without a consideration of the curtailment of production and circulation of products, is of doubtful value. Although the demand for money decreased during the Revolution, in at least one direction the demand increased. Speculation was rampant, which tended to keep prices down when no turnover of commodities and bills was involved.

Gold and silver were in circulation in varying amounts during the Revolution. Before the terrorist policies were successfully enforced, the Assignats had to compete with gold and silver to an appreciable extent. With the weakening of these policies, and finally with the repeal of the discriminatory legislation against gold and silver, the metals offered renewed competition to the Assignats. No final significance is to be attached to the statistics of paper money in circulation so long as an unknown quantity of gold and silver circulated in addition to the paper money.

Four factors that influenced the value of the paper money have been outlined above, viz., the land security, the state of the subsistence market, the supplies of commodities, and the competition of gold and silver. But I considered several other factors in Chapters VII and VIII: political, military and financial conditions, public discussions of depreciation, demonetisation practices (including "au cours" payments with its increased demands on the currency and the loss of confidence resulting from an official recognition of depreciation), and counterfeiting.

Three problems that owed their origin to the introduction of Assignats have been discussed — the problem of coping with depreciated exchanges, of adjusting creditor-debtor relations after and during the period of extreme depreciation, and of bringing back gold and silver. The movement of the exchanges, however, was not exclusively an effect of the issues of the Assignats; for such factors as capital movements, public control of gold movements, trade and the exchanges, and the inelastic demand for necessities on the part of the Government, all had independent effects. Of much interest today are the attempts of the Government to support the exchanges: control of imports and exports, the confiscation of all foreign credits, payment abroad with gold, silver and precious stones instead of by the purchase of foreign exchange, borrowing from foreign banks, payment abroad in Assignats, and requisitioning of luxuries for export purposes.

The Assignats were replaced first by gold and silver, then by the Mandats, and finally by gold and silver again. The attempt of the French Government to revise the contracts made during the period of paper money, forms a fascinating chapter in paper money history. Two problems were involved: first, the Government had to prevent attempts (during the periods of rapid depreciation) to repay in a worthless paper money for debts contracted in a more valuable money; and, second, it had to save debtors who had incurred obligations during the paper money régime from the unfair demands for metallic reimbursements. Payments to the Government, farm leases and the like also had to be revised.

The third problem was how to return to a metallic standard. A protracted period of hardships resulted from the failure of the precious metals to return from abroad and from private hoards as quickly as was expected. The stable value of the paper money fell to approximately one hundred million livres at the end of 1795. The more rapid consumption of monetary balances, the partial return of gold and silver, and a reduced demand for money scarcely offset this reduction of the pre-Revolutionary circulating media by 95 per cent. Prices fell; the Government found it difficult to collect its revenues; and a heterogeneous collection of new paper substitutes appeared.

BIBLIOGRAPHY

I. DOCUMENTS AND REPRINTS

Aside from the newspapers, parliamentary reports and the like, four valuable collections of documents relative to the French Revolution exist:

1. The Documents inédits sur l'Histoire de la Révolution Française include, for example, the notable collection of acts, letters, circulars, and the like of the Comité du Salut public. Aulard has recently issued the twenty-sixth volume of this particular collection.

2. The Documents inédits sur l'Histoire économique de la Révolution Française owe their origin to Jaurès. These documents contain the local legislation, transactions and the like pertaining to subsistence and land. But many other miscellaneous works are included.

3. The Publications of the Commission de Recherche include many valuable documents primarily on economic questions: The collection of laws, circulars, notes, and the like pertaining to money, commerce, industry, rural economy; the surveys of prices and industrial conditions undertaken by the Comité du Salut public — these are a few of the notable documents republished by the editors of this annual volume.

4. The Collection de Documents relatifs à l'Histoire de Paris pendant la Révolution Française contains such valuable material as the Cahiers of Paris, the laws of the Commune of Paris, and the Police Reports of Paris.

Archives Nationales. Conseil de Commerce et Bureau du Commerce, 1700–1791.

Inventaire analytique des Procès-Verbaux. Paris, 1900.

Archives parlémentaires de 1787 à 1860. Recueil complet des Débats législatifs et politiques des Chambres françaises (1787–1793). Première Série (1787 à 1799). 82 Vols. 2d Ed. Paris, 1879–1914.

BUCHEZ, P. J. B. et ROUX, P. C. Histoire parlémentaire de la Révolution Française. 40 Vols. Paris, 1834–1838.

Collection de Documents inédits sur l'Histoire de France.

1. Correspondance générale de Carnot. Publiée par E. Charavay. 4 Vols. Paris, 1892–1907.

2. Recueil des Actes du Directoire exécutif (Procès-Verbaux, Arrêtés, Instructions, Lettres et Actes Divers). Publié par A. Debidour. 4 Vols. Paris, 1910–1917.

3. Recueil des Actes du Comité de Salut public avec la Correspondance officielle des Représentants en Mission et le Registre du Conseil exécutif provisoire. Publié par F. A. Aulard. 26 Vols. Paris, 1889–1923.

Collection de Documents relatifs à l'Histoire de Paris pendant la Révolution Française.

1. Actes de la Commune de Paris pendant la Révolution. 1st Series, 7 Vols.; 2d Series, 8 Vols. Publiées par S. Lacroix. Paris, 1894–1914.

2. La Société des Jacobins. Par A. Aulard. 6 Vols. Paris, 1889.

3. L'État de Paris en 1789. Par H. Monin. Paris, 1889.

4. Les Élections et les Cahiers de Paris en 1789: Recueillis par C. L. Chassin. 4 Vols. Paris, 1888–1889.

5. Paris pendant la Réaction thermidorienne et sous le Directoire. Publié par A. Aulard. 5 Vols. Paris, 1898–1902.

Collection de Documents inédits sur l'Histoire économique de la Révolution Française.

1. Correspondance du Ministre de l'Intérieur (16 Avril–14 Octobre, 1792). Publiée par A. Tuetey. Paris, 1917.

2. Département des Bouches-du-Rhône. Documents relatifs à la Vente des Biens nationaux. Publiés par P. Moulin. 4 Vols. Marseilles, 1908–1911.

3. Département de la Gironde. Documents relatifs à la Vente des Biens nationaux. Publiés par M. Marion, J. Benzacar et Caudrillier. 2 Vols. Bordeaux, 1911.

4. Département de la Haute-Garonne. Documents relatifs à la Vente des Biens nationaux. District de Toulouse. Publiés par H. Martin. Toulouse, 1916.

5. Département de la Haute-Garonne. Le Comité des Subsistances de Toulouse. Correspondance et Délibérations. Publiés par J. Adher. Toulouse, 1912.

6. Département de la Haute-Marne. Les Subsistances dans le District de Chaumont. Publiés par C. Lorain. 2 Vols. Chaumont, 1911.

7. Département d'Ille-et-Vilain. Documents relatifs à la Vente des Biens nationaux. Publiés par A. Guillon et A. Rebillon. Rennes, 1911.

8. Département du Nord. Documents relatifs à l'Histoire des Subsistances dans le District de Bergues. Publiés par G. Lefebvre. 2 Vols. Lille, 1914–1921.

9. Département du Rhône. Documents relatifs à la Vente des Biens nationaux. Publiés par S. Charléty. Lyon, 1906.

10. Département de Seine-et-Oise. Les Subsistances dans le District de Versailles de 1788 à l'An V. Publiés par A. Defrèsne et F. Évard. 2 Vols. Rennes, 1921–1922.

11. Département des Vosges. Documents relatifs à la Vente des Biens nationaux. District de Remiremont. Publiés par L. Schwab. Épinal, 1913.

12. Département des Vosges. Documents relatifs à la Vente des Biens nationaux. District d'Épinal. Publiés par L. Schwab. Épinal, 1911.

13. Département de l'Yonne. Documents relatifs à la Vente des Biens nationaux dans le District de Sens. Publiés par C. Porée. 2 Vols. Auxerre, 1912.

14. Procès-Verbaux des Comités d'Agriculture et de Commerce de la

Constituante, de la Législative et de la Convention. Publiés par F. Gerbaux et C. Schmidt. 4 Vols. Paris, 1906–1910.
15. Procès-Verbaux du Comité des Finances de l'Assemblée constituante. Publiés par C. Bloch. Rennes, 1922.
16. Rapports du Comité de Mendicité de la Constituante. Publiés par C. Bloch et A. Tuetey. Paris, 1911.

Commission de Recherche et de Publication de Documents relatifs à la Vie économique de la Révolution.
1. Application du Maximum Général dans le District de Bergues. Par M. G. Lefebvre. 1913, 415–446.
2. Comité des Subsistances de Meulan et l'Approvisionnement de Paris. Par P. Caron et L. Raulet. 1907, 24–60.
3. Commerce Lyonnais et la Dépréciation des Assignats. Par P. Caron. 1913, 190–209.
4. Conséquences du Maximum pour l'Agriculture. Par P. Caron. 1908, 217–221.
5. Enquête du Comité de Salut Public sur le Draperie en l'An III. Par L. M. Schwab. 1913, 371–389.
6. Enquête sur la Récolte de 1792. Par P. Caron. 1915, 161–184.
7. Enquête sur les Prix après la Suppression du Maximum. Par P. Caron. 1910, 1–134, 303–412.
8. Essai de Statistique industrielle en l'An V. Par C. Schmidt. 1908, 11–205.
9. Instructions, Législation et Recueil des principaux Textes législatifs et administratifs sur le Commerce des Céréales de 1788 à l'An V. Par P. Caron. 1906, 104–320.
10. Instructions etc. concernant le Commerce de 1788 à l'An XI. Par C. Schmidt. 1912, 1–342.
11. Instructions etc. concernant l'Économie Rurale de 1788 à l'An VIII. Par G. Bourgin. 1907, 260–431.
12. Instructions etc. concernant l'Industrie de 1788 à l'An XI. Par C. Schmidt. 1909, 229–452.
13. Instructions etc. concernant la Monnaie et le Papier-Monnaie de 1789 à l'An XI. Par C. Bloch. 1911. (Entire.)
14. Mémoire du Conseil général du Département du Nord sur les Assignats. (1792.) Par P. Caron. 1908, 206–212.
15. La Préparation d'un Recueil de Documents sur les Subsistances pendant la Révolution. Par P. Caron. 1913, 395–414.
16. Oeuvre de la Municipalité de Toul pour assurer les Subsistances. Par M. Albert. 1913, 447–468.
17. Projet de Nationalisation des Mines d'Anzin en 1792. Par C. Schmidt. 1910, 225–243.
18. Rapports de Grivel et Siret sur les Subsistances et le Maximum. Par P. Caron. 1907, 67–231.
19. Revendications économiques et sociales des Assemblées primaires de Juillet, 1793. Par C. Reffatèrre. 1906, 321–380.
20. Statistiques révolutionnaires. L'Enquête de Delessart et de Roland. Par J. Bourgin. 1910, 244–302.

21. Subsistances en Céréales dans le Département de l'Eure de 1788 à l'An V. Par F. Évard. 1909, 1–96.

22. Subsistances à Reims pendant la Révolution. Par M. Laurent. 1913, 469–481.

23. Tableaux de Dépréciation du Papier-Monnaie. Réédités avec une Introduction. Par P. Caron. Paris, 1909.

24. Valeur et le Paiement des Biens nationaux dans les Vosges. Par L. Schmidt. 1913, 346–351.

25. Vérification des Caisses patriotiques. Par C. Bloch. 1910, 134–197.

Choix de Rapports, Opinions et Discours prononcés à la Tribune nationale depuis 1789 jusqu'à ce jour. 16 Vols. (1789–1798). Paris, 1818–1821.

Débats de la Convention nationale. Édité par Léon Thiessé. 6 Vols. Paris, 1828.

Instructions sur le Tableau général du Maximum. Paris, 1794.

Journal des Débats et des Décrets. Vols. 56–79 and 92–103 (1794–1795 and 1796–1797). Paris, 1794, 1795, 1796, 1797.

Journal politique national. 1789–1790. Publié par M. Salomon à Cambrai. Vol. I. Paris, 1789–1790.

Livre rouge. Paris, 1790.

Loi et Résolutions complettes sur les Transactions entre Particuliers contractées avant et depuis la Dépréciation du Papier-Monnaie. Paris, 1797.

MERCIER, L. S. Le nouveau Paris. 6 Vols. Brunswick, 1800.

Le Moniteur, Réimpression de l'Ancien. (Mai 1789–Novembre 1799.) Vols. 1–31. (1789–March 1797.) Paris, 1892.

Papiers de Barthélemy, Ambassadeur de France en Suisse, 1792–1797. Publiés sous les Auspices de la Commission des Archives diplomatiques. Par M. Jean Kaulek. 6 Vols. Paris, 1886.

Patriote François, Le. 7 Vols. July–December 1789. Édité par Brissot. Paris, 1789.

Procès-Verbaux des Signes charactéristiques auxquels On peut reconnoitre la Falsification des Assignats de 2,000, de 500 et de 200 livres. Le Couteulx, Gatteaux, Ilidot, Ferrier, Amelot. Paris, 1792.

Procès-Verbal de L'Assemblée nationale. Troisième Livraison. 45 Vols. 1789–February 1791. Paris, 1789–1791.

Procès-Verbal de l'Assemblée nationale. Douzième Livraison. Vols. 46–75. February 1791–September 1791. Paris, 1791.

Rapport et Projet du Décret fait et présenté à l'Assemblée nationale, au nom du Comité de l'Ordinaire des Finances sur la Suppression des Payeurs et Controleurs des Rentes établis à Paris. Par P. P. Bargnoux. Paris, 1792.

Rapport des Commissaires du District des Prémontrés. Paris, 1790.

Rapport des Plans et Projets présentés au Comité des Finances. Paris, 1789.

Rapport fait à l'Assemblée nationale par M. Ramel, Membre du Comité de Liquidation sur le Remboursement à faire du premier Cinquième des Capitaux de l'Emprunt fait à Gênes en 1785. 4 Février, 1792. Paris, 1792.

Rapport présenté à l'Assemblée nationale, au nom des Comités de l'Ordinaire et de l'Extraordinaire des Finances sur le Compte rendu par M. De Narbonne, Ministre de la Guerre. Paris, 1792.

Rapport sur la Banque de M. Pottin Vauvineux, fait au nom des Comités de l'Ordinaire et de l'Extraordinaire des Finances réunis. Le 24 Mars, 1792. Paris, 1792.

Recueil des Documents d'Ordre économique. Département de l'Orne. Vol. 1. Compilé par F. Mourlot. Alençon, 1907.

Révolution de Paris. Publiés par le Sieur Prudhomme. Vols. 1-2. Paris, 1789-1790.

Les Représentants du Peuple en Mission près les Armées, 1791-1794. Publié par Bonnal de Ganges. 4 Vols. Paris, 1898-1899.

SCHMIDT, A. Tableaux de la Révolution Française. 3 Vols. Leipzig, 1867.

Select Documents Illustrative of the History of the French Revolution. Edited by L. G. W. Legg. 2 Vols. Oxford, 1905.

TAILLANDIER, A. H. et MONGALVY, S. C. T. Recueil général des Lois et Arrêts concernant les Émigrés. Volume 1. Paris, 1825.

Third Report of the Committee of Secrecy on the outstanding demands of the Bank of England, April 21, 1797. Reports of the Committees of the House of Commons, Vol. II.

WALLON, H. Histoire du Tribunal révolutionnaire de Paris avec le Journal de ses Actes. 6 Vols. Paris, 1880-1882.

II. PAMPHLETS

Analyse de l'Ouvrage de M. Mirabeau sur la Constitution monétaire. Paris, 1791.

ANONYMOUS.

1. Appel à l'Honneur ou les Remboursements en Assignats. Paris, 1795 (?).

2. Courtes Réflexions sur l'Émission de près de deux Milliards d'Assignats-Monnaie. 1790.

3. Des Billets de l'État et du Profit qu'On en pourrait tirer pour le Service de la Finance. 1789.

4. L'État libéré et l'Impôt diminué. 1789.

5. Impossibilité de la Banqueroute. 1789.

6. La Fameuse Semaine, ou le Peuple de Paris Sept Fois heureux. Paris, 1790.

7. La Papillotte. 1790.

8. Lettre d'un Anglois à un François. Qu'est-ce que la Papier-Monnaie?

9. Le Sage Citoyen qui offre au Gouvernment le Moyen le plus simple et le plus facile pour remplir, le déficit des Finances, etc. En France, 1788.

10. Moyen de faire reparoître le Numéraire dans Paris. 1790.

11. Observations d'un Rentier viager. 1796?

12. Observations nécessaires sur la Partie du Mémoire de Finances relatifs au Subsides Qu'exige le Déficit de 1790.

13. Oh! Sauvons la France puisqu'On le peut encore. 1794 ou 1795.

14. Opinion et Profit de Décret sur les Assignats. Paris, 1792.

15. Opinion sur les Assignats et Proposition d'un autre Mode de Libération. Lille, 1790.

16. Parallèle entre les Effets de la nouvelle Émission d'Assignats et les Billets de Caisse nationale. 1790.

17. Projet pour l'Établissement d'une Caisse d'Escompte à Bordeaux. Bordeaux, 1790.

18. Prompte Liquidation de toutes les Dettes de l'État, avantageuse au Roi et aux Particuliers. 1789 (?).

19. Réflexions d'un Citoyen Jaloux. 1792.

20. Réflexions sur les Assignats-Monnaie. Paris, 1790.

21. Réflexions sur les Moyens de payer la Dette qu'On veut appeller la Dette nationale. Bruxelles, 1791.

22. Supplément aux Observations sur les Finances et sur les Assignats. 1792.

23. Suppression des Écus et des Louis d'Or. 1790 (?).

24. Sur l'Intérêt des Assignats-Monnaie. Paris, 1790.

ASSIGNATS, Discours prononcé le 3 Septembre 1790, à la Société de 1789. Paris, 1790.

BAILLEUL, A. Tableau complet de la Valeur des Assignats, des Rescriptions, et des Mandats, etc. 2d Ed. Paris, 1797.

BARING, SIR F. Observations on the Establishment of the Bank of England, etc. 2d Ed. London, 1797.

BARNAVE, A. P. Oeuvres mises en Ordre par M. Bérenger de la Drome. Vol. II. Paris, 1834.

BERGASSE, A. M. Sur les Assignats et les Biens du Clergé. Paris.

BERGASSE, N. Lettre à ses Commettans au sujet de sa Protestation contre les Assignats-Monnaie. Paris, 1790.

Observation sur un Article de Protestation de M. Brissot de Warville concernant ma Protestation contre les Assignats-Monnaie.

Protestation contre les Assignats-Monnaie. 2d. Ed. 1790.

Réponse au Mémoire de Montesquiou sur les Assignats. Paris, 1790.

Réplique à M. de Montesquiou.

BEYERLÉ, J. P. Avertissement aux 83 Départements ou Réflexions de J. P. L. Beyerlé. Paris, 1791.

BOISLANDRY, F. L. L. Observations sur les Dangers du Papier-Monnaie. Paris, 1789 or 1790.

BOISLANDRY, L. Considérations sur le Discrédit des Assignats. Paris, 1792.

BRISSOT, J. P. Discours sur la Nécessité de suspendre momentanément le Paiement des Liquidations au-dessus de 3,000. Paris, 1791.

Discours sur la Rareté du Numéraire et sur les Moyens d'y Remédier. Paris, 1790.

Point de Banqueroute ou Lettre à un Créancier de l'État. Londres, 1787.

CAILLE, D. Précis du Plan d'un Établissement. Paris, 1791.

CAPON, P. Observations sur le Mode de Paiement de quatrième quart des Biens nationaux. 1796.

CERUTTI, M.   Idées simples et précises sur le Papier-Monnaie, les Assignats forcés et les Biens ecclésiastiques.   Paris, 1790.
  Pièces diverses sur les Finances.   Paris, 1789–1790.
CLAVIÈRE, E.   De la Conjuration contre les Finances.   Paris, 1792.
  Du Numéraire métallique ou de la Nécessité d'une prompte Refonte des Monnoyes.   Paris, 1792.
  Lettre de M. Clavière à M. Beaumez sur l'Organisation du Trésor public (Décembre, 1790).   Paris, 1791.
  Lettres à M. Cerutti.   Paris, 1790.
  Opinions d'un Créancier de l'État sur quelques Matières de Finances importantes dans le Moment actuel.   London and Paris, 1789.
  Pétition à l'Assemblée Nationale sur le Remboursement des Créances publiques non vérifiées.   Paris, 1791.
  Réflexions sur les Formes et les Principes auxquels une Nation libre doit assujétir l'Administration des Finances.   Paris, 1791.

CONDORCET, M. J. A. N. C. (Oeuvres.)   Paris, 1847.
  1. Biens appertant au public, VII, 433–452.
  2. Caisses d'Accumulation, XI, 387–405.
  3. Caisses de la Disette du Numéraire, XI, 529–531.
  4. Dette publique, VIII, 523–559.
  5. Discours sur les Finances, XII, 69–104.
  6. Distribution des Assignats, X, 301–317.
  7. Examen des Causes de la Différence de Valeur entre l'Argent et les Assignats, XI, 531–536.
  8. Mémoire sur les Effets, XII, 43–51.
  9. Mémoires sur les Monnaies, XI, 585–673.
  10. Nouvelles Réflexions sur le Projet de payer la Dette exigible en Papier forcé.   1790, XI, 517–529.
  11. Opérations nécessaires pour rétablir les Finances.   1790, XI, 363–387.
  12. Plan d'un Emprunt public, avec des Hypothèques spéciales.   1789.   XI, 351–363.
  13. Proposition d'Acquitter la Dette Exigible en Assignats.   1791, XI, 485–517.
  14. Résultes de l'Émission de la nouvelle Monnaie de Cuivre, XII, 43–51.
Correspondance entre M. J. A. J. Cerutti et le Comte de Mirabeau sur le Rapport de M. Necker.   Paris, 1789.
CUSTINE, COMTE DE.   Réflexions sur la Proposition de Premier Ministre des Finances, de sanctionner, comme Caisse Nationale, la Caisse d'Escompte.   Paris, 1789.
D'ALLARDE, M.   Motion sur un Nouveau Régime de Finances.   Paris, 1789.
D'ÉPRÉMESNIL, M. D.   Projet d'un Décret pour la Restauration des Finances.   Paris, 1790.
De la Manière la plus favorable d'effectuer les Emprunts.   Par un Député du Baillage de Nemours à l'Assemblée Nationale.   Paris, 1789.

DE LONGCHAMP, J. F. D. À l'Assemblée Nationale. Résumé sur la Question des Assignats. Paris, 1790.

DE MACAYE, M. Plan pour l'Établissement d'une Banque Nationale. Paris, 1789.

DE MONTGAILLARD, M. État de la France au Mois de Mai 1794. Londres, 1794.

DE MONTLOSIER, F. D. Observations sur les Assignats. 1790.

DE NANCY, M. L'ÉVÊQUE. Opinion et Réclamation.

DERANT. Un dernier Mot en Faveur des Mandats. Paris, 1796.

DESLANDRES, G. Du Crédit public en France, ou Moyens de Réunion. Paris, 1792.

Sérieux et dernier Examen pour le Salut de la Chose publique. Paris, 1790.

DE VALENCE, C. M. A. Essai sur les Finances de la République française et sur les Moyens d'anéantir les Assignats. Hamburg, 1795.

Observations, Addressées au Directoire exé·utif. Hamburg, 1795.

DIJON ET CIE. Mémoire sur le Traité concernant les Mandats fait entre la Trésorerie Nationale et la Société connue sous le Nom de Dijon et Compagnie. Paris, 1798.

DIJON, Les Citoyens. Réflexions sur le Rapport fait au Conseil des Cinqcents par le citoyen Camus. Paris, 1797.

DILLON, L'ABBÉ À. Lettre à M. De Cazales. Paris, 1791.

D'IVERNOIS, F. A cursory View of the Assignats. Translated from the French. London, 1795.

État des Finances de la République française, pendant l'Année 1796. London, 1797.

DUBERNET (fils aîné). Projet de Finance ou Moyen pour les rétablir dans le Royaume. Bordeaux, 1789.

DUPORT, M. Des Assignats. Paris, 1790.

DUVAUCELLES, L. Observations sur les Moyens de faire circuler les Assignats. Paris, 1791.

DUVEYRIER, H. Observations générales sur le Projet de Loi relatif aux Transactions entre Particuliers. Paris, 1797.

Résumé de Cause pour la Compagnie Dijon. Paris, 1797.

Examen impartial du Projet d'une nouvelle Émission d'Assignats par un Négociant de Bordeaux. Bordeaux, 1790.

Extrait des Idées de M. Odet. Paris, 1790.

HOPE, M. Lettre à M. Le Couteulx de Canteleu. Amsterdam, 1790.

HUBERT. Erreurs et mauvaise Foi d'un Écrit intitulé: Observations importantes sur le Mode de Remboursement des Obligations contractées en Assignats. 1796.

KING, LORD P. Thoughts on the Restriction of Payments in Specie at the Banks of England and Ireland. London, 1803.

LACHEVARDIÈRE, A. L. Opinion sur cette Question, Est-il juste, est-il utile de fixer le Maximum du Prix des Grains? Paris, 1793.

LAPORTE. Organisation et Administration des Finances pour un Peuple libre. Paris, 1790.

LARCHER. Éclaircissemens sur le Citoyen Lamarche et sur Clavière. Paris, 1792.
LAVOISIER, A. L. De l'État des Finances de France au Premier Janvier 1792. Paris, 1791.
    In Oeuvres, VI, 464–513. Paris, 1833.
    Réflexions sur les Assignats et sur la Liquidation de la Dette exigible ou arriérée. Paris, 1790.
    In Oeuvres, VI, 364–402. Paris, 1833.
    Résultats extraits d'un Ouvrage intitulé de la Richesse territoriale du Royaume de France. Paris, 1791.
    In Oeuvres, Vol. VI, 403–463. Paris, 1833.
LEBRUN, P. A. J. Mémoire présenté à l'Assemblée nationale sur les Moyens de soutenir la Valeur des Assignats. Paris, 1792.
Lettre à M. Desmeuniers par l'Auteur des Observations sur les Deux Modes de Paiement, etc. 1790.
Lettre de Messieurs les Députés du Commerce de France, à Messieurs les Présidents et Commissaires du Commerce à Bordeaux. Bordeaux, 1790.
Le Vérificateur général des Assignats à ses Concitoyens. Paris, 1794.
LINGUET, M. S. N. Point de Banqueroute, plus d'Emprunts. Paris, 1789.
LUCADOU, P. AND C. J. Projet d'un Établissement patriotique. Bordeaux, 1790.
M. R. D., B. Mémoire présenté au Roi le 20 Avril, 1789. Amsterdam, 1789.
MARCHANT. Aux Gens de bonne Foi. Paris, 1796.
MARÉCHAL, M. R. Le Triomphe des Assignats sur l'Argent. Paris, 1791.
MIRABEAU, M. De la Constitution monétaire. Paris, 1790.
MONTESQUIOU, M. Lettre à M. Clavière sur son Ouvrage intitulé: de la Conjuration contre les Finances de l'État. Paris, 1792.
    Du Governement des Finances de France. Paris, 1797.
    Mémoires sur les Assignats ou Supplément aux Mémoires sur les Finances du Royaume. Paris, 1791.
    Réponse à la Réplique de M. Bergasse. Paris, 1791.
    Réponse à MM. Bergasse, Maury, etc. Paris, 1791.
Motion de M. Thouret sur les Propriétés de la Couronne du Clergé. 1789.
Motifs et Précis de la Motion de M. le Baron d'Allarde. Paris, 1790.
Moyens de faire baisser le Prix du Charge de l'Argent. Par l'Auteur des Réflexions sur les Assignats. Paris, 1790.
Mémoire sur la Vente des Biens ecclésiastiques. Extrait des Numéros de la Gazette de Paris. Paris, 1790.
Observations sur les Assignats par un Membre de la Société de 1789. Paris, 1790.
Observations sur les Moyens de retirer les Assignats de la Circulation Présentées par le Conseil,de Commerce au Comité de Salut public. Paris, 1795.
OLLIVIER. Observations sur le Rapport fait par Paradis, sur la Résolution du 19 Thermidor, An V. Paris, 1797.
    Rentiers de l'État. Paris, 1797.
    Réponse à l'Opinion de Duguet sur les Transactions. Paris, 1797.

Opinion sur les Assignats. Par M. L. Lu le 6 Septembre, 1790, dans la Société de 1789.

Opinion de la Chambre du Commerce de Lyon. Paris, 1790.

ORRY. Lettre à Monsieur le Comte de Mirabeau sur la Motion concernant la Caisse d'Escompte. 1789.

P., M. L. F. La France sauvée par le seul Moyen Qui soit au Pouvoir des Hommes. Paris, 1789.

Pankoucke, C. J. Nouveau Mémoire sur les Assignats ou Moyen de liquider sur le Champ la Dette nationale. 2d Ed. Corrigée. Paris, 1795.

PERISSE DULUC. Opinion sur le Papier-Monnaie ou Papier forcé en Circulation, sans Caisse ouverte. Paris, 1790.

Plan d'un Emprunt public avec des Hypothèques spéciales. Paris, 1789.

PLAYFAIR, W. Lettre II d'un Anglais à un Français sur les Assignats. 1790.

PRADÈRE, M. B. L'Impôt unique ou la Régéneration de la France chancelante. Toulouse, 1789.

Provinces, à l'Assemblée nationale sur l'Émission des Assignats-Monnaie. Paris, 1790.

PRUNELÉ, A. M. E. Fortunes, publique et particulières, Consolidées ou Plan rajeune sur les Assignats. Paris, 1795.

Rapport sur la Disproportion qui se trouve entre le Numéraire en Espèces et les Billets de Caisse. 1790.

Remboursement des Billets de la Caisse d'Escompte, Proposé en Motion par un Soldat Citoyen au District Sante-Opportune. 1790.

RIVES, J. B. Réflexions et Observations sur les Subsistances et sur le Retirement des Assignats. Paris, 1795.

ROCHON, A. M. Apperçu présenté au Comité des Monnaies. 1790.

ROCQUAIN, FÉLIX. L'État de la France au 18 Brumaire. Paris, 1874.

ROEDERER, COMTE DE. Oeuvres publiées par son Fils, Am. Roederer, Vol. 6. Paris, 1857.

SCHLEUCHER, M. Deuxième Projet de Finance. Paris, 1790.

SOLIGNAC, M. F. Observations de M. Mirabeau l'aîné relativement à l'Essai sur la Proportion de l'Or à l'Argent. Paris, 1790.

TASCHEREAU, P. A. J. Il en est Tems encore. 1796.

V. L. M. D. Réflexions sur les Assignats. 1790.

VERNIER, M. Élément de Finances. Paris, 1789.

Vues relatives à la Caisse d'Escompte, dans son Rapport avec les Finances, et le Commerce de France. Bordeaux, 1790.

III. BIOGRAPHY

BABEAU, A. La France et Paris sous le Directoire. Lettres d'une Voyageur anglaise. (1796–1797.) Paris, 1888.

BARÈRE, B. Mémoires publiés par H. Carnot et David (d'Angers). 4 Vols. Paris, 1842.

BELLEVILLE, R. Notes et Correspondance. Vol. 1. Paris, 1892.

BRADBY, E. D. The Life of Barnave. 2 Vols. Oxford, 1915.

BROWNING, O. The Dispatches of Earl Gower, English Ambassador at Paris from June 1790 to August 1792. Cambridge, 1885.

Correspondance de Napoléon Ier. Vols I–III (1796–1798). Paris, 1858–1859.
Correspondance originale des Émigrés. Édité par Alexandre C. Omer. 2 Vols. Paris, 1793.
Correspondance entre le Comte de Mirabeau et le Comte de la Marck pendant les Années 1789, 1790 et 1791. Recueillie et publié par M. Ad. de Bacourt. Vols. 1–3. Paris, 1851.
Du Pan, M. Mémoires et Correspondance, Recueillis par A. Sayons. 2 Vols. Paris, 1851.
Hesdin, R. The Journal of a Spy in Paris during the Reign of Terror, January–July, 1794. London, 1895.
Jung, T. L'Armée et la Révolution. Dubois-Crancé. 2 Vols. Paris, 1884.
Larevellière–Lépaux, L. M. Mémoires publiés par son Fils. Paris, 1895.
Mollien, F. N. Mémoires d'un Ministre du Trésor public. 1780–1815. 2 Vols. Paris, 1845.
Pariset, E. Journal de Gouverneur Morris. Paris, 1901.
Saint-Cyr, G. G. Mémoires sur les Campagnes des Armées du Rhin et de Rhin-et-Moselle. 4 Vols. Paris, 1829.
Thibaudeau, A. C. Mémoires sur la Convention et le Directoire. Vol. II, Directoire. Paris, 1824.
Turner, F. J. Correspondence of French Ministers 1791–1797 (Annual Report of American Historical Association, 1903). 2 Vols.

IV.　OTHER BOOKS AND PERIODICALS

Aftalion, A. Monnaie, Prix et Change. Paris, 1927.
Angell, J. W. The Theory of International Prices. Cambridge, 1926.
Anglade, M. De la Sécularisation des Biens du Clergé sous la Révolution. Paris, 1901.
Aulard, F. V. A. Études et Leçons sur la Révolution Française. 7e Série. L'Histoire économique de la Révolution. Paris, 1913.
Bienaymé, G. "La Fiscalité sur l'Éclairage à Paris," Journal de la Société de Statistique de Paris, XXXIV, 373–382.
"Le Cout de la Vie a Paris," XXXVI, 57–68, 355–360; XXXVII, 375–390; XXXVIII, 83–90; XL, 366–383.
Biollay, L. Les Prix en 1790. Paris, 1886.
Biré, A. "La Révolution et le Droit de Propriété," Revue de la Révolution, II, 146–152, 165–170, 277–282.
Biré, E. Journal d'un Bourgeois de Paris pendant la Terreur. Vols. 2–3. Paris, 1910.
Paris pendant la Terreur. Paris, 1890.
Blanc, L. Histoire de la Révolution Française. 2 Vols. Paris, 1872.
Boissonnade, P. Les Études relatives à l'Histoire économique de la Révolution Française. (1789–1804.) Paris, 1906.
Bornarel, F. "Étude sur les Assignats pendant la Révolution Française," La Révolution Française, XV, 498–530; XVI, 111–132, 209–229.
Bourdeau, H. Les Armées du Rhin au Début du Directoire. Vol. 1. Paris, 1905.
Bourne, H. E. "Maximum Prices in France 1793–1794," American Historical Review, XVIII, 107–113.

BOURNE, H. E. "Food Control and Price-Fixing in revolutionary France," Journal of Political Economy, XXVII, 73–95, 188–210.

BOUVIER, F. Bonaparte en Italie, 1796. Paris, 1899.

BURTON, R. G. Napoleon's Campaigns in Italy. 1796–1797 and 1800. London, 1912.

CALONNE, C. A. De l'État de la France. London, 1790.

CARON, P. Paris pendant la Terreur. Rapports des Agents secrets du Ministre de l'Intérieur. 2 Vols. Paris, 1910, 1914.

COLSON, A. "Tableaux des Billets de Confiance émis dans les 83 Départements et Qui ont eu Cours de Monnaie de 1790 à 1793." Revue Numismatique, 1852, 257–287, 384–468.

COURTOIS, A. "Histoire du Papier-Monnaie en France," Journal des Économists, 3d Series, XXXIII, 258–278.

Histoire des Banques en France. 2d Ed. Paris, 1881.

DAUBAN, C. A. Paris en 1794 et en 1795. Histoire de la Rue, du Club, de la Famine; composée d'après des Documents inédits. Paris, 1869.

La Démagogie en 1793 à Paris ou Histoire, Jour par Jour, de l'Année 1793. Paris, 1868.

DAUDET, E. Histoire de l'Émigration. Coblentz, 1789–1793. (D'après des Documents inédits.) Paris, 1889.

D'AVENEL, G. Histoire économique de la Propriété, des Salaires, des Denrées et de tous les Prix en général, depuis l'An 1200 jusqu'en l'An 1800. Vol. III. Paris, 1898.

DE FAYOLLE, M. E. "Documents relatifs à la Rareté du Numéraire en Guyenne en 1789 et 1790." Communiqués par Archives Historiques du Département de la Gironde, XXXVI, 470–494.

DE LA VERGNE, L. Les Économistes français du Dix-Huitième Siècle. Paris, 1870.

DE LA VERGNE, L. "De la Richesse et de la Population de la France au Dix-Huitième Siècle," Journal des Économistes, 2d Series, IV, 355–386.

DE NERVO, M. LE BARON. Les Finances françaises sous l'ancienne Monarchie, la République, le Consulat et l'Empire. 2 Vols. Paris, 1863.

Les Finances françaises sous la Restauration. Vols 1–3. Paris, 1865–1867.

DU CHATELLIER, M. V. "Les Assignats," Académie des Sciences morales, CXXIII, 843–861.

FALKNER, S. V. "Das Papiergeld der französischen Revolution 1789–1797." Aus dem russischen Übertragen von Friedrich Schlömer. Schriften des Vereins für Sozialpolitik, CLXV. Leipzig, 1914.

FERRARIS, C. F. Moneta e Corso Forzoso. Napoli, 1879.

FERVEL, J. N. Campagnes de la Révolution Française dans les Pyrénées orientales, 1793–1795. 2 Vols. Paris, 1851–1853.

FORNERON, H. Histoire générale des Émigrés pendant la Révolution Française. Vol. 1, 2d Ed. Paris, 1884–1890.

GIBON, F. "La Révolution dans les Finances," Revue de la Révolution, XIV, 268–287.

GOMEL, C. Histoire financière de l'Assemblée constituante. I. 1789. II. 1790–1791. Paris, 1896–1897.

GOMEL, C. Histoire financière de la législative et de la Convention. 2 Vols. Paris, 1905.

GUYOT, Y. et RAFFLOVICH, A. Inflation et Déflation. Paris, 1921.

GUYOT, R. Le Directoire et la Paix de l'Europe (1795–1799). Paris, 1911.

HARGREAVES, E. L. Restoring Currency Standards. London, 1926.

HAWTREY, R. G. Currency and Credit. 2d Ed. London, 1923.
"The Bank Restriction of 1797," The Economic Journal, XXVIII, 52–66.

HOFFMAN, V. Die Devalvierung des österreichischen Papiergeldes im Jahre 1811. München, 1923.

ILLIG, H. "Das Geldwesen Frankreichs zur Zeit der ersten Revolution bis zum Ende der Papiergeldwährung," Abhandlungen aus dem Staatswissenschaftlichen Seminar, XXI. Strassburg, 1914.

JAURÈS, J. Histoire socialiste de la Révolution Française. Éditions de la Libraire de l'Humanité. 5 Vols. Paris, 1923.

LECARPENTIER, G. La Vente des Biens ecclésiastiques pendant la Révolution Française. Paris, 1908.

LECOCQ, M. G. "Le Papier-Monnaie des Communes de France pendant la Révolution," La Révolution Française, III–IV, 649–653, 712–715, 834–837, 941–944, 1029–1032, 1127–1130.

LEVASSEUR, É. "Les Finances de la France sous la Révolution," L'Académie des Sciences morales, 3d Series, XXX, 103–147, 277–309; 4th Series, I, 21–74.
Histoire des Classes ouvrières et de l'Industrie en France de 1789 à 1870. 2d Ed. 2 Vols. Paris, 1904.
Histoire du Commerce de la France. 2 Vols. Paris, 1911 and 1920.
"Les Prix," Journal de la Société de Paris de Statistique, XXXIV, 383–401.

LOUTCHISKY, J. La petite Propriété en France avant la Révolution et la Vente des Biens nationaux. Paris, 1897.

MALLET, G. La Politique financière des Jacobins. Paris, 1913.

MARION, M. Histoire financière de la France depuis 1715. Vol. II: 1789 à 1792. Vol. III: 1792 à 1797. Paris, 1919–1921.
"Les Lois de Maximum et la Taxation des Salaires sous la Révolution," Extrait de la Revue Internationale de Sociologie. Paris, 1917.
La Vente des Biens nationaux pendant la Révolution avec Étude spéciale des Ventes dans les Départements de la Gironde et du Cher. Paris, 1908.

MATHIEZ, A. "Les Subsistances pendant la Révolution," Annales Révolutionnaires, IX. 1. "De Réglementation à la Liberté," 166–187. 2. "Un Essai de Taxation populaire au Printemps de 1792," 289–313. 3. "Les Enragés et la Lutte pour le Maximum," 456–483.
"Le Vote du premier Maximum (Avril-Mai 1793)," Annales Révolutionnaires, XI, 294–321. "L'Application du premier Maximum (Mars-Juillet 1793)," Annales Révolutionnaires, XI, 495–507.
"Les Enragés contre la Constitution de 1793" (Juin 1793). Annales Révolutionnaires, XIII, 297–321. "Les Enragés et les Troubles du Savon," Annales Révolutionnaires, XIII, 353–371. "La Mort de Marat

et le Vote de la Loi sur l'Accaparement" (Juillet 1793), XIII, 477–484.
"Le Banquier Boyd et ses Amis," Annales Révolutionnaires, XII, 218–231. "Encore le banquier Perregaux," *ibid.*, XII, 237–243. Études Robespierristes. 1. La Corruption parlémentaire sous la Terreur. Paris, 1917. 2. La Conspiration de l'Étranger. Paris, 1918. Procès de Corruption sous la Terreur. L'Affaire de la Compagnie des Indes. Paris, 1920. Question sociale, La. Paris, 1905. Révolution et les Étrangers, La. Paris, 1918.

MORTIMER-TERNAUX, L'Histoire de la Terreur, 1792–1794, d'après des Documents authentiques et inédits. 2d Ed. Vol. 4. Paris, 1864.

NECKER, J. A Treatise on the Administration of the Finances of France. 3 Vols. Translated by Thomas Mortimer. 3 Ed. London, 1787.

NOGARO, B. La Monnaie et les Phénomènes monétaires contemporains. Paris, 1924.

PEUCHET, M. J. Statistique élémentaire de la France. Paris, 1805.

POINSARD, LEON. "Le Crédit public pendant la Révolution Française," La Révolution Française, XV, 227–254, 312–333.

PORÉE, C. Les Subsistances dans l'Yonne et particulièrement dans le District d'Auxerre pendant la Révolution. Auxerre et Paris, 1903.

ROUSSEL, P. L. Le Système des Mandats territoriaux. (1796–1797.) Paris, 1920.

SCHMIDT, A. Paris pendant la Révolution, d'après les Rapports de la Police secrète. 1789–1800. Traduction française par Viollet. Vols. 2 and 3. Paris, 1885–1890.

SCHMIDT, C. "La Crise industrielle de 1788 en France," Revue Historique, XCVII, 78–91.

SÉE, H. "Doctorate de M. Léon Dubreuil. La Vente des Biens nationaux dans le Département des Côtes-Du-Nord," Révolution Français, LXIII, 148–156.

SENIOR, N. W. Three Lectures on the Cost of obtaining Money and on some Effects of private and Government Paper Money. London, 1830.

SHAW, W. A. The History of Currency 1252–1894. London, 1895.

SILBERLING, N. J. Theories of Money and Credit, 1776–1848. (Harvard Doctorate Thesis, 1919.)

STOURM, R. Les Finances de l'ancien Régime et de la Révolution. 2 Vols. Paris, 1885.
　　Bibliographie historique des Finances de la France au Dix-Huitième Siècle. Paris, 1895.

TAINE, H. A. The French Revolution. Translated by John Durand. Vol. 3. New York, 1885.

THORNTON, H. An Enquiry into the Nature and Effects of the Paper Credit of Great Britain. London, 1802.

WAGNER, A. Die russische Papierwährung. Riga, 1868.
　　Theoretische Sozialökonomik, Part II, Vol. 2. Leipzig, 1909.

WHITE, A. D. Paper Money Inflation in France. New York, 1876.

YOUNG, A. Travels during the Years 1787, 1788 and 1789. 2d Ed. London, 1794.

INDEX

INDEX OF SUBJECTS

AGRICULTURE, state of, 3
AMERICAN DEBT, repayment of, 240
ASSIGNATS See also Paper Money
  attacks on in 1790 and 1791, 170
  bill for improving mechanical features, 38
  brief résumé of history of value, 206
  decree of April 1790, 14
  demand for according to Clavière, 23
  demands for in 1790–91, 169–170; in 1792, 172–173; in 1793–94, 183–184
  demonetization proposed in 1795, 198–201
  destroyed, 39, 58, 70–71
  each unit the equivalent of a decreasing quantity of land, 65
  financial tool, a, 59, 63, 262
  first decree, 12
  in circulation, large increases legalized by change in wording of law, 54–55
  issues for exchange purposes, 58
  issues under the Convention, 56–57
  issues under the Directorate, 57–58
  issues under the National Assembly, 55–56
  justification for a study of, vii–viii
  law for attaching it to specific parcels of land, 66–68
  new role of, 1791–92, 64–65
  non-acceptance of, 207–208
  not a proposal for increasing the sale of lands, 12, 62–63
  proposals to reduce circulation, 178–180
  quantities erroneously reported, 39–40
  stable value of, 208–209
  versus quittances de Finance, 13
"AU COURS" PAYMENTS See also Contracts
  all contracts not subjected to terms of law of 5 Messidor 5, 217
  attempts in recent years, 217
  demanded by government, 210
  Directory demands for lands, 229
  effect on depreciation, 187–188

  evolution of, law of 5 Messidor 5, 215–216
  introduced for contracts made in the Assignat period, 214–215
  opinions of authorities, 218
  problems involved, 266–267
  right of state to interfere questioned, 216–217
  tax collection and, 46

BILLETS DE CONFIANCE, 24–26

CAHIERS, on paper money, 8
CAISSE D'ESCOMPTE, criticism unwarranted, 7
CAPITAL REIMBURSEMENTS, suspended in July, 1796 owing to depreciation, 215
CÉDULES D'HYPOTHÈQUE, issue proposed, 196
CHAMBER OF COMMERCE OF LYONS, protest against Assignat, 19
CHURCH LANDS, proposals to confiscate, 9–10
CODE NAPOLÉON, 218
COMMISSIONERS, report on bank and paper money, 11
COMMITTEE OF FINANCE, 13, 24
COMMITTEE ON MONEY, proposal to reduce value of gold, 7
COMPAGNIE CROZE, 248
CONTRACTS. See also "au cours" payments
  Adjustment of, xi
  Private, modification of, xii
COURAJOD ET CIE, 207

DEBTORS, relieved of burden of metallic reimbursements, 215–216
DECREES OF MANUFACTURE — confusion with decrees of issue, 59
DEFICITS See also Taxation
  estimates by Gomel, 35–36, by Marion, 36–37
  for 1790–95, 37–38
  of 1791, 60–61
  repayment of public debt an important factor, 35

Revolution, before the, 28
DEPRECIATION See also Assignats, Exchanges, Land, Maximum Laws, Paper Money
according to local tables and Treasury tables, 120
advantageous for debtors, 213–214
attributed to Billets de Confiance, 25
attributed to large denominations and fear for land security, 69–70
causes of xii, 194
comments by Boislandry, 22–23, 174
consideration of measures of by contemporaries, 94–95
explanations by Falkner and Hawtrey, 202
explanations by Lavoisier, 22
explanations by present day writers, 164
explanations on the basis of the quantity theory, 202
fatalistic attitude of French writers, 163–164
financial policy in 1794–95 and, 195–200
foreign exchange as measures of, 97–98
gold and silver as a measure of, 95–97
land security and, 204–205
loss of confidence in 1792, 172–173
measure of, x, 95–102
measures of, appropriateness of measures used, 262–263
neglected factors in explanation, 203–205
noticed by many writers in 1792, 173–174
political conditions and, 195, 201–203
previous consideration of measures of, 92–93
price quotations most satisfactory measure of, 101–102
question of reduction in, 1794, 181–182
rapid in first 8 months of 1793, 176
rate of advance in 1795, 186
rate of more rapid than increase in total amount of money, 220–221
recognition by government, 208–209, 211
reduced by Billets de Confiance, 25–26
second half of 1792, not a period of appreciation, 175
significance of the state of the subsistence market and, 265

subsistence question and, 204
unhealthy political conditions in first 8 months of 1793, 176
unsatisfactory conditions of supplies early in 1793, 177
DIJON AND CO., disreputable contract with to destroy paper money, 232–234

ECONOMIC FEDERALISM, 203
EMISSIONS, errors in interpretation of figures, 53–54
excess over deficits, 38–41
facts concealed, 54
not in excess of notes withdrawn, 54
EXCHANGES
See also Depreciation, Gold and Silver
comparison of quotations in 1795 with prices of gold and silver, 260–261
control of foreign assets, 245
control of rates, 245–247
control of trade, 247–255
depreciation accounted for in early years of Revolution, 236–238
depreciation and early purchases of gold and silver, 244
depreciation explained in part by a movement of gold points, 250
effect of interference with gold and silver markets, 243–244
effect of purchases abroad, 243
explanation of depreciation during the Terror, 258–260
external and internal values do not move together, 235–236
external depreciation preceded internal depreciation, 255
movements in, xiii
not a matter of indifference which quotations are used, 255
quotations compared to prices of gold and silver, 256–258
quotations improved by heroic measures of Committee of Public Safety, 260
EXPORTATION OF CAPITAL, 238–240
EXPORTS, prohibition of, 240–241

FARM LEASES, adjustments for depreciation, 213–214
FINANCES, under Directorate, 47
proposals for improving in 1795, 199–201
Reign of Terror, during, 44–45

Summary, 47
FIRST COMMITTEE ON MONEY, 5
FORCED LOANS, 46–47
FOREIGN TRADE, estimates of, 242–243
    statistics and, 4

GERMAN MARK, depreciation more extreme than of Assignat, 227
GOLD AND SILVER
    competition with Assignat once more in 1795, 186–187
    competition with paper money, 265–266
    convictions for exporting, 239
    dealings in prohbited outside of bourses, 193
    effectiveness of legislation against use of in 1793–94, 182–183
    free dealings again in 1795, 196–197
    measures against use of, 177–178
    official purchases lucrative, 244–245
    substitutes for Assignats, 1790–91, 167
    Treasury quotations, 108–110
GRAINS
    See also Maximum Laws
    debate on free movements in 1792, 135–136
    decisive discourse for freedom by Creuzé-Latouche, 138
    effects of disorders on supplies in 1792, 134–135
    explanation of scarcity in, by Committee of Agriculture and Commerce, 135
    free movements of attacked by Robespierre, 137
    measures taken to assure adequate supplies, 133–134
    proposal for a census of, 136–137
    system demoralized by excessive issues of money, 136

INDUSTRY, depression in, 3

LAND See also Depreciation
    amounts received from sales, 85–87
    disastrous law of 10 Prairial, 198
    estimates of value, 76, 79–81, 84
    estimate of values by Montesquiou, 81
    estimates of values by Stourm and Cambon criticised, 82–84
    opinions as to success of sales 73–74
    optimistic estimates of value by authorities, 78–79
    payments on and anticipation of depreciation, 75–78

possibilities as a support for the Assignat, 71–73
    receipts from contingent on depreciation, 84–85
    receipts independent of time of sale, 89
    restitution of and value of Assignat, 194–195
    sales in Departments of Yonne and Vosges, 88–89
    sales price compared to price of estimation, 74–77
    source of increased confidence in the paper money, 68–70
    subsidiary to the Assignat, 64
    Land and the Value of the Assignat, x, 70, 202
    Land Fallacy, criticism carried too far, 90–91
LOANS, failure of, 28
LOCAL DEPRECIATION
    construction of tables of, 112–114
    in contiguous departments, explanation of, 128–130
    differences partly fictitious, 263
    explanation of, 126–131
    extent of, 111
    in Paris, explanation of, 127–128
    in South, explanation of, 126
    in West, explanation of, 127
LOCAL TABLES, instructions for constructing, 131
    significance of, 131–132
    weights of commodity prices, 119
    weights of land prices, 118

MANDATS, low yield from, 226–227
    popular acceptance not obtained, 225–226
    proposal to issue, 225
MAXIMUM LAWS See also Depreciation and Grains
    administrative difficulties, 143–144
    debate on repeal, 146
    effect on commodities not controlled, 152
    effect on consumption of necessities, 154
    effect on foreign trade, 241–242
    effect on meat supplies, 152–153
    effect on quality of commodities sold, 153
    effect on supplies, 149–150
    effectiveness, 264–265
    effects in 1795, 155–157

explanation of passage of by Mathiez, 139
failure of requisitions under, 157–158
futile attempts to prevent passage of, 141–142
modifications not proof of failure, 147
necessity of introducing requisitioning, 151–152
new legislation for general maximum in September, 144–145
opinions of writers as to effectiveness, 147
principle accepted early in 1793, 142–143
proposal to Committee of Commerce and Agriculture, 140–141
reaction against in 1794, 145–146
revocation disastrous, 187
significance for goverment, 159
significance for value of Assignat, 159–160, 264
violations of, 145, 150–151
MAXIMUM LAWS and the Value of the Assignat, xi
MAXIMUM PRICES, justification of, 52
METALLIC STANDARD, plan for return to in 1794, 184–185
MONETARY THEORY, recent developments and the Assignats, viii
MONEY, contemporaries conscious of scarcity, 223
estimates of pre-Revolutionary circulation, 5
in hoards and in circulation, 5
limitations to increase in rate of consumption of balances, 222
loss of, 6
scarcity exaggerated in period of rapid depreciation, 222
Scarcity of, 4

NUMÉRAIRE, explanations of scarcity, 27
requirements for export, 27
scarcity of, 26–27

PAPER MONEY See also Assignats
attack on by Du Pont, 11
Cahiers, 8
education of public as to advantages, 8–9
Falkner's estimate of receipts in stable value, 53 n. 1
Mirabeau on, 9 n. 6, 10

Necker on, 10
Paris on, 15
Provinces on, 16, 17
stable value less than that of land security, 65–66
PATENTE TAX introduced to curb speculation, 193
PRICES See also Maximum Laws
Bergues, in, 105–106
commodities, of, rise more rapid than prices of gold and silver early in 1795, 117–118
causes of high prices in 1795 explained by agents of Committee of Public Safety, 189
confusion of market and official, 99 – 100, 107
explanation of in 1789, 133
high in 1792 owing to reductions of supplies, 103
local variation in, 118
quotations invalidated by control, 100
satisfactory quotations not available, 99
stability of, 1790–91, 102
survey by Committee of Public Safety, 114–117
PUBLIC DEBT, classification of, 30
definition of "dette exigible," 30–31
estimates of "dette exigible," 30–32
government agreement to repay, 29–30
proposal of Mirabeau to use Assignat to pay, 14
repayment before 1792, 32–34
significance for Assignats, 29
PUBLIC EMPLOYEES, treatment of by government, 211

QUANTITY THEORY, recent formulations of, 205
QUITTANCE DE FINANCE, favored by Talleyrand, 17–18

RENTENMARK, similarity to Assignat, 91
RENTIERS, treatment of by government, 211–212

SAVINGS, availability questioned, 84–85
SILVER, loss of, 6
SMALL DENOMINATIONS, law of May 6, 1790, 26

measures taken in 1790 and 1791 to overcome shortage of, 26

scarcity of, 24

SPECULATION, flourishing conditions in 1795, 192–194

SUBSISTENCE, history of and depreciation, 161–162

SUPPLIES, effects of war and Revolution in 1795, 190–192

inadequate in 1795, 188–189

TAXATION See Deficits

estimate of receipts from, 48–53

improvement in 1792, 43, 50

low yield, 1790–92, 42

nominal and stable receipts, 51–52

not a negligible factor, 52–53

radical measures, 1793, 43–44

suppression of, 41–42

system unsuitable for period of depreciation, 50

TAX IN KIND, proposals for in 1795, 197–198

TRANSITION TO A METALLIC STANDARD, difficulties of Treasury in period of extreme depreciation, 224–225, 228–229

early proposals of, 223–224

ease exaggerated, 127, 218–219

heterogeneous collection of types of money, 230–232

low prices 1795–1797, 236

return of gold and silver, 219–220

scarcity of gold and silver, 220

supplies of money available in June, 1796, 227

VOTES OF CREDIT, 45

INDEX OF NAMES

Abbema, 247
Abbema et Fils, 253
Abbot of Abbecourt, 11
Abbot of Cazalès, 13
Abbot of Maury, 13
Aftalion, 205, 222
Amelot, 240
Anderson, 219 n. 2
André, 254
Angley, d', 11
Anson, 11, 13, 14, 15, 24
Arnould, 5, 242
Aulard, 247

Bailleul, 255
Balland, 66
Barbaroux, 138
Barère, 145, 184, 185
Beaumez, 16, 26
Beffroy, 137, 141
Bendixen, 90 n. 1
Benzacar, 73
Bergasse, 81, 168 n. 2, 170, 237
Bishop of Aix, 13
Blanc, 148, 159, 160, 163
Boislandry, 22, 174, 236
Boissy d'Angas, 192
Bonn, 220 n. 1
Bonnet, 205
Borel et Frères, 253
Bornarel, 92
Bortkiewicz, 90 n. 1
Bourdon, 66, 197
Brissot, 30
Buzot, 142

Cailhasson, 55, 173
Caille, 23
Calonne, 5, 6, 31, 64, 76, 79, 170
Cambacères, 66
Cambon, 30, 31, 32, 33, 39, 40, 43, 44, 78,
    79, 80, 81, 82, 83, 177, 178, 179, 183,
    184 n. 1, 185, 188, 195, 196, 237, 245,
    246.
Camus, 81
Cannan, 91

Caron, 97 n. 1, 207
Cerutti, 20
Chapelier, 15
Charles, 142
Clavière, 5, 6, 23, 30, 43, 173, 176 n. 1,
    179, 236, 237
Colson, 163
Combe, 253
Condorcet, 9, 94, 170, 173, 238
Count of Custine, 237
Creuzé-Latouche, 138, 139, 141

Dallard, 26
Danton, 144
d'Arcy, 10, 14
de Cernon, 13
Delamorre, 247
Desjardins, 248
Deslandres, 176 n. 1, 213, 214, 238
Desvars, 142
de Valence, 199, 201
Dianyère, 104
d'Ivernois, 79 n. 1, 195
de Montlosier, 11
Dubois-Crancé, 66, 67, 197, 198, 224,
    243 n. 2
Du Chatelier, 147
Ducos, 141, 142
Dumas, 252, 254
Durazzo, 254
Du Pont de Nemours, 11, 13, 46
Dupont, Jacob, 154

Eschassériaux, 80, 81, 83, 84, 188, 193

Fabre, 237
Faipoult, 47
Falkner, xiv, 53 n. 1, 92, 93, 99, 165, 166,
    202, 219, 227, 255
Fanno, 97 n. 4
Fauchet, 249
Fer, 250
Féraud, 135
Ferraris, 94 n. 2, 202, 203
Frécine, 38

Garnier, 149, 255
Gartner, 218
Gaston, 223
Gennissieux, 142
Genz, 219 n. 1
Géraud, 146
Gerod, 212
Gide, 205
Gomel, vii, xv, 35, 47, 56, 63, 68, 147, 163
Gower, 245
Grandpré, 142

Hahn, 205, 235 n. 1
Hargreaves, 206 n. 1, 208 n. 1
Hawtrey, vii, xiv, xv, x, 68, 69, 70, 84, 90,
    91, 92, 93, 95, 162, 164, 169, 178, 202,
    264
Herrmann, 205

Illig, 92, 97, 164
Isoré, 153

Jaurès, 92, 169
Johannot, 78, 79, 80, 81, 188, 196, 197,
    198, 202, 208
Jourdan, 158

Katzellenbaum, 90 n. 1
Kaufman, 214
Keynes, 90 n. 1, 222
Knapp, 218

Lablanche, 16
Lafon-Ladébat, 174, 200, 216, 223
Larevillière-Lépaux, 208
La Rochefoucauld, 14
Lataché, 216
Lavoisier, 31, 32, 76, 94, 168 n. 1, 202, 238
Law, 8, 169
Lebrun, 223, 224
Le Carpentier, 74
Lecointre, 142, 157
Lefèbvre, 148
Lehardy, 193
Lejeune, 137
Levan, 250
Levasseur, xvi, 55, 56, 67, 68, 69, 70, 90,
    99, 147, 163, 169
Lotz, 97 n. 2
Loutchisky, 84
Luobert, 252, 254
Lucadore, 23

Macaye, 10
Mallarmé, 97 n. 1
Mallet du Pan, 44
Maréchal, 23
Marion, vii, xiv, 34, 36, 47, 68, 73, 84, 85,
    147, 159, 164, 264
Marx, 222
Mathiez, 139, 148, 176 n. 2, 177 n. 4,
    239
Mill, xvi, 68, 90
Mirabeau, xvi, 10, 15, 64
Mises, 90 n. 1, 203, 219 n. 3, 235 n. 1
Mitchell, 203
Mollévaut, 131, 216
Mollien, 230, 231
Momoro, 140
Montesquiou, 20, 24, 31, 32, 41, 64, 76, 79,
    81, 82, 238
Montgilbert, 142
Mosmiron, 174

Napoleon, 228
Necker, 5, 6, 7, 10, 13, 28, 63, 242
Nogaro, 235, 236
Nowak, 195

Odet, 23
Ollivier, 212

Pancoucke, 199, 230
Pelet, 190
Perrière, 104
Pétion, 14, 15
Peuchet, 242
Philibert, 173
Philippeaux, 141
Pierpont, 253
Poinsard, 169
Porée, 77
Pribram, 111 n. 3
Prunélé, 79 n. 2, 223

Rabaut, 26
Raffron, 143, 144
Ramel, 47, 54, 55, 85, 185
Réal, 142
Rheinhold, 91
Rewbell, 66, 222
Ricardo, 97 n. 4, 235 n. 1
Robespierre, 137, 186
Roland, 136
Roederer, 14
Rousseau, 140

Saint-André, 198
Saint-Cyr, 228
Saint Just, 136
Savary, 223
Schmidt, 97 n. 3, 226
Sennebier, 9
Senior, 68, 90
Serré, 137
Shaw, 6
Siret, 144, 154
Smith, 135, 136, 137
Solignac, 27, 236
Stourm, xv, 28, 55, 56, 68, 80, 81, 82, 83, 84, 85, 163
Subercasseaux, 263 n. 1
Swan and Schwitzer, 253

Taine, 147
Talleyrand, 9, 10, 11, 76, 79
Taschereau, 230
Thibeaudeau, 219
Thiers, 219 n. 3
Thornton, 68
Thuriot, 70, 142, 144
Turgot, 135, 137

Vernier, 43, 66, 70, 142
Viger, 137

Wagner, 94 n. 2, 98 n. 3, 202, 203, 263 n. 1
White, 169

Young, 5, 31, 169